# Socialist Iraq
## A Study in Iraqi Politics Since 1968

# Socialist Iraq
## A Study in Iraqi Politics Since 1968

Majid Khadduri

THE MIDDLE EAST INSTITUTE
WASHINGTON, D.C.
1978

Copyright 1978 by The Middle East Institute
Library of Congress Catalogue Card Number 78-51916.
ISBN 0-916808-16-5
Printed in the United States of America

Dedicated
In Friendship
to
Francis O. Wilcox

# THE WRITER'S BOOKS IN ENGLISH

*Islamic and Legal Studies:*

War and Peace in the Law of Islam
  The Johns Hopkins University Press

Law in the Middle East
  Edited, in collaboration with H. J. Liebesny, for the Middle East Institute

Islamic Jurisprudence
  The Johns Hopkins University Press

The Islamic Law of Nations
  The Johns Hopkins University Press

Major Middle Eastern Problems in International Law
  Editor and Contributor, the American Enterprise Institute for Public Policy

*Studies on the Modern Arab World:*

Independent Iraq: A Study in Iraqi Politics, 1932–1958
  Oxford University Press

Republican Iraq: A Study in Iraqi Politics Since the Revolution of 1958
  Oxford University Press

Socialist Iraq: A Study in Iraqi Politics Since 1968
  The Middle East Institute

Modern Libya: A Study in Political Development
  The Johns Hopkins University Press

Political Trends in the Arab World: The Role of Ideas and Ideals in Politics
  The Johns Hopkins University Press

Arab Contemporaries: The Role of Personalities in Politics
  The Johns Hopkins University Press

# Contents

| | | |
|---|---|---|
| Preface | | IX |
| Chapter I: | The Arab Socialist Movement | 1 |
| Chapter II: | The Arab Socialist Revolution | 13 |
| Chapter III: | Arab Socialists in Power | 31 |
| Chapter IV: | Struggle for Power among Socialist Leaders | 49 |
| Chapter V: | Struggle Among Ideological Groups | 77 |
| Chapter VI: | Social and Economic Development | 111 |
| Chapter VII: | Foreign Policy | 141 |
| Chapter VIII: | Conclusion | 177 |
| Appendix A: | The Interim Constitution | 183 |
| Appendix B: | The National Action Charter | 199 |
| Appendix C: | March 11 Manifesto on the Peaceful Settlement of the Kurdish Issue in Iraq | 231 |
| Appendix D: | The Iraqi-Soviet Treaty of Friendship and Cooperation | 241 |
| Appendix E: | Iran-Iraq Treaty on International Borders and Good Neighbourly Relations | 245 |
| Index | | 261 |

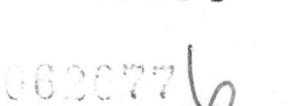

# Preface

THIS WORK is a sequel to *Independent Iraq* and *Republican Iraq*; the first dealt with Iraqi politics under the Monarchy and the second with the Revolution of 1958 and its aftermath. This volume, more closely connected with the latter, is essentially a study of the Revolution of 1968 with a special emphasis on political and economic development under Arab Socialist rule. The three volumes, though each appears as a separate study, cover a span of Iraqi political development extending to almost half a century and may well be regarded as a single work in three tomes. Coincidentally, the first volume begins with the year I entered public life—it is indeed the year Iraq had formally been declared independent—and the third roughly ends with the year I retired as an academician.

As in the earlier volumes, I tried not only to verify published material with oral interviews but also to obtain information not found in print from the *dramatis personae* with whom I had the privilege to meet and discuss fundamental questions of policy and other matters connected with the country's development. I should like to mention in particular Field Marshal Ahmad Hasan al-Bakr, President of the Republic; Saddam Husayn, Vice President of the Revolutionary Command Council; and a number of Cabinet Ministers, high Government officials, and other public men who have provided me with invaluable material. To Michel 'Aflaq, Secretary General of the National Command of the Ba'th Party and his staff, and a number of leading members of the Iraqi Regional Command, I am grateful for their assistance and counsel. I should also thank the University of Baghdad and the

Ministry of Information for the invitations they extended to me to visit Iraq in the summer of 1974 and in January 1976 and January 1977 and in making available all published material and in extending to me other facilities during my visits to Iraq. Though it is impossible to cite by name all others, in official or unofficial capacities, who have readily provided me with material or given me counsel, it is a pleasure to acknowledge their kindnesses. Some have preferred to remain anonymous, but the names of others are cited in the text or footnotes. The index was compiled by John Cahill. Needless to say, none is responsible for any error of fact or opinion which the work may contain.

Majid Khadduri
The School of Advanced International Studies
The Johns Hopkins University
January 15, 1978

Chapter I

# The Arab Socialist Movement

THE ARAB SOCIALIST movement in Iraq is part of a larger socialist movement which began to spread in Arab lands after World War II and to affect the structure and dynamics of Arab society in varying degrees of intensity. Broadly speaking, the Arab Socialist movement in Iraq may not be different in theoretical framework from the other Arab Socialist movements, but the impact and the course of development of each movement varied from land to land.[1]

The Arab Socialist movement, often called the Ba'th or the Arab Resurrection, emerged first in Syria in response to Arab nationalist demands as seen from Syrian perspectives, but after spreading to Iraq in conditions different from Syria, its goals and directions appeared not altogether similar to those in Syria or in other Arab lands. Though the Arab Socialist movement in Iraq appeared almost a decade after it had arisen in Syria, some of the influences that affected its scope and direction may be traced back to the intellectual and political activities of pre-war years as well as to the events and new conditions which gave rise to social upheavals that swept the country after the war. As a result, the Arab Socialist movement in Iraq has acquired a local coloring and the country's principal political figures stamped it with their own imprint and identified it with their own local interests and traditions.[2]

---

1. For the nature and drives of the general Arab Socialist movement, see my *Political Trends in the Arab World* (Baltimore, 1970), Chaps. 6–7.
2. For a critical study of social conditions in Iraq that are likely to affect political opinion, see the works of the Iraqi sociologist 'Ali al-Wardi, especially his *Dirasa Fi*

## THE DRIVES AND AIMS OF THE ARAB SOCIALIST MOVEMENT

Like the socialist movements in other Arab lands, the Iraqi Arab Socialist movement sought progress, social justice and prosperity which were not possible to achieve under the Old Regime. As I have already had occasion to explain in other works, the pre-Revolutionary political system of Iraq which had been laid down under foreign control was a form of parliamentary democracy modelled on Western European patterns.[3] It was hoped that in time that system would mature into a stable and truly parliamentary form of government which would provide the legitimate basis for political participation and opportunities for welfare and prosperity for all. Soon after independence, however, this system began to appear meaningless, because the ruling élite betrayed authoritarian tendencies and had little or no respect for parliamentary processes. The people soon began to learn how scandalously these processes could be misused by unscrupulous leaders; no effective opposition to check these trends existed. After World War II, when a "new generation" began to grow and sought participation in the political system, they were denied the freedom necessary for political participation. Failure of the ruling oligarchy to accommodate itself to the new social conditions prompted the new generation to resist the monopoly of power, by force if necessary. When the young civilian leaders were unable to achieve power, the young officers felt compelled to overthrow the Old Regime, for these officers shared the same ideas and aspirations as their civilian contemporaries. They sought to achieve by the armed forces of the state what civilian leaders could not do by strikes and street demonstrations.

But the military achieved only a political revolution which rid the country of the ruling oligarchy; the social revolution which reformers had dreamed of had yet to be achieved. The new generation was divided on what sort of "social revolution" it should seek and what method it should pursue to achieve it. Some, disappointed with the military, urged the revival of traditional symbols and values, because the social changes achieved by military methods did not measure up to

---

*Tabi'at al-Mujtama' al-'Iraqi* [A Study of the Character of Iraqi Society] (Baghdad, 1965); and the social history of Iraq, entitled *Lamahat Min Ta'rikh al-'Iraq al-Hadith* [Some Aspects of the Modern History of Iraq] (Baghdad, 1969- ). Only five volumes have been published to date (1977).

3. See my *Independent Iraq* (London, 2nd. ed., 1960), Chap. 2; and *Republican Iraq* (London, 1969), Chap. 1.

expectations. Others preached radical ideologies which sought basic changes in social conditions. In Iraq—indeed in several other Arab countries—only the Arab Socialist Party (the Ba'th) seems to excite young Arabs more than other radical groups, because it sought to harmonize the Arab heritage with modern social and economic doctrines considered necessary to modernize Arab society. Though for over half a century the Communists have been trying to achieve these objectives, they have not yet made much headway.

## ANTECEDENTS OF THE ARAB SOCIALIST MOVEMENT

Apart from the fact that it was an offshoot of the general Arab Socialist movement, the Iraqi Arab Socialist movement may be said to have been influenced, directly or indirectly, by three diverse though not necessarily conflicting forces. Since these forces have either originally stemmed from or adapted to the Iraqi social milieu, their impact on the Arab Socialist movement has rendered easier the task of the Iraqi leaders to adapt their ideology to local conditions. The impact of these forces may be summed up as follows:

First, the Ahali (Populist) movement, whose origins and ideas have been discussed elsewhere,[4] made its appearance in the early thirties, first as an intellectual movement and then as a political party called the National Democratic Party. It was the first successful effort by a small group of thinkers and political leaders to break new ground in an essentially traditional Islamic society for socialist teachings. The Ahali program was both moderate and inoffensive—it disclaimed any pretension to undermine traditional values, moral or religious, and often paid high tribute to patriotic and nationalist symbols.[5] Even the word socialism, which was often confused with communism and atheism, was at first avoided to escape criticism, and the main emphasis was laid on liberal social and economic doctrines expounded in a manner considered not incompatible with the country's national and social institutions. After World War II when political parties were licensed, the Ahali group organized a political party which though identified with socialist (and to its opponents with communist) doctrines, never officially included in its platform socialist principles.

---

4. See my *Independent Iraq*, pp. 69ff; *Republican Iraq*, pp. 132–137; *Political Trends in the Arab World*, pp. 106–109; and *Arab Contemporaries* (Baltimore, 1973), pp. 128–142.
5. In early Ahali circulars there was an emphasis on patriotism rather than nationalism, but later under the impact of the rising tide of nationalism, the Ahali leaders adopted the nationalist symbol.

Only Kamil al-Chadirchi, leader of the party, openly declared himself to be a socialist. It may therefore seem strange indeed that when the Arab Socialist Party (the Ba'th) was established in Iraq, the two parties never really made an attempt to cooperate, even though both often found themselves in the same camp as opponents to the ruling oligarchy.[6] The principal objection of the Ba'th to the Ahali group was its reluctance to include in its program Pan-Arab ideas which were, in Ba'thist eyes, overriding. Had the Ahali leaders been united after 1958, their program might have been appealing to the Revolutionary Regime which was not in favor of radical ideologies at the outset. Failure to agree on a moderate program of action set the stage for the appearance and future competition between two radical groups—the Ba'th and Communist parties.[7]

Yet the impact of the Ahali teachings on radical groups—Communists and Arab Socialists—was farreaching despite barriers that separated the Ahali from the other groups.[8] The Ahali was the earliest set of thinkers in the country who had the courage to expound socialist ideas at a time when the very word "socialism" was anathema to the public.[9] They proved successful in interpreting socialist ideas in a manner not incompatible with the country's national heritage and traditions. After the war, when political parties were organized, socialist candidates of various denominations (Ahali and others) could participate in general elections and address themselves to national issues as patriotically as any other leaders. True, the public was still far from being sold on collectivist slogans, but socialist leaders were no

6. Only once, shortly before the Revolution of 1958, did the Ahali and Arab Socialist leaders agree to cooperate within the framework of a United National Front, but never again was this attempt repeated.

7. For disagreement among the Ahali leaders, see my *Republican Iraq*, pp. 132–137.

8. Though most Ahali leaders have often blamed Chadirchi for his failure to get along with other leftist leaders, they all must share the blame. For Chadirchi's inability to cooperate with his own group, let alone other leaders, see my *Arab Contemporaries*, pp. 139–142.

9. Before the Ahali thinkers, Mahmud Ahmad used to write in the twenties about the wretched conditions of the poor in the cities and the countryside in order to arouse public sympathy with them, but he never openly advocated socialist doctrines (see my *Political Trends in the Arab World*, pp. 104–105). According to 'Abd al-Qadir Isma'il, one of the early Iraqi Communists and a member of the Ahali group (see my *Independent Iraq*, pp. 64, 73, 83, 117, 358–359), the first who began to preach socialism in Iraq was Husayn al-Rahhal. A member of an old Turkoman family in Iraq, he went to Germany before World War I and fell under the influence of German socialist thought during the Weimar Republic. Upon his return to Baghdad early in the twenties, he began to talk about socialism and his ideas attracted a number of young Iraqi thinkers such as Mahmud Ahmad and others, including 'Abd al-Qadir Isma'il, who formed the Ahali group (the writer's interview with 'Abd al-Qadir Isma'il, Baghdad, January 1, 1977).

longer considered as traitors and their views were taken very seriously. When some of the Ahali leaders organized the National Democratic Party, whose platform consisted of national as well as socialist symbols, a few liberal nationalists who had certain reservations about Ahali teachings joined this newly organized party on the ground that the Ahali socialist ideas were modified by the inclusion of national and democratic symbols. To some Ahali leaders, however, the platform of the National Democratic Party was a step backward in the process toward ultimate Socialism; but it was a step in the right direction because it compelled some conservative national groups (Pan-Arabs and others) to follow the example of the National Democratic Party by adopting in their programs certain socialist measures.

Second, communist teachings, though considered more destructive to national traditions and values than the Ahali's, have had a pervasive effect on the Iraqi public. Unlike the Ahali group, whose influence was confined essentially to intellectual circles, the Communists were able to penetrate into the poorer and working classes. Though the Ahali thinkers found it often difficult to persuade young men to accept views considered opposed to national traditions, it was even more difficult for Communists to prevail on the illiterate masses of the lower stratum of society to accept doctrines the essence of which, they were constantly told, was blasphemy and the denial of God. Yet in time the Communists were able to put across to the public the notion that their teachings were not all treason and blasphemy and many a believing Muslim became convinced that the Communist creed was not incompatible with Islam.

Perhaps more important was the persecution and harsh treatment which the Old Regime had inflicted on the Communists and other left-wing groups. The tenacity and endurance with which these groups resisted authority aroused the sympathy of the masses and made them appear almost as martyrs in the public eye. Upon the collapse of the Monarchy in 1958, the initial response to Communist propaganda after their reappearance from hiding or imprisonment was indeed overwhelming. The Communist creed no longer remained anathema to the masses.[10]

No less significant was the cooperation of Communists and nationalists in their opposition to Western defense plans and to all forms of colonialism and exploitation which had become not only the national demands of Iraq but of all other Arab countries. True,

---

10. See pp. 79–91, below; and my *Republican Iraq*, p. 117ff.

Communists and nationalists have often come into conflict on a number of issues, but Communist leaders appeared no less patriotic than others and they no longer were denounced as traitors. These inhibitions and mental reservations that the Ahali and Communist leaders were able to overcome, rendered easier the task of spreading the brand of socialism which the Arab Socialists expounded.

Third, the Pan-Arab movement, though confined essentially to national symbols, had perhaps the greatest influence on Arab Socialist teachings. Beginning as a liberal nationalist movement, advocating the achievement of independence and unity for the Arabs, it gradually became conservative and totalitarian in outlook when its goals were frustrated by Western European policies. In Iraq that frustration prompted the Pan-Arabs to go to war with Britain in 1941 and the movement was discredited after the victory of the democracies over totalitarianism. In the postwar years, when new political parties were organized, their programs were formulated under the impact of the ideologies which the national liberation movements advocated, stressing nationalism, democracy and socialism as basic principles. The Pan-Arab leaders took it for granted that in addition to nationalist symbols their party platform should include such social and economic principles as socialism. The adoption of collectivist principles by the Pan-Arabs was a triumph of socialism as Pan-Arab leaders had shown no interest in socialism before World War II. For this reason, the Istiqlal (independence) Party, which the neo Pan-Arabs had organized in Iraq in 1946, proved instrumental in spreading socialist ideas in conservative circles, because they upheld principles the elder Pan-Arabs had repudiated before the war.

However, though they adopted liberal principles to attract the new generation, the neo Pan-Arabs failed to impress young nationalists because they could not correlate — much less synthesize — Arab nationalist ideas with socialist principles and create a coherent system. To liberals, the neo Pan-Arabs appeared to differ but little in outlook from the pre-war leaders, as most of those who had advocated totalitarian ideas reappeared to provide guidance for the Istiqlal Party. To young nationalists, the neo Pan-Arab leaders seemed outmoded and compromising with the Old Regime, of which they were more trenchantly critical before the war.

There was accordingly the need for a more vital and articulate Pan-Arab movement which would combine nationalist with socialist doctrines and champion the cause of a new generation of nationalists against older leaders who mouthed empty slogans and represented vested interests. In an attempt to achieve these goals in Iraq, the Arab Socialists succeeded where the Pan-Arabs, old and new, had failed.

## THE BA'TH PARTY

Although this work is devoted to a study of Ba'thist rule in Iraq, a brief account of the principles and background of the Ba'th Party as a whole might be illuminating.

As has been seen, the Arab Socialist movement was a new departure in Arab politics aiming at creating a new "social order" out of the diverse streams of thought that have become the subject of public debate among reformers during and after World War II. Several intellectual groups toyed with the idea of blending these streams, especially socialism with Arab nationalism, but only one proved capable of giving it an articulate expression and presenting it to the public with coherence, greater vigor and a deeper sense of conviction than others. This group, under the dual leadership of Michel 'Aflaq and Salah al-Din al-Baytar, to mention only two principal leaders, was able to embark on a new venture in politics and to exploit the developing climate of opinion. Following the war, some nationalists and socialists began to cooperate and formulate nationalist-socialist platforms. Both agreed on a neutralist foreign policy, based essentially on the conviction that the Arabs were not prepared to be drawn into international conflicts involving issues of no concern to them. Very soon, however, cooperation among them went beyond the realm of foreign policy. Both nationalists and socialists, finding themselves concerned with the same social problems, came to a tacit agreement that nationalism and socialism were equally relevent to Arab society. The Ba'th Party, consisting essentially of active young men, who were in favor of the marriage between Arab nationalism and socialism, was both mentally and emotionally prepared to break with older leaders considered to have failed in their national duty. What helped the Ba'th to emerge as the most active Arab Socialist Party was its appeal to the new generation and its stress on Arab unity at a time when dissension in the Arab world and rivalries among Arab rulers were regarded as the root cause for Arab defeat in the Palestine wars. In its platform of "One Arab nation with an eternal message," the Ba'th seemingly offered the Arab World a panacea.[11] It is deemed outside the scope of this work to discuss the origins and the political thought of the Ba'th Party, as these have been discussed elsewhere; only the rôle of this party in Iraq will be the subject of this study.[12]

## EMERGENCE OF THE BA'TH PARTY IN IRAQ

As an ideology, the Ba'th began to spread in Iraq long before the party came into existence. Conditions in the country were favorable, as the new political parties that made their appearance after the war failed in Ba'thist eyes to meet the country's needs and aspirations and the Istiqlal Party, the embodiment of the neo Pan-Arab movement, differed but little from other parties. More specifically, the Istiqlal leaders appeared complacent and ready to compromise with the ruling oligarchy which was considered reactionary and corrupt and therefore unworthy of survival. Nor did the Istiqlal make a serious effort to bridge the gap between the new and old nationalists; it was therefore not unnatural that a more dynamic nationalist organization should become the center of attraction to young nationalists.

Ba'thist teachings began to enter into Iraq in a steady though unorganized way, first by Syrian students and teachers who went either to study or teach in Iraq, and then by Iraqi students who went to study in Syria and Lebanon. The earliest missionaries were a few young men from Alexandretta who, after their homeland had been annexed by Turkey in 1939, went to Iraq to study or settle there in a possible new home. They were welcomed by the Iraqi Government—some, who had been in high schools, enrolled in Government secondary schools to complete their education; others, who reached college level, entered Iraqi colleges; still others, who held college degrees, were appointed to

---

11. For a background on the origins and the ideas of the Ba'th, see K. S. Abu Jaber, *The Arab Ba'th Socialist Party* (Syracuse, 1966); Gordon H. Torrey, "The Ba'th—Ideology and Practice," *The Middle East Journal,* Vol. 23 (Autumn 1969), pp. 445–70; and John F. Devlin, *The Ba'th Party: A History From Its Origins to 1966* (Stanford, 1976).

12. The principal sources of Ba'thist teachings are to be found in the Ba'th Party's compilation of the proceedings of official meetings and decisions, circulars and ideological exposition by the party's leaders reprinted in *Nidal al-Ba'th* (Bayrut, 1963). For the writings of the founder of the party, see Michel 'Aflaq, *Fi Sabil al-Ba'th* (Damascus and Bayrut, 1959 and 1962); and *Ma'rakat al-Masir al-Wahid* (Damascus and Bayrut, 1958, 1959, and 1963). For the writings of other party leaders, see Munif al-Razzaz, *Ma'alim al-Hayat al-'Arabiya al-Jadida* (Cairo and Bayrut, 4th ed., 1960), *al-Tajriba al-Murra* (Bayrut, 1967); Shibli al-'Aysami, *Hizb al-Ba'th al-'Arabi al-Ishtiraki* (Baghdad, 1974), *Fi al-Thawra al-'Arabiya* (Bayrut, 1973); and Ilyas Farah, *Dirasat Fi al-Fikr al-Ishtiraki* (Bayrut, 1974), *al-Watan al-'Arabi Ba'd al-Harb al-'Alamiya al-Thaniya* (Bayrut, 1975).

teach in Government schools. True, not all Alexandrettans were Ba'thist in sympathy or affiliation—indeed, they displayed a variety of political opinions—but almost all were fervent nationalists in outlook. Fa'iz Isma'il, a student in the Law College,[13] Adham Mustafa, Sulayman al-'Isa and Wasfi al-Ghanim,[14] students at the Higher Teachers College, and Muhammad Jamil, a student in the College of Commerce and Economics were among the most active Ba'thist forerunners. Zaki al-Arsuzi, though not a member of the Ba'th Party, was very active in Arab nationalist circles in Alexandretta, before he went to teach in Baghdad and preach ultranationalist ideas not unlike Ba'thist views held by the founders of the Ba'th Party in Damascus.[15] Outside classrooms, he used to meet young men in coffee shops and private houses where, though he harangued them with anti-colonial slogans, he inspired them above all with such lofty principles as Arab unity, liberty and socialism.[16] These and other Alexandrettan nationalists inspired Iraqi students with Ba'thist ideas and participated later in the establishment of the Ba'th Party.

But it was not only Alexandrettans who preached the Ba'th gospel in Iraq. There were Arabs from other Arab countries who expounded Ba'th ideas and participated in the activities of the Ba'th Party. Some were from Trans-Jordan, where the Ba'th Party was active;[17] others came from various other Arab lands.[18] Abu al-Qasim Muhammad Karu, who left Tunisia to complete his college education in Baghdad, joined the Ba'th Party while he was still a student at the Higher

13. He was perhaps the most active Alexandrettan student in Iraq. He often travelled in the country and encouraged Iraqi students to organize Ba'thist units in various parts of the country. Hr returned to Syria in 1950 to become a member of the Ba'th Party in Damascus and rose to a Cabinet position in 1973.

14. They returned to work in Syria after graduation from college. Of these three, Mustafa became active in politics and al-'Isa, a poet, pursued a literary career.

15. Syrian Ba'th leaders today claim to derive their original inspiration from Arsuzi rather than from 'Aflaq and he is now regarded as the original initiator of the Ba'th ideology because of their disagreement with 'Aflaq and his followers. To acknowledge him as a founding father, the Syrian leaders have erected a statue near his home in Damascus in memory of his work and contribution to the party (the writer's interview with George Saddiqni, a member of the Syrian Ba'th National Command and one of the leading intellectuals of the Ba'th Party).

16. Meeting him during the war in the house of Darwish al-Miqdadi, a leading Palestinian nationalist and educator in Baghdad, I recall how with deep respect young men listened to his outspoken views about national unity and colonial "conspiracies." For a brief account of Arsuzi's ideas, see my *Political Trends in the Arab World,* pp. 206–207.

17. Ba'thists who came from Trans-Jordan were 'Adnan Lutfi, Yusuf Khurays and Mustafa Khasawna.

18. There was one from Saudi Arabia—Taha 'Ali Rashid. Originally born in southern Iraq, he became a Ba'thist member when he studied in Baghdad and returned to work in the Saudi Foreign Office in 1952.

Teachers College. He served as Secretary General of the Party for over a year (1951–1952) before he returned to become active in his country's literary life.[19]

But there was another channel through which Ba'thist ideas entered into Iraq. A number of Iraqi young men who went either for short visits or study in Damascus were naturally exposed to Ba'thist propaganda during their stay there. Some came into direct contact with 'Aflaq and Baytar who encouraged them to spread Ba'th teachings in their country. Among those who distinguished themselves as early converts and who after their return to Iraq participated in the establishment of the Iraqi Ba'th Party were 'Abd al-Rahman al-Damin and 'Abd al-Khaliq al-Khudayri. While in Damascus, they attended the first Congress to establish the Ba'th Party in 1947. Becoming Party members, they returned to organize officially an Iraqi Ba'th Party. Al-Damin was its first Secretary General who four years later left the party for health reasons.[20] Among those who went to Syria and Lebanon for study and joined the Ba'th Party while still in college, were 'Izzat Mustafa, who studied medicine in the Syrian University, Sa'dun Hamadi and Su'ad Khalil Isma'il who studied at the American University of Bayrut.

Under the influence of these early Ba'th missionaries, other young men in colleges or high schools were persuaded to adopt Ba'th teachings and in time became active members. It is exceedingly difficult to cite the names of all who became early party members, as some preferred to remain *incognito* while others, who participated in overt activities, naturally became well-known to the public. Most of them were recruited while they were still studying at one or another college. One of those who distinguished himself as an active member was Fakhri Qadduri (then a student at the College of Commerce and Economics), who became the Secretary General of the Ba'th Party in 1953, after Karu had returned to Tunisia. He relinquished the Secretaryship of and membership in the party when he left the country for study in England in 1954.[21] Others were recruited from the Colleges of Arts, Medicine,

---

19. Meeting him in Tunis (June 1966) he expressed broad nationalist views and reproached Tunisian leaders for stressing local against Pan-Arab teaching. Like other Ba'th thinkers, he advocates democracy, socialism and Arab unity.

20. He seems indeed to have been in poor health; during his absence and before he was succeeded by Karu in 1951, as Secretary General, Yahya Yasin, later Chief of Office of the Republican Palace, acted as his deputy.

21. He is now Governor of the Central Bank; he served in the Government as an economic adviser and held a Cabinet position. Among his classmates at the College of Commerce and Economics who participated in Ba'th activities and later joined the party were Shamsi Kazim, Muhammad Sa'id al-Aswad and 'Ali Salih al-Sa'di. The latter played a prominent part when the party achieved power in 1963 (see pp. 15–16, below; and my *Republican Iraq*, Chap. 8).

and Law; and from the Higher Teachers College.[22] Still others were Army officers who became party members or high school students who entered the Military College as Ba'th members and influenced classmates to enter the Party. The most important officers who became members of the Ba'th Party early in the 1950s were Ahmad Hasan al-Bakr, Salih Mahdi 'Ammash and 'Abd-Allah Sultan.[23] Fuad al-Rikabi, a graduate of the Engineering College, played an active role under the Qasim regime, as noted in another work.[24]

Rikabi, who succeeded Qadduri as Secretary General, was born in Nasiriya, a town in southern Iraq, in 1931 and joined the Ba'th Party while still in College. He became a member of the National Command when he attended the party's second congress in Damascus in 1954 and served in that capacity for the next five years. Under Rikabi's leadership, the party became increasingly restive and its teachings spread among the young generation. Some party members had already participated in the uprising of 1952 and were subsequently arrested on the ground that they professed radical views. Unknown to the authorities as Arab Socialists, they were considered as Communists in disguise. But after their participation in the abortive coup of 1956, following the tripartite attack on Egypt, their identity became known and some were arrested and detained for subversive activities. In 1957, when the opposition parties formed the United National Front, the Ba'th Party was invited to join and it participated in the underground activities which led to the eventual downfall of the Old Regime in 1958.

After the July Revolution of 1958, the Ba'th Party's activities were no longer clandestine and its leaders suddenly appeared to support the drive for Arab unity under the leadership of Egypt, of which 'Abd al-Salam 'Arif, co-author of the July Revolution, had become chief advocate in Iraq. The story of 'Arif's conflict with 'Abd al-Karim Qasim, the principal leader of the Revolution of 1958, and 'Arif's fall

---

22. Ba'thists from the College of Arts were: Ja'far Qasim Hammudi, 'Abd al-Sattar al-Duri, Karim Shintaf and Shafiq al-Kamali; from the Law College: 'Abd al-Rahman Munif and Jawad Abu al-Hub; from the Higher Teachers College (later the College of Education): Hamid al-Khalkhal, Hamdi 'Abd al-Majid, Hazim Jawad, Dahham al-Alusi, 'Abd al-Ghaffar al-Sa'igh, 'Abd-Allah Sallum and Kamil al-Sahhaf; from the Colleges of Medicine and Pharmacy: Tahsin Mu'alla and Tahir al-Rubay'i. Still others came from various schools in the countryside like Na'im Haddad, former Minister of Youth and Secretary of the Progressive National Front, studied at the Primary Teachers College of Nasiriya.

23. Other officers, like Sa'dun Ghaydan, Hardan al-Tikriti, Hasan al-Naqib and others, joined after the Revolution of 1958. Among the early Ba'th students who entered the Military College were Mundhir al-Wandawi, Muhammad 'Ali Sipahi and Salim al-Sa'di.

24. See my *Republican Iraq*, pp. 115–116, 126ff.

from power, has already been related elsewhere.[25] In that work, the Ba'th leaders' attempt on Qasim's life, the fall of Qasim and the short period in which the Ba'th Party achieved power in 1963, have been dealt with. In the present work, an account of the events and forces that brought the Ba'th Party again to power, the structure of the Ba'th regime and its working and achievements will be discussed.

25. *Ibid.*, Chap. 5

Chapter II

# The Arab Socialist Revolution

THE REVOLUTION OF 1958, carried out by the army, transferred power from civil to military hands. Had they been united, the civilian leaders who cooperated with the military might have taken responsibility, but rivalry and dissension prevented them from taking a firm stand against military rule. Despite public dissatisfaction, the military continued to rule the country. Nor was dissension confined to civilian leadership. The military, influenced by dissident civilian groups, developed their own factions. As a result, factionalism—alike in civil and military ranks—prevented any group from surviving and no regime was able to maintain stability and do constructive work.

After the fall of the Monarchy, the military leaders who carried out the Revolution of 1958 began to fall under the influence of competing parties and groups and each tried to influence the revolutionary process along one ideological line or another. Rivalry between the two top leaders—'Abd al-Karim Qasim and 'Abd al-Salam 'Arif—led to the division of civilian leaders into two camps, the Nationalists (essentially Ba'th and other Pan-Arab elements) and Communists, supported by left-wing groups. Moderate leaders who might have played a constructive role failed to reconcile the two camps and the gap between them became ever wider. Since the Nationalists supported 'Arif, who championed the cause of Arab unity, Qasim sought the support of Communists who, though in favor of Arab unity in principle, were against unity with the United Arab Republic.

After the fall of 'Arif, Qasim tried to keep a balance between Nationalists and Communists, as he was not at heart ideologically committed to Communism, but the Ba'th Party was not prepared to come to terms with Qasim and in due time became the sworn enemy of his regime. Qasim sought the support of other groups and tried by a careful balancing of forces, aptly called Qasimism (derived from his name, which literally means the "divider") to hold together the regime over which he presided by playing off one group against another. But this policy had its own limitations, as it eventually turned all elements against him and his personal rule had to depend only on the Army. Perhaps only the Communists showed readiness to support him when the Ba'th Party pursued an uncompromising opposition to his regime and the Nationalists as a whole began to regain power.

The Ba'th ringleaders were determined to overthrow the Qasim Regime at any cost, even by an attempt on Qasim's life if necessary. The first attempt in 1959, made by a few young members of the party under Rikabi's direction, failed. Not only did this incident alert Qasim into taking precautions for his safety, but it also led to an eventual disagreement on strategy and other matters among top Party leaders and to the expulsion of Rikabi from leadership of the Party.[1] It took the Ba'th leaders three or four more years before the party could recover from the setback and make another attempt to overthrow the Qasim Regime.

The Revolution of 1963, carried out by a dissident military group in league with Ba'thist leaders, replaced Qasim by his arch opponent 'Arif, who had championed the cause of Arab unity in his struggle for power with Qasim. After seizing power, 'Arif proceeded to erect his own regime irrespective of Ba'th principles and guidelines, though the Ba'th leaders were instrumental in soliciting military support for his candidacy to the highest position in the new Government.

## A TWILIGHT BA'TH RULE

As we pointed out before, it is deemed outside the scope of this work to give an account of the first Ba'th regime (February 8 to November 18,

---

1. Although Rikabi told me (December 18, 1966) that he obtained approval of the National Command leaders for his plan to assassinate Qasim (see *Republican Iraq*, p. 128, note 36), his claim has been denied by top Ba'th leaders. After he left Baghdad, Rikabi went to Cairo and became an advocate of Nasirite socialism. In the Ba'th Party's Fourth Congress in Bayrut (1960), Rikabi, who attended the meetings, was dropped from membership of the National Command. Upon reproaching the Ba'th for deviationism, he was expelled from the party (the writer's interview with 'Ali Salih al-Sa'di, who led the drive against him, and Tariq 'Aziz [Baghdad, January 1977]).

1963), since it has been dealt with in another work;² but the impact of Ba'th cooperation with 'Arif on subsequent events calls for a re-assessment. Young and inexperienced, the Ba'th leaders contended that because 'Arif had taken a stand against the Qasim regime, cooperation with him after they achieved power would enhance the prestige of their party even though he had never professed to be a member of the Ba'th Party nor did he contemplate joining it after that party achieved power. He had, it is true, come into conflict with Qasim on the question of Arab unity—a matter on which he shared the views of the Ba'th Party—but he never really accepted any other Ba'th principle, least of all its social and economic doctrines. After he became President, even his ideas on Arab unity had undergone important changes. Like Qasim, he became more interested in liquidating opponents and consolidating his rule than in carrying out abstract principles.³

'Ali Salih al-Sa'di, perhaps the principal leader who brought about collaboration between 'Arif and the Ba'th, discovered only after the events how unwittingly he had acted at 'Arif's instance to antagonize Communists who were more opposed to 'Arif's reactionary ideas than to his party's ideology. Sa'di's moves, though supported by some Ba'th leaders, were opposed by the majority who rightly considered them too vindictive and contrary to the party's best interests as it aroused unwarranted opposition at a time when the party's position was still precarious.⁴

But 'Arif, who proved more calculating than his collaboraters had realized, turned out to be a greater danger to the Ba'th Party than the Communists. His regime—first under his rule and then under his older brother's—won such ready support of the military that the Ba'th leaders were dropped from power without much difficulty. The inherent weakness of the Ba'th Party was perennial dissension and the ensuing struggle for power among the top Ba'th leaders. Consequently the younger 'Arif was able to govern the country for the next three years without serious opposition and only too late did they realize that their

---

2. See my *Republican Iraq* (London, 1969), Chap. 8.

3. Even his attachment to Arab unity, to which he continued to pay lip service, began to fade. Despite an outward cordiality to Nasir, he privately made derogatory remarks about him and went as far as to show, as Tariq 'Aziz once told me (January 12, 1977), more dislike for him than Qasim.

4. In an interview with the writer (January 17, 1977), Sa'di said that he had his own reasons and was not motivated by 'Arif's personal reasons for his opposition to the Communists. He also said that he suggested 'Arif for the Presidency in 1963 to be only a figurehead of the Ba'th regime.

real opponents were not the Communists but the 'Arif brothers and vested interests.

After its fall from power, the Ba'th Party suffered an internal crisis which became for a while the chief preoccupation of its leaders. Two major events might be singled out as the most important which prolonged the crisis. First, Sa'di's hold over the Iraqi Regional Command and his collaboration with the Syrian leaders encouraged 'Arif to exploit the rivalry among the Ba'th ringleaders in order to weaken the party as a whole. Second, Jamal 'Abd al-Nasir, President of the United Arab Republic, showed readiness to cooperate with the Syrian leaders as a whole but not with Syrian Ba'th leaders who supported Syria's secession from unity with Egypt in 1961. Sa'di, in a drive to dominate the National Command, supported the pro-Nasirite Syrian leaders who contributed to the fall of 'Aflaq and Baytar from leadership of the party in 1964, presumably because they have fallen into disfavor with President Nasir.[5] In Iraq, 'Arif gave indirect encouragement to Sa'di's followers by restricting the activities of his opponents. As a result, the struggle for power among the Iraqi Ba'th leaders was intensified, especially between Sa'di and his opponents, led by Ahmad Hasan al-Bakr. The dissension within the party was not easily resolved—it took two party congresses held in 1964 and 1965 to patch up differences and purge the group led by Sa'di. At first, the National Command appointed a temporary Regional Command for Iraq under the leadership of 'Abd al-Karim al-Shaykhli, an active member who had taken part in the attempt on Qasim's life, until the two rival factions could be reconciled. Needless to say, the struggle for power continued unabated.

In 1964 Ahmad Hasan al-Bakr, perhaps the most highly respected member in the party, was elected member of the National Command at the party's Seventh Congress. This step, enhancing the position of the Bakr faction, brought the struggle with Sa'di almost to an end. Meanwhile, Saddam Husayn, a vigilant member of the party, who had also taken part in the attempt on Qasim's life, became member of the Regional Command and acted as its Secretary. He proved to be instrumental first in lining up support for Bakr's leadership and then in virtually putting an end to internal dissension. In May 1965, the National Command appointed Bakr Secretary General of the Iraqi

---

5. 'Aflaq and Baytar were subsequently expelled from the country and condemned to death *in absentia*.

Regional Command and Saʻdi was expelled from the party. This step, signaling the closure of internal dissension, gave an opportunity to other younger leaders to make their way up in the party's hierarchy. Upon his release from prison in 1966, Saddam Husayn became deputy Secretary General of the Regional Command.

### EVENTS LEADING UP TO THE REVOLUTION OF 1968

Under the first ʻArif regime (1963-1966), a wide-spread feeling in the country began publicly to be expressed that the time had come for ending military rule and that the appointment of ʻAbd al-Rahman Bazzaz as first civilian Premier since the downfall of the Monarchy was a step in the right direction. ʻArif, though he entered politics by resort to the Army, was himself in favor of a civilian regime; he was able to neutralize rival military factions by a careful balancing of power and acted as a civilian head of state.[6] The regime over which he presided received the support of the business community partly because of the relaxation of collectivist measures that had been introduced earlier and partly because the agreement with Mulla Mustafa of Barzan to end the Kurdish war was satisfactory to both Kurds and Arabs.

But ʻArif's rule was shortlived. He died in a helicopter accident,[7] and was succeeded by his older brother who possessed neither his ability nor his prestige. The second ʻArif's elevation to the presidency was partly due to the fact that he was a brother of the late President and partly because he was the only figure rival candidates in the Army could agree upon. Consequently, the military, who had been brought under control by the first ʻArif, resumed their ascendency under his brother's benign regime. One of the factions, the military Nasirites, that moved to overthrow the second ʻArif regime by force, was headed by Brigadier ʻArif ʻAbd al-Razzaq, but the attempt in June 1966 was quickly foiled and President ʻArif began to feel more confident of his position. Meanwhile, Premier Bazzaz proved more independent in his actions than the military had expected and began to talk about the need to hold elections for a representative Assembly to reestablish legitimacy and parliamentary rule. Thereupon the military began to bring pressure on

---

6. I have it on the authority of some who knew ʻArif intimately that because he had been the victim of rivalry among military factions under the Qasim regime, he was determined to keep the Army out of politics. It is also possible that he desired personal rule by selecting a civilian Premier who enjoyed some popularity among the intelligentsia but who was also ultimately dependent on his support.

7. For a brief account of this tragic event, see my *Republican Iraq*, pp. 262–264.

'Arif to remove Bazzaz and the relations between President and Premier were necessarily affected. It did not take long for Bazzaz, after a stormy meeting with 'Arif, to tender his resignation in August 1966.

Conditions began to deteriorate under the second 'Arif regime soon after Bazzaz's fall. The reasons for this deterioration were not hard to seek. Not only power remained in military hands, but factionalism in the Army was accentuated and leadership changed hands, not always in accordance with what was in the country's best interests. Bazzaz was succeeded by Colonel Naji Talib who, though conciliatory to rival groups and moderate in outlook, was inactive and no constructive work was done during his tenure of office. He was succeeded by General Tahir Yahya in 1967 who had held the Premiership under the first 'Arif regime and proved to be an ineffective administrator. Very soon, however, he was charged with corruption and economic conditions were far from improving.

The defeat in the Arab-Israeli war led to intense unrest and to demands for fundamental changes in political and economic policies. Rival factions, led by General 'Abd al-'Aziz al-'Uqayli, former Minister of Defense, and 'Abd al-Ghani al-Rawi, former Deputy Premier, and others put forth demands for free elections, relaxations of restrictive collectivist measures, and a policy independent of the United Arab Republic. In an attempt to control military factions opposed to the regime, all retired senior Army officers were carefully watched, but these measures could by no means stop the military from agitation and clandestine activities.

Meanwhile, outside military circles, the Ba'th Party had become restive. However, splits within the party, resulting from the action of Syrian leaders to expel Michel 'Aflaq and his supporters from the National Command, affected the attitude of the Iraqi Ba'th leaders towards the Syrian Ba'th regime. Since Salah Jadid, Syria's new strong man, advocated a Marxist policy, the Iraqi Ba'th leaders were divided on the issue. Some, led by Bakr and Saddam, were opposed to Jadid and supported 'Aflaq. Others, in favor of Marxism, and opposed to 'Aflaq, supported Jadid. After successive purges in which dissident elements were eliminated, Bakr and Saddam were able to control the Regional Command and the crisis was finally resolved. By 1967, the Ba'th Party was at last ready to participate actively in opposition activities. In the fall of 1967 the political atmosphere in the country became very tense.

As a reaction to the resolutions taken at Khartum (September 1967) concerning the Arab-Israeli conflict, considered by Iraqi leaders to have been ineffective, demonstrations began to take place in Baghdad. In one of these demonstrations (September 6, 1967) the resumption of war with Israel was demanded. The Ba'th Party, more outspoken in its criticism of Western policies, organized a demonstration which proceeded through Baghdad's main street, and Ahmad Hasan al-Bakr, carried by some of his admirers, made a speech at the Southern Gate, in which he criticized the Government's attitude toward the West and toward Israel in particular, and charged Iraq's rulers with corruption and inefficiency. Meanwhile, five Ministers, in protest against the decision to resume oil supplies to Western countries, and a sixth, dissatisfied with the policy towards the Kurds, resigned. President 'Arif, who was outside the country, cancelled an official visit to Algeria in order to fly back to Baghdad and persuade the six Ministers to withdraw their resignations. In order to tighten control over the opposition, a new press law was issued on December 3 restricting freedom of the press and licenses of 16 privately-owned Baghdad papers were revoked, replaced by five papers controlled by the Government.[8]

Despite these actions opposition to the regime continued. On January 12, 1968, students at the University of Baghdad, inspired by the opposition, went on strike presumably on the ground of need for changes in the administrative process of the University, but they also demanded a return to parliamentary government. It was reported that four students had been injured in clashes between supporters and opponents of the strike.[9] On January 13 six Ministers, without publicly giving a reason, resigned. Though they were replaced without much difficulty, President 'Arif declared at the swearing-in of the new Ministers that the resignations were connected with a wave of opposition to the regime, and warned against conspiracies inspired by imperialists and foreign oil companies. It was rumored that the Government had decided to grant a Western firm a concession to exploit sulphur and to sign a new agreement with the Iraq Petroleum Company (IPC) granting it certain privileges considered virtually to

---

8. The five papers were issued under the auspices of the Ministry of Culture and National Guidance. Only one privately owned paper, the Kurdish paper *al-Ta'akhi*, issued in Arabic, was allowed to reappear in February 1968.

9. Although the President of the University was on good terms with the Prime Minister, the faculty and the students were divided resulting in clashes between the two factions.

nullify Public Law 80.[10] Six Ministers threatened to resign to stop action by the Government to sign the agreement.

Meanwhile, the Ba'th Party, joined by other opposition leaders, including Nasirites and other right-wing nationalists and a dozen retired army officers, issued a statement on April 16 demanding the removal of Premier Tahir Yahya, the formation of a coalition Government and the reestablishment of a National Assembly with powers to legislate and control the Government. In a petition to the President, embodying these demands, it was stated that "it is no longer possible for Iraq to carry out political and economic reforms without returning to constitutional life, with an Assembly, elected by universal suffrage."[11] In June it was rumored that two or three Ministers resigned because of a disagreement with Premier Yahya's policies. Thereupon General Yahya himself resigned on July 15, but was asked to continue in office and rejected the demands of those who petitioned for his dismissal.

In response to calls for the restoration of a parliamentary system, the Government promised that general elections would be held in 1968, a year after the three-year period declared by the former regime in 1964. But the 'Arif regime declared in 1968 that it would be extended for another two years—until 1970.[12] In a conversation with President 'Arif in the summer of 1968, the writer learned that the Government had no intention to return to a parliamentary regime operated by a multiple party system as the opposition leaders demanded, but that a National Assembly composed of members drawn from a single party organized as a Socialist Union, after the pattern of Egypt, was contemplated.[13] To meet reiterated demands for an elected Assembly, it was announced that an appointed provisional Legislative Council was under consideration which would draft an electoral law and a permanent Constitution for submission to the elected Assembly. Once convened, this Assembly was to take over the Cabinet's legislative powers. But these announcements, carrying no conviction, were not taken seriously.

Meanwhile, unrest continued among the Kurds who resented the Government's failure to implement the agreement of 1966. Clashes

10. This law, issued under the Qasim regime in 1961, deprived the IPC of all land except the fields under actual operation by IPC. For Law 80 see my *Republican Iraq*, p. 164.
11. Copies of the petition were made public in memographed circulars.
12. The reasons for the postponement, it was then announced, were the difficult circumstances through which the Arab nation was passing and the need for a more accurate calculation of those eligible to vote.
13. The writer's interview with President 'Arif (Baghdad, June 18, 1968).

occurred between Mulla Mustafa and some of his young Kurdish opponents—Jalal al-Talabani and Ibrahim Ahmad—leaders of the Kurdish Democratic Party.[14] An attempt on Talabani's life was made in December 1967, and some 19 Kurds were killed in the inter-factional clashes in March 1968. When President 'Arif went to France for a visit in February to conclude an agreement on the sale of arms, Mulla Mustafa sent a letter to President de Gaulle appealing to him not to supply arms to Iraq because the Kurds feared the possibility of a new offensive against them by the Iraqi Government. Thereupon, a request urging the French Government to supply arms only on condition that it would not be used against the Kurds was echoed in certain French circles. President 'Arif dismissed the suggestion that the French arms would be used against the Kurds as absurd. Although no important arms agreement was concluded, it was understood that France agreed to supply Iraq with some 70 light armored cars. A number of trade agreements, considered as encouraging signs of cooperation between France and Iraq, were concluded while 'Arif was in the French capital.

Criticism of corruption was directed in the main against the Yahya Government, but since President 'Arif could do nothing constructive to inspire confidence, the regime as a whole was undermined and its replacement by another was expected at any moment. Protests and agitations, however, though arousing public concern, could not effect a change in the system. The opposition leaders therefore had only one weapon at their disposal—the Army.

## THE REVOLUTION OF 1968

On July 17, 1968, ten years almost to the day after the July Revolution of 1958, the regime was overthrown for the fourth time by the military which indicates that the revolutionary process had not yet reached its full development. The reasons given for the change—Premier Yahya's corruption, Kurdish protests and dissatisfaction, submission to foreign pressures, etc.—were only circumstantial events and affectations that triggered the process of violent change, but the root cause lies in the fact that the regime had neither been sufficiently consolidated nor attained legitimacy by popular consent. Both in the Army and outside official circles, there existed certain groups that were determined to effect a change by force if their demands to participate in the political process were not heeded. Since the regime was not prepared to tolerate

---

14. See pp. 91ff., below.

the opposition its tenure of office ultimately depended on the loyalty of the Army. Indeed, the Army had already become the arbiter between the group in power and the opposition. If the Army—more specifically the leading officers who controlled the Army—ever defected, the fate of the regime was sealed.

The major military units on which the 'Arif regime depended were the Republican Guard, the Baghdad Garrison and Military Intelligence. The first was headed by Colonel 'Abd al-Rahman Ibrahim al-Dawud, a protégé of President 'Arif, and assisted by Colonel Sa'dun Ghaydan, Commander of a Tank Brigade. The principal task of these two officers was to shield the Republican Palace from a sudden attack and protect the President's own life. The second, under the command of Colonel Hammad Shihab, seemingly a neutral officer, was stationed at the outskirts of the nation's capital to defend it from an attack against any possible uprising in other military units. The third, under the control of Colonel 'Abd al-Razzaq al-Nayif, presumably a protégé of President 'Arif, was to keep an eye on and report to the President on all military activities; he was indeed in a position to know if there was any plot—or even the rumor of a plot—in any of the units throughout the country. The influence of these officers who had direct access to the President, had increased considerably because it was indeed upon them that the 'Arif regime ultimately depended. Nor had President 'Arif, who was personally responsible for their appointment, any doubt about the loyalty of his Praetorian Guard.

But these arch officers, occupying such an important position in the regime, had not been immune to outside influences. They had often been approached by various ideological leaders, each competing to tempt them to shift their loyalty in favor of causes considered more worthy of support than the 'Arif throne. They were warned that if the regime with which they were identified was ever overthrown by mutiny in military units outside the capital, they would not merely be relieved and disgraced but might also undergo trial for having given support to a regime that was considered corrupt and inefficient. These and other persuasive arguments were put forth to them by a number of the Government's opponents to induce them to defect from 'Arif. And these officers, especially Nayif and Dawud, who had already become conscious of their power, had their own ambitions and plans for the future. They seem to have tacitly come to the conclusion that if 'Arif were ever overthrown, they would be the successors on whose shoulders the mantle of the 'Arif regime should fall. Keenly feeling that they were in need of a front that would disguise their naked personal ambition, they agreed to cooperate with the Ba'th Party because it was thought it might provide legitimacy for their rule. With a poor record under the first 'Arif regime, they felt the Ba'th Party would be the ideal tool in their hands. For this reason they agreed to cooperate with its leaders. Not aware of the real intentions of Nayif and Dawud, the Ba'th leaders agreed to cooperate only as a means to achieve power. Once they were in the saddle, it was tacitly agreed among them that they would bridle Nayif and Dawud at the earliest possible moment.

However, on the eve of the contemplated date of the uprising (intended to be on July 14, in order to identify the aims of the July Revolution of 1968 with the July Revolution of 1958), Nayif and Dawud seem to have had second thoughts and informed Bakr that they had changed their minds about the feasibility of a military uprising. It was conjectured that the two arch officers either decided to mutiny single-handed, without collaboration with the Ba'th Party, or that they merely contended that they would be better off if they remained loyal to the 'Arif regime. Perhaps they also suspected that some Ba'th leaders did not quite feel the need for cooperation with them and, therefore, tried to let the Ba'th Party know that no action could possibly be undertaken without their support. Bakr is reported to have replied that his followers were not prepared to call off action and that they were determined to carry out the plan without their assistance.[15] The date of the uprising, however, was changed from July 14 to July 17 for logistical reasons.

On July 16, while the Ba'th leaders were reviewing the situation in a secret meeting at Bakr's house, Dawud sent word intimating that he and Nayif were now quite prepared to cooperate with the Ba'th Party if Nayif were offered the Premiership of the new regime. Dawud, who seems to have enjoyed the confidence of Bakr, had prevailed over Nayif to change his opinion and promised to secure for him the Premiership if he cooperated with the Ba'th in the joint venture. Bakr and the ringleaders, without sounding out the opinion of other party members (some seem to have been opposed to Nayif but not necessarily to Dawud) accepted Dawud's offer on the ground that its rejection might prompt Nayif, Chief of Military Intelligence, to reveal the plot to higher authorities and precipitate their arrest. Accordingly, they felt they were bound to accept the offer as an

---

15. The writer's interview with President Bakr (Baghdad, August 14, 1974).

expediency if they were ever to achieve power, but they were determined to get rid of Nayif and Dawud once they had consolidated their position.[16]

From a military point of view, the plan proved a master stroke, as the regime over which 'Arif had presided quickly collapsed without resistance. The uprising started in the wee hours of July 17, when a few young Ba'thists in military uniform led by Bakr, Hardan al-Tikriti and Anwar 'Abd al-Qadir, were allowed to enter the Republican Palace because Colonel Dawud, Commander of the Republican Guard, had given instructions to throw open the doors for them. At the same time Dawud had put the Brigade under his command on the alert and at 3:00 a.m. ordered the Brigade to surround the Palace and fire four shots to announce the launching of the military uprising. Meanwhile, Tikriti and 'Abd al-Qadir were on their way to the Republican Palace to see President 'Arif. He was awakened to receive visitors who called to break the news to him that a military uprising was underway. He was told that if he surrendered without opposition and left the country, his life would be spared and his pension guaranteed. Perhaps mentally unprepared to accept this sudden shift of fortune, 'Arif tried in vain to contact officers likely to support him; he called Dawud and Ghaydan who told him that it was hopeless to resist and that the Army was in revolt. It is said that Bakr assured him on the telephone both the safety of his life and payment of his pension if he left the country. Alone and helpless, 'Arif immediately surrendered. Tikriti offered to take him to his (Tikriti's) home and a few hours later he escorted him to the airport where a plane was ready to take him outside the country. He first went to London, where his wife had been undergoing medical treatment, and shortly afterward to Istanbul, where he was given asylum, to live in retirement.

It might, indeed, seem strange that 'Arif had been taken by surprise, completely unaware of the move against him. Some held that 'Arif was not unaware of Ba'th clandestine activities, but he could do nothing to stop it as he failed to command respect in high military circles. Once called by 'Arif to his office, Dawud denied that he had any intention of conspiring against the regime. Bakr and some of his followers, it is said, had also been questioned by 'Arif and they also denied that they had anything to do with alleged conspiracies against the regime. President 'Arif is said to have warned against intrigues, but his warnings had little or no impact on his opponents.

16. Cf. *Taqrir al-Siyasi al-Sadir 'An al-Mu'tamar al-Qatri al-Thamin* [Political Report of the Eighth Regional Congress], January 1974 (Baghdad, 1974), p. 34.

## A Coalition Government

In accordance with a prior agreement between the Ba'th leaders and the Nayif-Dawud group the new regime was envisioned to be a form of a National Government or a coalition in which various shades of opinion would be represented. All the so-called "progressive" elements were invited to cooperate on the basis of a program acceptable to all. Negotiations resulted in an agreement only between the Ba'th and the Nayif-Dawud group, supported by a few independent political figures.

The first official step taken after 'Arif had been deposed was the establishment of a Revolutionary Command Council (RCC) which assumed supreme authority. It was a self-appointed body whose members were drawn partly from the Regional Command of the Ba'th Party and partly from the Nayif-Dawud group.[17] The first communiqué issued by the RCC was to relieve 'Arif of his position as President, replaced by Ahmad Hasan al-Bakr. His candidacy was pressed by Ba'th leaders against others who would have joined or given support to the new regime, but Bakr was the only candidate acceptable to all because of his seniority, prestige and congenial character.[18]

Having been installed as President, Bakr invited Nayif to form the new Government. The Cabinet, consisting essentially of Ba'thist and right-wing elements, was not a truly National Government, as was perhaps expected, but a coalition of two groups—the Ba'th and the Nayif-Dawud group. Though the Ba'th was given the highest position in the state—the Presidency—the most important portfolios were reserved to the Nayif-Dawud group.[19]

---

17. The Ba'thist members were: General Ahmad Hasan al-Bakr, Gen. Hardan al-Tikriti, Lieut. Gen. Salih Mahdi 'Ammash. The Nayif-Dawud group was represented by Col. Nayif and Col. Dawud. Col. Hammad Shihab and Col. Sa'dun Ghaydan were considered independents. Bakr was entrusted with the Presidency of the RCC. See the *Official Gazette*, Baghdad, July 18, 1968.

18. The present writer learned that, in a meeting between leaders of various shades of opinion on the morrow of the "Revolution," Brig. 'Abd al-Aziz al-'Uqayli, an officer who had a few army supporters and had been a former contender to the Presidency, offered support if he were considered as a possible candidate. Gen. Hardan al-Tikriti, who enjoyed perhaps higher prestige in military circles, was another candidate.

19. The composition of the Cabinet was as follows:

| | |
|---|---|
| 'Abd al-Razzaq al-Nayif: Prime Minister | (Nayif-Dawud group) |
| Nasir al-Hani: Foreign Affairs | (Nayif-Dawud group) |
| Ibrahim 'Abd al-Rahman al-Dawud: Defense | (Nayif-Dawud group) |
| Salih Kubba: Finance | (Independent, sympathetic to Nayif and Dawud) |
| Salih Mahdi 'Ammash: Interior | (Ba'th) |
| Muslih Naqshbandi: Justice | (Kurd) |
| Ahmad 'Abd al-Sattar al-Jawari: Education | (Ba'th) |

No sooner did the Government begin to function than a conflict between the Ba'th and the Nayif-Dawud group ensued, both inside and outside official circles. Only on negative matters did they agree—opposition to leaders of the former regime, most of whom were arrested, and an attempt to put an end to exploitation and corrupt practices—but on essential issues they seem to have reached no agreement. Premier Nayif made several statements to the press unfavorable to socialism which were unacceptable to Ba'th leaders—he declared that his country's experiment with certain socialist measures had failed and that the whole question of continuing them was under study by the Government. President Bakr, on the other hand, pointed out that the new regime was in favor of an Arab nationalist and socialist policy to which his party was committed and would expect its representatives in the Government to carry out. No less significant was the conflict on foreign affairs. The Nayif-Dawud group was inclined to cooperate with Western Powers and paid lip service to Arab unity while the Ba'th leaders were opposed to cooperation with Nasir and demanded a neutralist foreign policy (though Nasir al-Hani, Foreign Minister, said that the Government was not considering the resumption of diplomatic relations with the United States because of its support of Israel against Arab interests.) Apart from official statements, Nayif was rightly identified as friendly toward Britain and his Foreign Minister friendly toward the United States.[20] However, the Ba'th leaders,

| | |
|---|---|
| Anwar 'Abd al-Qadir al-Hadithi: Labor & Social Affairs | (Ba'th) |
| 'Izzat Mustafa: Health | (Ba'th) |
| Taha al-Haj Ilyas: Culture and National Guidance | (Independent) |
| Mahmud Shith Khattab: Communication | (Independent) |
| Muhsin al-Qazwini: Agriculture | (Independent) |
| 'Abd al-Majid al-Jumayli: Agrarian Reform | (Independent) |
| Ihsan Shirazad: Public Works and Housing | (Kurd) |
| Muhammad Ya'qub al-Sa'idi: Planning | (Independent) |
| 'Abd-Allah al-Naqshbandi: Economy | (Kurd) |
| Khalid Makki al-Hashimi: Industry | (Ba'th) |
| Mahdi Hantush: Oil and Mineral Resources | (Independent) |
| Gha'ib Mawlud Mukhlis: Municipal and Rural Affairs | (Ba'th) |
| Dhiyab al-'Alkawi: Youth Affairs | (Ba'th) |
| Muhsin Diza'i: Development of Northern Iraq | (Kurd) |
| 'Abd al-Karim Zaydan: Minister of State for Waqf | (Independent) |
| Jasim Kazim al-'Azzawi: Arab Unity Affairs | (Ba'th) |
| Rashid al-Rifa'i: Minister of State for Presidential Affairs | (Ba'th) |
| Naji 'Isa al-Khalaf: Minister of State | (Independent) |
| Kazim Mu'alla: Minister of State for Liaison With the RCC | (Ba'th) |

20. Nasir al-Hani, Foreign Minister, made a statement to the press that the agreement for exploitation of promising Iraqi oil fields made a year earlier with a French company was still valid, though the man who negotiated the agreement, Adib al-Jadir, President of the Iraqi National Oil Co., was arrested for bribery, presumably in connection with the oil negotiations.

ideological in outlook, sought to counteract Western influence on matters considered harmful to Arab interests.

In domestic affairs, Nayif declared that he was in favor of an understanding with Mulla Mustafa of Barzan as a step to settle the Kurdish question on terms agreeable to Kurds and Arabs. For this reason, he included four Kurds in the Cabinet in order to win Kurdish goodwill. The Ba'th leaders, unwilling to give the Kurds concessions likely to affect national unity, demanded a firm stand on the Kurdish question. As a result, an atmosphere of suspicion surrounded the relationships between the Ba'th and the Nayif-Dawud group and a struggle for power between them ensued. Nayif was confident that his position was strong enough not to concede to Ba'thist demands since the portfolios of Defense, Finance and Foreign Affairs were under the control of his group. He may have also been led to believe that public opinion was in favor of his policy. Above all, he felt that it was, after all, he and Dawud who were instrumental in carrying out the coup against the 'Arif regime and that the Ba'th Party had merely been the beneficiary of the July Revolution (1968) which, without his efforts, would not have been possible to achieve.

However, the Ba'th leaders felt differently about the matter. True, they cooperated with Dawud, whom they found more agreeable and hoped that he might eventually become sympathetic to their party; but they had grave misgivings about Nayif whom they considered as too ambitious, vain and opportunistic. Against their wishes, the Ba'th leaders held, Dawud disclosed the secret plan of the July Revolution to Nayif and consequently brought about his participation by entrusting him with the Premiership. For this reason, the top Ba'th leaders were taken to task by some who were opposed to the Nayif-Dawud group and were pressed to assure the party that they would purge the regime of the Nayif-Dawud group at the earliest possible moment.[21]

Matters came to a head on the question of reinstating over one hundred young officers either members of the Ba'th Party or sympathetic to it who had been purged from the Army following the fall of the Ba'th Party from power in November 1963. Because the return of these officers to duty would enhance the influence of the Ba'th Party in the armed forces, Nayif naturally refused. Negotiations with the IPC were partly opposed by the Ba'th leaders as a matter of principle and partly to retaliate against Nayif's opposition to Ba'thist attempts at infiltrating the Army and the bureaucracy. Nayif's desire to come to an

---

21. Al-Taqrir al-Siyasi, *op. cit.*, pp. 36–37.

understanding with the IPC resulted in the spread of a rumor that he was prepared to give the IPC certain privileges considered contrary to Public Law 80 which transferred full control of oil affairs to the Iraqi National Oil Co. The Ba'th, opposed to any settlement that would limit the country's rights as defined under Public Law 80, criticized Nayif for compromising the national interest. Indeed, the Ba'th Party was on record that it was in favor of the nationalization of the oil industry in principle. Nayif's willingness to cooperate with the IPC was construed as a gesture to obtain Western support for his group against the Ba'th Party. But neither the Ba'th nor the Nayif-Dawud group seems to have won public support in this controversy.

## FALL OF THE NAYIF-DAWUD GROUP FROM POWER

To change a regime by the polls or civil resistance has become almost impossible ever since the Army moved to overthrow the monarchy in 1958 and took control of authority. Since the Ba'th Party twice succeeded in seizing power by military action—in 1963 and 1968—it was clear that no group could stay long in power without military support. Therefore, to purge the regime of the Nayif-Dawud group was impossible as long as the key positions, political and military, were held by its leaders, even though the Ba'th Party held a number of important posts, including the Presidency and the post of Chief of the General Staff. Consequently, the Ba'th leaders deemed it necessary to oust the Nayif-Dawud group by an essentially tactical maneuver and avoid a military conflict, the outcome of which was uncertain.

The Ba'th purge was carried out in two steps. The first was by sending Dawud, Minister of Defense, on a mission out of the country. Because the Iraqi Government had committed itself to send a force to Jordan, as noted before, the Ba'th leaders declared that the time had come to carry out this commitment. Dawud, unaware of the real motive, was persuaded to proceed to Jordan on July 29 for a three-day visit to inspect the Iraqi force as a sign of moral support to Jordan against Israeli pressures. As a result, Hardan al-Tikriti, Chief of Staff, was able to take full control of the Army during the absence of the Minister of Defense.

The next step was to keep Prime Minister Nayif away from his office while a military takeover by the Ba'th would be carried out. On July 30, a day after Dawud had arrived in Jordan, Nayif was invited to lunch with President Bakr at the Republican Palace. To give the impression that nothing unusual was expected to happen, Salih Kubba, Minister of Finance, was called to discuss the budget and other financial matters with the President on the morning of the same day. On his way out, the Minister of Finance saw Premier Nayif before he entered the Presidential Palace and reported to him with great satisfaction his conversations with President Bakr.

Upon entering the Palace, Nayif was warmly received by the President with whom he had a long conversation during the luncheon. After lunch, Nayif was shown into a waiting room before he was to take leave from the President. No sooner had he entered than four officers led by Saddam Husayn broke into the room and, with pistols pointed at him, he was told that he was under arrest. Alone and overwhelmed, he surrendered at once. Meanwhile, Colonel Sa'dun Ghaydan, Commander of the Republican Palace Guard, issued an order to place the Brigade on the alert.[22]

Nayif, unaware of what was going on outside the Palace, was kept waiting under arrest for the next three or four hours. It is said that word was sent back and forth between him and the top Ba'th leaders. It was agreed that he would be entrusted with a special mission abroad, and that his life would be spared if he left the country. From the Palace he was taken directly to the Military Airport. A cable was dispatched to the Moroccan Government to the effect that Nayif was on his way to Morocco as the head of a special mission. Nayif, though accepting the appointment, went first to Madrid for a visit. Dawud was given instructions first to remain in Jordan as head of the military mission and soon after, both he and Nayif, were first appointed as Ambassadors in residence abroad and then retired in 1970.

The coup was bloodless and caused no disturbances in running the business of the Government. Since both Nayif and Dawud were out of the country, their followers accepted the *fait accompli* without lifting a finger. At last, the Ba'th leaders were able to have full control of authority; they moved at once to detain or arrest all opponents whom they considered dangerous to the regime. In accordance with a law to cleanse the bureaucracy of corruption, a host of civil servants considered unfriendly to the Ba'th Party were either retired or relieved of duty.

## "THE REVOLUTION OF JULY 30, 1968"

Although the July Revolution of 1968 was a joint venture with the Nayif-Dawud group, the majority of Ba'th members were critical of the

---

22. It is said that General Hardan al-Tikriti, Chief of Staff, also issued orders to the Army to be on the alert.

arrangement and demanded a wholly Ba'thist regime. Some top leaders seem to have given the impression that their initial cooperation with the Nayif-Dawud group was dictated by the force of circumstances and that purging of the Nayif-Dawud group from the regime had already been decided upon before the Revolution of July 17, 1968. Though this rationale may have been given after the events, official records confirm that the Ba'th Party accepted cooperation with Nayif and Dawud only temporarily until it had taken full control. In his speech to the nation on July 30, 1968, President Bakr declared that opposition to Ba'th principles prompted the Ba'th leaders to drop from power Nayif and Dawud. He went on to denounce Nayif and Dawud as corrupt elements and opposed to liberal reforms to which the Ba'th Party was committed. The time to carry out the Party's goals, he said, had come and the march of events led at last to "The Revolution of July 30, 1968."[23]

The ideological reasons for the purge may well be a rationalization for an underlying struggle for power between two rival groups. Nayif and Dawud were not members of the Ba'th Party nor did they intend to join it. They advocated free enterprise rather than collectivist doctrines and though they agreed to follow a neutralist policy, they leaned at heart toward the Western rather than the Eastern Powers. Their cooperation with the Ba'th Party was intended to provide a political justification for their rebellion against the 'Arif regime and were indeed waiting for the opportunity to purge the Ba'th leaders from the coalition. It was to this matter that Bakr, in his speech of July 30, 1968, pointed out that Nayif and Dawud were conspiring to subordinate the RCC to the Cabinet and concentrate power in their hands. Nayif and Dawud, to be sure, tried to entrust responsible positions to an increasing number of their own followers and to reduce Ba'thist elements in the regime. But these moves, in Ba'thist eyes, were but a step to overthrow the Ba'th Party from power. For these and other reasons the Ba'th leaders decided to act promptly and drop Nayif and Dawud before they acted against them. It was a bloodless Revolution. Some have called it the White Revolution.[24]

23. For text of the speech, see the *Official Gazette*, Baghdad, August 10, 1968.
24. Ibid., p. 394; and *al-Taqrir al-Siyasi*, op cit., p. 39. For a discussion of the pattern of revolutionary changes, see Phebe Ann Marr, "The Iraqi Revolution: A Case Study of Army Rule," *Orbis* Vol. 14 (1970) pp. 714–39.

Chapter III

# Arab Socialists in Power

THE DOOR was now thrown open to the Ba'th Party to take full control and to develop the country in accordance with the party's goals and guidelines. President Ahmad Hasan al-Bakr, holding the post of Prime Minister in addition to the Presidency, became nominally the head of all branches of Government and the national forces. He also presided over the RCC and the Regional Command of the Ba'th Party. Most of the Cabinet posts, especially those vacated by the Nayif-Dawud group, were given to Ba'th leaders.[1] Though not a member of the Ba'th Party, Ibrahim Faysal al-Ansari was appointed Chief of Staff. Since President

---

1. The composition of the Cabinet was as follows:
Ahmad Hasan al-Bakr: President and Prime Minister
Hardan al-Tikriti: Defense
'Abd al-Karim al-Shaykhli: Foreign Affairs
Amin 'Abd al-Karim: Finance
'Abd-Allah Sallum: Culture
'Abd al-Husayn al-'Attiya: Agriculture
Jasim Kazim al-'Azzawi: Agrarian Reform
Mahdi al-Dula'i: Justice
Jawad Hashim: Planning
Fakhri Yasin Qadduri: Economy
Rashid al-Rifa'i: Oil
Shafiq al-Kamali: Youth
'Abd-Allah al-Khudayr: Unity
'Adnan Ayyub Sabri: Minister of State
Hamid al-Juburi: Minister of State
Taha Muhyi al-Din: Minister of State
Muhammad al-Karbuli: Minister of State
See *The Official Gazette*, Baghdad, July 18, 1968.

Bakr was Commander in Chief, Hardan al-Tikriti, Minister of Defense, and al-Ansari, Chief of Staff, it became clear that the Army passed under Ba'thist control. In December 1968, Ansari was replaced by Lieut. General Hammad Shihab.[2] Elements opposed to the new regime were either purged or retired from service, but those who were considered *personae non-gratae*, estimated to have numbered over a hundred, were either arrested or detained pending trial. It became clear that under no circumstances were the Ba'th leaders prepared to allow political opponents to conspire against the new regime, not even under the guise of "loyal opposition," before their position had been completely consolidated.

## THE TEMPORARY CONSTITUTIONS

Under socialist rule, two temporary Constitutions have to date been promulgated. They were designed to define the framework of the country's evolving political structure, based on Ba'thist teachings and experiences, and to become ultimately the basis of the country's permanent Constitution. The ultimate form of government, envisioned as enshrining Ba'thist principles and goals, would be democratic and socialist under which the individual would be able to develop his personality, cultivate the Arab heritage, and live in freedom unfettered by social and economic differentials.

The first temporary Constitution was issued on September 21, 1968. It was prepared by a committee of three jurists, well-known for their integrity and experience, appointed by the President of the Republic.[3] The three jurists, meeting under the chairmanship of President Bakr, prepared a draft constitution drawn essentially from previous constitutions and the country's constitutional experiences within the framework of Ba'thist guidelines.[4] Before it was submitted to the RCC for approval, the draft provided for a parliamentary form of government, but the legislative and executive powers were temporarily entrusted to the RCC until Parliament was convened. Only decrees, not laws, were in principle to be issued by the RCC, pending final approval of

---

2. Lack of cooperation with Tikriti, Minister of Defense, resulted in the dismissal of Ansari. He was, soon afterward, accused of conspiracy against the regime and sentenced to 12 years in prison.

3. In addition to President Bakr, the three members were Husayn Muhyi al-Din, Dia' Shith Khattab and Badi' Sharif. The first two were members of the Court of Appeal and the third was Chief of the Republican Palace. The last named was soon relieved from his work when he retired. None of the three jurists was a member of the Ba'th Party.

4. Other Arab constitutions, especially the Constitution of Egypt, were examined.

Parliament.⁵ After a thorough scrutiny by the RCC, the draft was considerably revised to meet immediate needs. After the first temporary Constitution came into force on September 21, 1968, it was four times revised before it was replaced by another Constitution. The second temporary Constitution, based on a thorough revision of the first, was promulgated on July 16, 1970. This Constitution was twice revised in 1973 and 1974.⁶ The political structure that emerged from these charters may be summed up as follows:

In principle, Iraq was considered a portion of the Arab homeland and its people part of the Arab nation.⁷ At the present, however, Iraq stands as a sovereign state whose independence and territorial integrity are preserved. The second temporary Constitution, reflecting three years of Ba'thist experience, reaffirmed internal unity as a priority and declared the people of Iraq to be composed of "two major nationalities"—Arab and Kurdish. The rights of all, regardless of race or religion, were to be equally protected. While the Arabic language was recognized as official for the entire country, Kurdish was declared equally official in the Kurdish provinces. The rights of other nationalities, ethnic or religious, were given full recognition by allowing Syriac and other minority languages to be used in religious and academic institutions and in special radio broadcasts. It is interesting to note that perhaps for the first time in the modern history of Iraq were societies for the study of the cultural heritages of minority groups given special encouragement.⁸

Islam, the religion of the majority, is declared to be the official religion of the state; however, religious freedom to other groups is also recognized. In the first temporary Constitution, not only was Islam recognized as the official religion but also as "the fundamental source of the Constitution" and Islamic jurisprudence as the law governing

---

5. In an interview with Dia' Shith Khattab (Baghdad, Aug. 13, 1974), the writer learned that the Government laid down no special restrictions on the committee. However, it was taken for granted that the RCC, which came into existence on the same day of the Revolution (July 17, 1968), was empowered to exercise supreme authority.

6. For text of the first temporary Constitution, see *The Official Gazette*, Sept. 21, 1968 and Dec. 24, 1969. For text of the second temporary Constitution, see Appendix A.

7. In the Constitution of 1968, the same principle embodying the Ba'th Party's slogan "One Arab nation with an eternal message," was more clearly stated than in the second temporary Constitution (1970) which merely stated that "Iraq is part of the Arab nation." The clause stating that the Government was obligated to realize it was deleted.

8. These rights were given full expression in decrees issued by the RCC. The decrees concerning the Kurdish language were issued in 1970 and the decrees concerning the Syriac language and Syriac Academy in 1972.

inheritance.[9] In the second temporary Constitution, reflecting a step forward toward secularism, only lip service was paid to Islam by stating merely that "Islam is the religion of the state" (Article 4), deleting the reference to Islam as "the fundamental source of the Constitution" and to "Islamic jurisprudence as the law governing inheritance."[10]

In the second temporary Constitution nationalist and socialist principles (derived essentially from Ba'thist teachings) were more strongly emphasized than in the first temporary Constitution. Society is envisioned to be ultimately composed of equal and responsible individuals, presumably to be a classless society maintained by social solidarity. The function of the state is to help establish this society structured on the findings of science and achieved through a revolutionary process. The state undertakes to achieve these objectives by continuous planning and regulating the social and economic system. The country's natural resources and the instruments of production were declared to be owned collectively by the nation—the state undertakes to exploit them for the benefit of the people as a whole. Private ownership, however, was recognized and a private sector allowed.

No confiscation of private ownership was permitted unless it came into conflict with public ownership. Maximum ownership of agricultural land was limited, the extent of the limitation was to be defined by law, not to exceed 200 *dunams*.[11] Except in extraordinary cases, land ownership was denied to foreigners. A bill of rights, as in earlier constitutions, was provided, including a specific clause recognizing human dignity and prohibiting any kind of torture, physical or psychological. This prohibition was considered essential in view of the rising popular criticism of torture imposed under former regimes. Of special interest, especially to Ba'th leaders, the Constitution guaranteed protection of persons seeking asylum in Iraq who suffered persecution in other Arab countries. Organizations known to be opposed to the principles enshrined in the Constitution, especially those considered dangerous to national unity or known to stir ethnic or sectarian antagonism, were prohibited.

The machinery of government is composed of four principal branches: the Revolutionary Command Council (RCC), the National Assembly, the Presidency and the Judiciary. The first is the supreme

---

9. The law of personal status as a whole is essentially based on Islamic law.
10. These were left to be spelled out in the new civil codes which were to apply to all the people without regard to religious or ethno-cultural differences.
11. See p. 119, below.

authority in the land; until the National Assembly is convened, the RCC exercises not only executive but also legislative powers. It elects from its own members the President of the Republic, who presides over its meetings; and a Vice President, who acts as Head of State during the President's absence and succeeds him as President in case of death. The RCC is composed of 22 members elected from the Regional Command by a majority.[12] These members enjoy full immunity; they cannot be arrested or brought to trial save by decision of the RCC itself. The RCC meets *in camera* by a request of the President or the Vice President or by one third of its members. Its functions include the formulation of general policy and the approval of plans and projects for development. More specifically, it discusses all matters relating to the budget, defense, foreign policy, approval of treaties and other international agreements, the use of national forces for defense and the maintenance of public order.

The National Assembly, composed of corporate representation, will exercise legislative power when convened. The manner in which the Assembly would be elected and how it would conduct its business was left to a special law which would specify in detail its composition as well as how the elections would be held. Its primary function would be to enact laws submitted to it as bills either by the RCC, by the President of the Republic or by one-fourth of its members. The Assembly will meet in two sessions each year and it may meet in an extraordinary session if there were need for it.

---

12. The RCC, originally appointed by the Regional Command, is in practice the highest official organ in the state. Each time a member has been dropped, no new member has been appointed to replace him. Only one—Col. Sa'dun Ghaydan—is not a member of the Regional Command. Originally not a member of the Ba'th Party, he has recently joined and is a member of the military unit of Baghdad. Composition of the RCC is as follows:
1. Ahmad Hasan al-Bakr, Secretary General of the Regional Command and President of the Republic
2. Saddam Husayn, Assistant Secretary General of the Regional Command and Vice President of the RCC
3. 'Izzat Ibrahim al-Duri
4. Taha al-Jazrawi
5. 'Izzat Mustafa Ahmad*
6. Sa'dun Ghaydan.

\* At a meeting of the Regional Congress (March 22, 1977) attended by members of the National and Regional Commands, 'Izzat Mustafa Ahmad, Minister of Municipalities, was expelled from the Ba'th Party and dropped from membership of the RCC and the Regional Command for negligence and failure to fulfill official duties.

On September 5, 1977, the 17 members of the Regional Communal were made members of the Revolutionary Command Council, raising the number of that body to 22.

The President of the Republic is the Chief Executive and Commander in Chief of the national forces. He presides over the Cabinet and is entrusted with carrying out laws and decrees, assisted by Vice Presidents and Ministers. He meets with his Ministers to discuss matters connected with the various departments, and all decisions would be carried out by decrees issued in his name. Before its approval by the RCC, the budget and all other projects must be first discussed by the Cabinet. All appointments—Vice Presidents, Cabinet Ministers and all high Government functionaries—are either directly made by the President or by heads of departments in the name of the President. The President also issues orders of pardon and appoints and receives heads of diplomatic missions.

The Judiciary, composed of all judges, is designed to be separate from other branches of the Government and considered immune from political influence. Its composition was left to a special law regulating the operation of the judicial processes. Judges are appointed by the President, and their functions and the manner in which they are transferred were left to a special law.

The second temporary Constitution was designed to remain in force until a permanent Constitution, presumably to be prepared and approved by the National Assembly, is promulgated. No time, however, was specified when the temporary Constitution would be replaced by a permanent Constitution.[13]

## THE ROLE OF THE BA'TH PARTY

The Ba'th Party considers itself entrusted with a national duty—a duty equal to almost a transcendental or a sacred message—which it undertakes to fulfill by official and unofficial acts. No matter how effective the state might be, it is considered as only one instrument among others by virtue of which the Party can achieve its goals. After they came to power, only a few of the Ba'th leaders have become engaged in official acts, because the Party sought to influence and guide not only official but also other national organizations. For this reason, the Party operates as a separate entity, never to merge with or to become a part of any other organization. It merely intends to influence men and organizations to adopt Ba'thist principles and guidelines, each in its field or fields of endeavors, but not to be responsible for their

---

13. For texts of the two temporary Constitutions, see footnote 6 above.

acts. If they fail, the Ba'th Party offers to help them correct or improve their methods.

The state is the most important organization which the Ba'th Party endeavors to influence because it has at its disposal the most effective means to achieve Party goals. Though its leaders may hold key positions, the Party itself operates as a separate unit and makes no attempt to become part of or merge with the state. The state, in Ba'thist eyes, is only means toward an end, while the Party is the agency which provides leadership and direction for action. Thus, the Party serves as a midwife or a link between state and people and provides plans and policies for the state in accordance with Party guidelines. If the state fails in its duty, the Ba'th leaders in the service of the state would be held accountable for failure before the Party. For this reason, not all Ba'th leaders are allowed to serve in the state—some are required to remain in key Party posts and act as watchdogs to prevent those in the service of the state from falling into an error or deviating from Party directions and guidelines.[14]

There are several reasons why the Party would not permit too many of its top leaders to serve in the state. First, because the Party would be deprived of many experienced leaders whose service is necessary for the Party's activities. Second, because service in the state might tempt some leaders to identify state acts with their own acts and might feel bound to defend them just as the leaders of old regimes had done. For, if leaders in the service of the state should ever become apologetic for their acts, the Party would become subordinate to the state rather than the state to the Party. Third, perhaps the most dangerous, is because of the possible subordination of the state to the leaders' own personal interests.

The only way to check these propensities, in Ba'thist eyes, is to keep Party and state apart and to allow the Party leaders in power to be censored by the Party. In order to achieve these objectives, the Ba'th Party decided to allow a maximum of one-third of Cabinet positions to be held by Party members, provided that the others who serve in high Government positions would be either sympathetic or at least not opposed to Ba'thist principles.

14. National Command, "How the Party Achieves a Balance Between Guidance of the Public and Guidance of Authority After Seizure of Power," *al-Thawra al-'Arabiya*, Vol. II (1971), pp. 19–26; and *al-Hizb wa al-Sulta*, Bayrut, 1974, pp. 3–13. See also Sahib al-Samawi, "al-Thawra wa al-Dawla" [The Revolution and the State], *al-Thawra*, Baghdad, January 18, 1976.

Moreover, the Ba'th Party has set up in each Government department, including the Army, a unit composed of Ba'th members working in that department who would be held responsible for anything that may take place in it. These units are regarded as arms of the Party and not parts of the Government's administrative structure. The units, though meeting in the headquarters of the department concerned, are presided over not necessarily by the Minister or a high ranking official (who may or may not be members of the Ba'th Party), but by the highest ranking member of the Ba'th Party in each department. The units meet regularly to weigh the work of each department in the scale of Party principles and guidelines and submit reports and recommendations to the Party's headquarters. These reports are examined by the Regional Command with a view to indicating the extent to which Party objectives and goals were carried out. If some of the departments appear to lag behind others or if the impact of the Party is undermined, an explanation is called for by the members directly concerned and instructions from the Regional Command issued to repair the situation.

Perhaps even more extensively dispersed outside official organizations are Party units in unofficial organizations—indeed, these may be found in almost every walk of life. They are set up in private enterprises, trade unions, associations—lawyers, teachers, medical and otherwise—in cities and towns as well as in the countryside. Although the Ba'th Party does not yet claim to have completed the network to perfection, it certainly intends to achieve it at the earliest possible moment.

The discipline maintained by the Ba'th Party is indeed praiseworthy. This is evidenced not only in the dedication, strength of character and high morale of members but also in the efficiency of work and distribution of responsibility. The Regional Command provides the Party's highest responsible leadership for the country. The National Command, composed of representatives of the various Regional Commands in Arab lands, provides the Ba'th Party's highest responsible leadership for the Arab homeland as a whole.[15] In Iraq, as in

---

15. The National Command, elected by the Ba'th Party's periodical congresses, is composed of representatives of the Arab homeland and not necessarily by all Arab countries as the Ba'th Party has not been active in all Arab lands. Originating in Syria, the National Command was first established in Damascus. Because of the conflict today between the Iraqi and Syrian Ba'th leaders, there are now two National Commands—one in Baghdad and the other in Damascus. The latter is headed by

other Arab countries, the National Command is represented by an Assistant Secretary General of the National Command who serves as the liaison between the Iraqi Regional Command and the Secretary General of the Ba'th Party. Before he moved to Baghdad in 1975, Michel 'Aflaq, Secretary General of the National Command, often visited Iraq for consultations and his assistant, Shibli al-'Aysami, served as the executive head of the National Command. After the Ba'th leaders achieved power in Iraq, the headquarters of the Party was transferred to Baghdad.[16] Receiving support of the Iraqi Ba'th leaders, Michel 'Aflaq was reelected Secretary General of the National Command. Because of ill health, 'Aflaq preferred to reside in Bayrut, but he moved to Baghdad after the civil war broke out in Lebanon. As head of the National Command, he is officially called the Founder and the Secretary General of the Party. In his absence, he is officially represented by the Assistant Secretary General. Although in agreement on general principles, al-'Aysami often tended to follow his own interpretation of Party guidelines. The National Command, concerned with matters affecting the Arab homeland as a whole, meets periodically (once every three years) and the Regional Command, concerned with matters of Iraqi character, meets annually. In Iraq, the Regional Command, composed of leaders elected by the Iraqi members of the Ba'th Party, provides in practice the backbone of the Ba'th Party. Ahmad Hasan al-Bakr, President of the Republic and head of the RCC,

---

President Asad of Syria, combining leadership of the National and Regional commands. In Iraq, the National Command is headed by Michel 'Aflaq, founder of the Ba'th Party and Secretary General of the National Command of Iraq. Composition varies from one congress to another. Members are today as follows:
 1. Michel 'Aflaq, Secretary General
 2. Ahmad Hasan al-Bakr, Deputy Secretary General
 3. Saddam Husayn, Assistant Secretary General
 4. Shibli al-'Aysami, Assistant Secretary General
 5. Munif al-Razzaz, Assistant Secretary General
 6. Abd al-Majid al-Rafi'i
 7. 'Ali Ghannam
 8. Qasim Salam
 9. Badr al-Din Mudaffar
 10. 'Izzat Ibrahim al-Duri
 11. Taha Yasin al-Jazrawi
 12. Na'im Haddad
 13. Tariq 'Aziz

The identity of five other members is concealed, as some of them are Syrians who still reside in that country and lead an opposition against the present Syrian regime.

16. Though the original seat of the National Command was in Damascus, it was transferred to Bayrut after the conflict between the faction that seized power in Damascus and Michel 'Aflaq, Secretary General of the Party, in 1964.

is the Secretary General of the Regional Command and Saddam Husayn, Vice President of the RCC, is Assistant Secretary General of the Regional Command.[17]

The Regional Command is composed of representatives of all party "units" (*far'*—pl. *furu'*). There are 16 units in the country, one in each province. Members of the unit are elected by the "section" (*shu'ba*—pl. *shu'ab*). In each province there are several sections, operating in various towns and centers. Each section is composed of two or more "groups" (*firqa*—pl. *firaq*) organized in each town or locality. The group is made up of two or more "circles" (*halqa*—pl. *halaqat*) organized in several parts of the urban areas. The circle is composed of two or more "cells" (*khaliya*—pl. *khalaya*). The cells are scattered throughout the country in both rural and urban areas. Each cell is headed by a party member of the circle and meets to discuss the affairs of the locality, to enlist the support of the people on all levels and echo grievances and demands to higher authorities through formal channels.[18]

---

17. The Iraqi Regional Command, elected every two years by the Iraqi Ba'th Party's periodical congresses, is the highest authority within the Iraqi region. Its composition varies from time to time—it was 17 when the Ba'th Party came to power in 1968 and dropped to 13 in 1975 either because some expelled or appointed to diplomatic posts abroad. In 1977 the number has been increased to 21. In 1975 the tenure of office was extended to five years to supervise the five year development plan of 1976–80 and undertake responsibility for its implementation. The members are as follows:
1. Ahmad Hasan al-Bakr, Secretary General
2. Saddam Husayn, Assistant Secretary General
3. 'Izzat Ibrahim al-Duri
4. Taha Yasin Ramadan al-Jazrawi
5. Na'im Haddad
6. Tayih 'Abd al-Karim
7. Muhammad Mahjub
8. 'Adnan Husayn al-Hamdani
9. Ghanim 'Abd al-Jalil
10. Tahir Tawfiq al-'Ani
11. Hasan 'Ali al-'Amiri
12. 'Abd al-Fattah Muhammad Amin
13. Sa'dun Shakir
14. Ja'far Qasim Hammudi
15. 'Abd-Allah Fadil
16. Tariq 'Aziz
17. 'Adnan Khayr-Allah
18. Hikmat Ibrahim
19. Muhammad 'A'ish
20. Burhan al-Din 'Abd al-Rahman
21. Muhyi al-Din 'Abd al-Husayn

18. The structure of the Ba'th Party may be sketched as follows:
*al-far'* (unit): one in each province.
*al-shu'ba* (section): each *shu'ba* composed of a minimum of two groups.

Although it recognized the existence of more than one political party in principle, the Ba'th Party operates as one party in a single party system presumably on the ground that a multiple party system would be feasible only when society had become truly socialist and democratic. During the transition period, the Ba'th Party is not opposed to cooperation with other parties that have like principles and objectives. For this reason, the Iraqi Regional Command decided to form a Progressive National Front in 1973 composed essentially of the Ba'th, the Communist and the Kurdish Democratic parties.[19]

Self-criticism is not only allowed but encouraged by the Ba'th Party in principle, though discipline and obedience are considered in practice as more important in order to avoid factionalism and splits among leaders who often tend to disagree on secondary and procedural matters. Some have gone so far as to call for full agreement and solidarity within Party ranks on all matters but this view is by no means acceptable to the majority.[20] The Iraqi Ba'th leadership has been able to maintain on the whole a high degree of stability and continuity by applying various means of conformity, including disciplinary actions.[21]

## THE BUREAUCRACY

As a revolutionary party, the Ba'th sought a sweeping change in the political and the administrative systems in order to create a new polity based on Ba'thist teachings. It was a relatively easy task to change the political structure and to lay down the foundation of a new regime, presided over by Ba'th leaders; to change the administrative system, however, proved an exceedingly more difficult task, for if the business of Government were to be carried out without interruption the bureaucracy of the old regime had to be preserved, purged only of elements hostile to the new regime. Since the creation of a new administrative system requires not only a change in form but also in substance, a complete break with the past can only lead to anarchy and paralysis of the machinery of Government which responsible

---

*al-firqa* (group): each group composed of a minimum of two circles.
*al-halqa* (circle): each circle composed of a minimum of two cells.
*al-khaliya* (cell): each cell composed of several persons headed by a member of the circle.
19. See Chapter 6, below.
20. CF. *Tanzim al-Qa'ida al-Hizbiya* [Organization of the Party Cadre] (Bayrut, dar al-Tali'a, 1974).
21. For a general outline of the duties of party members, see Salah al-Din al-Baytar "al-Nidal al-'Aqa' idi Fi al-Hizb" [Ideological Struggle of the Party], in *al-Sha'biya wa al-Nidal al-Hizbi* [Populism and Party Struggle] (Bayrut, 1974), pp. 65ff.

leaders cannot afford, at any rate in the initial stage of the revolutionary process.

Neither in the political nor in the administrative posts did the Baʻth Party intend to fill all vacancies with Baʻth members. The principal objective of the Party was first to cleanse the administration of corrupt and inefficient functionaries and then to control them by party "units" implanted into each department which would raise the standard and morale of the administrative system and guide all Government officials and functionaries in accordance with Baʻthist goals and guidelines.

The first step—to cleanse the administration of corrupt elements—was not a very difficult one, but to provide new and efficient civil servants proved exceedingly more complex and difficult to achieve. Some of the old and experienced civil servants who were dismissed or retired on political grounds could not be easily replaced. True, the young functionaries who replaced the old displayed greater efficiency and enthusiasm, but they lacked the skill and professional experience which can be obtained only after long tenure of office. Even if it takes a very long time, the Baʻth leaders seem to be determined eventually to achieve administrative efficiency. Above all, they aim at inspiring the bureaucracy with integrity and a sense of duty which are essential for running the business of Government with efficiency.[22]

## THE REVOLUTIONARY COURT

On the morrow of the Revolution of 1958, a "revolutionary court," operating side by side with ordinary courts, was established to deal promptly and more effectively with cases directly connected with the security of the regime. Since it is described as "revolutionary," the jurisprudence that governs the proceedings and decisions of the court must be a special or extra-constitutional in nature in order to fulfill functions deemed necessary under a revolutionary regime.[23]

Since a law for the establishment of a Special Revolutionary Court has already been in existence since 1958,[24] the Baʻth regime merely

---

22. See Sahib al-Samawi, *al-Jihaz al-Idari wa Muhimmat al-Taghyir* [The Administrative System and the Need for Change] (Baghdad: *al-Thawra* Publications, 1974). See also Sabah Salman, "al-Buruqratiya" [Bureaucracy], *al-Thawra*, Baghdad, July 12, 1975.

23. The term "revolutionary jurisprudence" has been used to account for extra-constitutional rulings on the ground that security necessitated such actions, dictated by *raison d'état* (see an article on the subject by Husayn Jamil in *al-Bilad*, Baghdad, July 18, 1958, p. 4). The term "revolutionary jurisprudence" was first used in the Arab world by the Egyptian lawyer Sayyid Sabri (see an article by Sabri in *al-Ahram*, Cairo, July 24, 1958).

issued a decree revising that law to provide the establishment of a Revolutionary Court on December 9, 1968.[25] The court, composed of three judges, was presided over by a civilian judge—Jar-Allah al-'Allaf. Once established, the Court dealt with cases involving persons charged not only with conspiracy against the Government such as rebels and spies but also others whose actions were considered to have undermined the regime, such as corruption and trade in narcotics. The decisions of the Court, though often harsh, proved instrumental in the maintenance of public order by dealing promptly and effectively with adventurers who had been politically motivated to create disorder and jeopardize the leadership.

Two extraordinary trials, each involving a relatively large group of persons charged with an attempt at overthrowing the regime—the first in 1970 and the second in 1973—were referred to a Special Revolutionary Court set up to investigate the culprits rather than to the permanent Revolutionary Court. As noted before, these trials were conducted under special circumstances and exemplary verdicts were given and carried out on the same day. However, these courts were by their very nature temporary; they were set up to investigate special cases and their *raison d'être* came to an end when the task for which they were called was completed.[26]

## THE POPULAR MILITIA

In an effort to enlist popular support for the regime, the Ba'th Party has organized units composed essentially of young men inspired by the principles of the Ba'th Party and trained in military methods to maintain public order and other tasks deemed necessary for the security of the regime. Since the Revolution of 1958, paramilitary units have been organized to secure popular support for military regimes—the Popular Resistance Force in 1958, the National Guard under the first Ba'th regime in 1963, and now the Popular Militia under the second Ba'th regime, organized in 1974.[27] The purpose of the Militia is to strengthen the position of the Ba'th Party in the country and to carry out orders deemed necessary by the Ba'th to achieve national objectives. The Militia, trained by well-selected army officers, is under the command of

---

24. See my *Republican Iraq*, pp. 79–82.
25. See the *Official Gazette*, Baghdad (December 9, 1968), pp. 1–2.
26. See pp. 54 and 66, below.
27. See my *Republican Iraq*, pp. 82–84, 198–99.

a leading member of the Ba'th Party who is held ultimately responsible for the Militia's activities to the Regional Command.[28] The Militia, consisting of well-trained paramilitary formations, has branches all over the country and is considered an arm of the Ba'th Party and not a branch of the armed forces.[29] In 1975, some members of the Militia took part in the fighting on the side of the Palestinians in the Lebanese civil war. Although trained in military methods, their function seems primarily to be to enlist the support of young men for the Ba'th Party rather than to use it as a counterpart force against the Army. In case of war, the Militia might be used to carry out a task that would relieve the regular armed force from some duties.

### MILITARY OR POPULAR AUTHORITARIANISM?

The Ba'th leaders have always asserted in public and private pronouncements that they derived their mandate to govern the country from the people and sought popular support to achieve party objectives on the ground that these objectives serve not only Iraq but the Arab world as a whole. Whenever the Ba'th leaders were questioned on what basis can they speak on behalf of the people, they invariably replied that their rule would eventually be legitimized by popular expression through democratic processes. Yet in practice the Ba'th Party has achieved power twice in Iraq (and, indeed, several times in Syria) by means far from democratic—by military interventions.

The rationale for their action, Ba'th leaders argue, is that the people have long been ruled by oligarchic regimes and that they have not yet been freed from traditional fetters—tribal, feudal and otherwise—to be able to exercise their rights freely. Nor has the individual been able to be free from social and economic deprivations which made him a slave of a society composed essentially of a small rich class and a large poor class. Unless the individual is freed from all these fetters, he would not be able to participate in the democratic processes. The Ba'th Party, accordingly, maintained that it was bound to resort to revolutionary means in order to eliminate the obstacles that have prevented the individual from exercising his rights by peaceful methods. The Ba'th appealed to the Army for support, because the Army has always been

---

28. Today, Taha al-Jazrawi is the head and the Party member responsible for the Militia's activities.

29. It is said that the number of young men who joined is in the neighborhood of 50,000; but this is merely an estimate and not an official figure.

considered part of the people and opposed to the repressive measures the leaders of old regimes had imposed on their opponents.[30]

After they achieved power, the Ba'th leaders continued to invoke military intervention whenever the opposition challenged their rule. But their ultimate objective is to establish a popular base for their regime and to legitimize it through democratic processes. To achieve this objective, they have approached young men who responded more readily to their appeal than older people.

Nor is that all. They have established contacts with national organizations outside official circles, like trade unions, professional associations and others, to enlist their support. These have been injected with cells whose principal aims were to explain goals and objectives and to find out what were their demands and expectations in order to include them in the party's programs and slogans. Trade unions and other corporate organizations will form, in Ba'thist eyes, important sections of the electorate when general elections would be held for the National Assembly. When this Assembly is convened the Ba'th Party expects that these organizations would return representatives in favor of Ba'thist rule. And yet the Army will perhaps remain for a very long time the single most important factor in governmental changes; for, if the Army's loyalty ever shifted to the opposition, the established regime would be in grave danger.[31]

## LEADERSHIP

Broadly speaking, there are two schools of thought concerning the role of leadership in society. One school stresses the creative and dynamic aspects and assumes that the person who is endowed with certain leadership qualities, social and otherwise, can impose his will and create a social movement. The other considers the leader as a product of social forces and assumes that whenever a certain movement is in progress the person or persons who happen to ride the crest of the wave become the leader or leaders of the movement. It is also assumed that in relatively advanced societies, the latter kind of leadership develops while in primitive or less advanced societies the former type is likely to exist. It has also been observed that in democratic societies the leader tends to be the spokesman either for the group in power, or for any one of a

---

30. See Sa'dun Hamadi, *Qadaya al-Thawra al-'Arabiya* (Bayrut, 1968), pp. 241–67.
31. For the Ba'th Party's views about the Army, see *al-Taqrir al-Siyasi, op.cit.,* pp. 143–151.

number of groups contesting for power; in authoritarian systems, political power and political leadership are the monopoly of one or a few at the top.[32]

Neither one of these views, however, fully accounts for the nature of Arab leadership and the role it has played in Arab society. In the modern age, a plethora of Arab leaders made their appearance in periods of stirring events—national revival, two world wars, and social and political upheavals. These events created opportunities for many men to be drawn into politics, but only a few rose to the occasion to play a constructive role. Most of them failed either because their ideas or platforms were not relevant to Arab conditions or because they lacked leadership qualities. In order to succeed, the leader must possess certain requisite qualities relevant to Arab society. The Arabs yearn for a "strong" leader to preside over their destiny; if he possesses integrity, straightforwardness, and strength of character, he is likely to receive the support and confidence of the people and to enjoy a long period of political survival. Competent men who possess these qualities must play their role in accordance with the conditions in which the Arabs find themselves. The Arabs are highly individualistic and parochial in character. In ordinary circumstances, they manifest narrow loyalties, tribal or local in nature. Contrary to their apparent submissiveness and polite manners, they are a robust, violent and highly sensitive people whose volatile emotions may rise to a very high pitch in moments of excitement. In normal circumstances, the Arabs tend to relapse into local jealousies or inter-tribal warfare, but when circumstances shift and are met with the man who can inspire them with a moving ideal, their imaginations are fired by the leader's call and their narrow loyalties are at once submerged, even superseded, and they can rise to the task they are called to fulfill.[33] It follows that both qualifications and circumstances are necessary for a leader to succeed. Neither the man nor the circumstances alone can produce the successful leader, as noted in the study of Arab leadership in another work; it is the confluence of the man's requisite qualifications with the relevant circumstances.[34]

While Ba'th leaders are not unaware that the Arabs desire strong leadership and they themselves have paid high tribute to heroic leadership—such as that exemplified in the life of the Prophet

---

32. For a general discussion of the various kinds of leadership and their relevance to social movements, see Sidney Hook, *The Hero in History* (Boston, 1955).
33. Cf. my *Political Trends in the Arab World* (Baltimore, 1970), p. 24.
34. See my *Arab Contemporaries* (Baltimore, 1971), pp. 227–28.

Muhammad in the past and of charismatic leaders in modern time[35]—they subscribe to the doctrine of collective leadership and maintain that the party rather than the man plays the role of the strong leader and presides over the destiny of the Arab nation. The Ba'th Party is opposed to personality cult in principle and urges Party members to give the credit for their work to the Party and not to themselves. Like the Communist Party in theory, the Ba'th does not acknowledge the rule of one leader; it recognizes the collective leadership of the National Command for the Arab homeland and Regional Command for each Arab country separately, but no single person should be entrusted with supreme leadership as exemplified in the pre-war totalitarian dictatorships. As a democratic organization, the Ba'th Party recognizes only a Secretary General for the National Command and a Secretary General for each Regional Command; but all these leaders are viewed as instruments who carry out decisions reached by collective actions in regional or national congresses.

Despite commitment to collective leadership, the Ba'th Party fell under the influence of a strong leader like President Nasir of Egypt who could fire the imagination of the Arabs and call for some ideals, like Arab unity and socialism, which the Ba'th Party advocated. Nor was the enthusiasm which the Ba'th ideology aroused among young men enough to solicit public support through collective leadership without the fascination of charismatic leadership. On the contrary, collective leadership proved a source of conflicts and dissension which often led to a struggle for power among party leaders. It was for these and other circumstantial reasons that the Ba'th Party sought Nasir's leadership.

True, Nasir might have been the ideal leader for the Ba'th Party; but he was not interested in the Ba'th as a political party and suggested, after the establishment of the United Arab Republic, the self-liquidation of all political parties, including the Ba'th. Very soon he appeared in Ba'thist eyes as the dictator who refused to be guided by Ba'thist teachings. For this reason, the Ba'th leaders supported Syria's secession from Egypt in 1961, though they continued to call for unity as a basic principle of the Party.

Reverting to collective leadership, the Ba'th Party continued to experience conflicts and dissension both on the national and regional levels. Conflicts among leaders on the national level (the National

---

35. See Michel 'Aflaq, "Dhikra al-Rasul al-'Arabi" *Fi Sabil al-Ba'th* (Bayrut: Dar al-Tali'a, 1959, 1963), pp. 50–61.

Command) resulted in virtually splitting the Party into two—both are now in the saddle in Iraq and Syria but each is governing independently of the other as two separate parties. Dissension within each on the regional level (the Regional Command) led to a struggle for power among rival leaders resulting in the rise of a "strong" man in each country. Whether as Secretary General of the Party on both the National and Regional levels, as in the case of Syria, or as merely the second in rank on the Regional level, as in the case of Iraq, the rise of a strong leader in each country accounts for the success of the two Parties to operate independently in accordance with the needs and aspirations of each country irrespective of the existence of a National Command in each one. Thus, the tacit acceptance of strong leadership on the regional level reveals the Ba'th recognition of Arab need for strong leadership, though the Party still asserts the simulacrum of collective leadership. Since Iraq and Syria are governed separately, the perennial leadership crisis seems so far to have been resolved on the regional level, but if the two countries were ever to agree on a unified National Command, the leadership crisis on the national level will have to await a similar accommodation to realities as on the regional level.

Since this work is essentially a study of Ba'thist rule in Iraq, only a discussion of how the Party resolved the leadership crisis on the regional level will be attempted here. How the matter was dealt with in Syria will have to await another work.[36]

36. In a forthcoming sequel to my *Arab Contemporaries*, I propose to contribute an essay on Hafiz al-Asad as leader of the Syrian Ba'th Party. For a study of leadership in Iraq from an educational, ethno-cultural and professional backgrounds, see Phebe A. Marr, "The Political Elite in Iraq," *Political Elites in the Middle East*, ed. George Lenczowski (Washington, D. C. 1975), pp. 109–49.

## Chapter IV

# Struggle for Power among Socialist Leaders

As THE experiences of Iraq and other Arab countries demonstrated, the absence of a multiple party system and the concentration of power in a single party is likely to give rise to factionalism leading to rivalry and conflict among leaders within that party. In Iraq, the conflict first centered around the question whether the socialist regime was to fall under civil or military leadership. Since the military were responsible for seizure of power by the Ba'th Party, they were perforce in the ascendancy as long as they remained united. Very soon, however, rivalry ensued among the top leaders which undermined the position of the military in civilian eyes and induced the Ba'th Party's civilian leaders to warn against the effects of dissension on the regime. By invoking the principle of collective leadership, to which the Ba'th Party was committed, the civilian leaders were able to assert their role on the ground that collective leadership is likely to provide greater stability and progress for the country than military authoritarianism.

However, once the military ascendancy began to recede, conflict among civilian leaders vying for power was bound to develop as collective leadership did not provide for the Ba'th Party the support of a public yearning for a strong leader, as we noted earlier. Before dissension and factionalism in civil or military ranks came to the surface solidarity among the Ba'th leaders had been maintained for over two years after they achieved power, because the Ba'th Party as a whole was confronted by opponents who seem to have been determined to undermine or overthrow the regime by peaceful or violent methods. Rising to the occasion, the Ba'th leaders showed remarkable solidarity and resourcefulness in frustrating the opposition and foiling plots to overthrow the regime. It is deemed necessary to discuss first the manner in which the Ba'th leaders dealt with their opponents before we turn to examine the civil-military rivalry within the party and the struggle for power among top leaders.

## SPORADIC ASSAULTS AGAINST ARAB SOCIALIST RULE

After they achieved power, the elements opposed to Ba'th rule spared no time in showing dissatisfaction, whether by passive or active resistance. The initial opposition naturally came from the Nayif-Dawud group, but very soon it subsided; another from the former regime, who proved more dangerous, and still another from politicians of the pre-revolutionary period, some of whom joined hands with revolutionary leaders.

After Nayif and Dawud left the country—at first both were offered diplomatic posts but preferred self-exile—their followers took an initial negative attitude. Some, like Nasir al-Hani, who agreed to serve as special adviser to the President on foreign affairs, made a number of statements construed by Ba'th leaders to be critical of the regime's policy. On November 12, 1968, it was suddenly announced on the Baghdad Radio that Hani was assassinated by unknown persons[1] and that the President, on behalf of the Government, asked Hardan al-Tikriti, Deputy Prime Minister and Minister of Defense, to attend the funeral. Hani was an ambitious politician who began his career under the Monarchy, first as a junior academician in a teacher's college. Becoming a protégé of Khalil Kanna, then Minister of Education, he was appointed Cultural Attaché at the Iraqi Embassy in Washington in 1955 and returned to Baghdad shortly after the Revolution of 1958. While he was in the United States, he had made the acquaintance of Hashim Jawad, the Iraqi delegate to the United Nations, who appointed him Ambassador to the United States in 1960 upon becoming Minister of Foreign Affairs under the Qasim regime. Shifting loyalty from one prospective group to another, Hani was able to climb the political ladder until he became Minister of Foreign Affairs under Nayif. After the fall of Nayif, President Bakr appointed him as personal adviser on foreign affairs. Suspecting surreptious contacts with

---

1. Some said they were five; others three.

opponents, some Ba'th leaders were dubious about his appointment as a Presidential adviser. Hani's tenure of office was not expected to last long, though the Ba'th Party denied any connection with the assassination and the persons involved have never been identified.

There were other opponents who seemed more dangerous in clandestine activities. While these were preoccupied with their plans the Government suddenly announced in January 1969, that it had uncovered spy networks which seemed to have been passing on intelligence to Israel. The culprits were arrested and the trials were shown on television. The principal initiators were Iraqi Jews who sought the assistance of a few compatriots to provide information on Soviet military assistance to Iraq. The trial resulted in the conviction of 14 persons, of whom nine were Jews. All were put to death by hanging in public which stirred a storm of protests, mainly by Jewish organizations in Western countries on the grounds of ethnic and religious discrimination.[2] The Iraqi authorities maintained that the Jews involved were Iraqi citizens and that the others, Muslims and Christians alike, were executed regardless of religious or ethnic affiliations.[3] The Grand Rabbi of Baghdad, disturbed by Jewish overreaction in the West, made public statements in which he declared that the trial was fair and that the Jewish community in the country enjoyed freedom and security under the Iraqi regime.[4]

In the course of one of the spy network trials, the testimony of 'Abd al-Hadi al-Bajari (al-Bachari), a former member of Parliament, broadcast by the Baghdad Radio on January 24, 1969, revealed that several opposition leaders were involved in clandestine activities against the regime. Al-Bajari, disclaiming any part in the plots, said that he had obtained his information from a certain 'Abd al-Hamid al-Damarji, an export-import merchant, who acted as a liaison between opposition leaders inside and outside the country. Al-Bajari went on to say that, according to Damarji, a secret organization composed of 'Abd al-Rahman al-Bazzaz, former Prime Minister, 'Abd al-'Aziz al-'Uqayli, former Minister of Defense (both under the 'Arif regime) and Khalil

---

2. For statements of protests from American and some European governments as well as from the Secretary General of the United Nations, see *The New York Times,* January 28, 29, 30, and February 1, 2, 1969.
3. See *al-Jumhuriya,* Baghdad, January 31, 1969.
4. For text of the Rabbi's public statement, see *al-Jumhuriya,* Baghdad, January 31, 1969. Since criticism continued in the West, especially following further trials, the Grand Rabbi of Baghdad sent a letter, dated April 28, 1971 to the Secretary General of the United Nations in which he assured him of the freedom and equality enjoyed by Jews in Iraq (See *Action,* New York, May 17, 1971).

Kanna, protégé of General Nuri al-Saʻid and former Minister of Education under the Monarchy, was formed with the avowed purpose of overthrowing the Baʻth regime and establishing a new Government headed by Bazzaz and composed of ʻUqayli, Kanna and others representing Arabs and Kurds. Its form was to be a parliamentary democracy, based on free enterprise under which all moderate groups would be represented. The plot, al-Bajari said, was to be carried out first by the resumption of Kurdish military operations in the north and then a military uprising in the south instigated by Army officers in secret contact with ʻUqayli and his group. Meanwhile, Khalil Kanna, then residing in Bayrut, offered to coordinate the activities of political leaders outside the country, of whom some were in secret contacts with Western Powers and others with Israel. The latter country, in order to give support to the military uprising in southern Iraq, was expected to mobilize a force near Jordan's frontiers to divert part of the Iraqi forces from action against opposition leaders. In the cross-examination of al-Bajari during the trial, he was asked: "How was it possible for Bazzaz, a socialist, to cooperate with politicians like Kanna, a Monarchist, ʻUqayli, an anti-Kurdish officer, and Mulla Mustafa, leader of the Kurdish rebellion?" Al-Bajari is reported to have replied that Bazzaz's socialism was so diluted that it could be reconciled with free enterprise, and ʻUqayli, though opposed to Kurdish autonomy in principle, was prepared to cooperate with Mulla Mustafa as a means to achieving power.[5] This explanation, satisfactory to the court for possible cooperation among opposition leaders, was taken at its face value to verify the evidence against the culprits.

As a sequence to the trial, investigations uncovered further activities and exposed other leaders, both civil and military, with which they had been involved. Some were given various prison sentences and others capital punishment.[6] Some who were condemned to death seem to have confessed that they had been involved in spying for Israel or working for the CIA.[7] Despite alleged connections with spy networks, the principal political leaders—Bazzaz, ʻUqayli and others—were given various prison rather than death sentences presumably on the ground that their activities were essentially political and not criminal. Bazzaz, after a long illness in prison, was released in 1971 and despite medical treatment died a year later; but ʻUqayli and several others,

---

5. For testimony of al-Bajari, see *al-Jumhuriya,* Baghdad, January 26, 1969.
6. For the trial, see *al-Jumhuriya,* February–March 1969.
7. See *The New York Times,* April 14, 1969.

considered too dangerous, have not been released. Although these trials by no means nipped all clandestine activities in the bud, the Ba'th leaders slowly but steadily moved to consolidate their regime and silence all possible opponents. Outside military circles only two organized groups remained as potential sources of opposition—the Communists and the Kurds. The Ba'th leaders tried at first to resolve the Kurdish problem peacefully. From 1970 to 1972, there was an uneasy truce with Mulla Mustafa; the agreement on the implementation of "autonomy" collapsed and war broke out in 1974. Faced with a possible showdown with the Kurds, the Ba'th leaders prudently reconciled their differences with the Communists and set up the Progressive National Front in 1973. But to these subjects we shall return later.[8]

## THE ABORTIVE COUP OF 1970

Perhaps more dangerous than previous attempts, a projected coup against the regime was carried out on January 20, 1970, by military leaders inside and outside official circles. The principal authors were Major-General 'Abd al-Ghani al-Rawi, a retired senior officer and a protégé of the 'Arif brothers, and Colonel Salih Mahdi al-Samarra'i, former Military Attaché at the Iraqi Embassy in Bayrut under the Monarchy. This unholy alliance between two retired officers of opposing regimes may seem strange indeed, but the readiness of these two officers to cooperate is indicative of the kaleidoscopic shift of loyalty in military circles regardless of political affiliation. True, the Ba'th Party tried to influence a few officers who showed readiness to accept its ideology, but the majority paid little or no attention to ideological differences. Consequently, some officers—indeed, a few civilian leaders too, as noted before—who had supported opposing regimes in the past were now ready to work together against the Ba'th regime because they aspired to occupy high political posts. Thus, General Rawi, it is said, with his eyes fixed on the Presidency, was able to lure a number of officers in active service to side with him by offering them high Government posts.

The news of this coup was made public on January 21, 1970.[9] Baghdad Radio interrupted its broadcast at noon to announce that a conspiracy to overthrow the regime had been crushed the previous

---

8. See Chapter 5, below.
9. For text of the Government announcement, see *al-Jumhuriya*, Baghdad, January 22, 1970.

night and that the conspirators had been arrested. A Special Court, presided over by Captain Taha al-Jazrawi, member of the RCC, and consisting of two other members, Nazim Kazzar, Chief of the Security Policy, and 'Ali Rida, Director of the RCC Public Relations, was set up on January 21 to begin trying the culprits at once. Those condemned to death were executed immediately, the military by shooting and the civilians by hanging. Four groups, consisting of 18 military and 4 civilians, were executed on January 21; three, consisting of 8 military and 4 civilians, on January 22; and the last of one military and two civilians, on January 24. The number of persons brought to trial has been estimated roughly about 90, but only some 50 had been convicted—37 executed and 15 imprisoned—and the rest (about 20) were released on the ground that no evidence existed to prove their participation in the plot.[10] On January 24 Taha al-Jazrawi announced that the Special Court had completed its work for the time being only, but in reality its work had come to an end.

In a conversation with the writer,[11] Jazrawi said that the Government became aware of the preparation to carry out a military uprising nearly a year before it was crushed.[12] He said that intelligence reached the authorities that the plotters had received weapons from the Iranian authorities to enable them to overthrow the regime because of the conflict over the Shatt al-Arab.[13] The Ba'th Government made no move to arrest the conspirators, because it was deemed essential to arrest them *in flagrante delicto;* for if evidence was insufficient and the authorities announced only that they had learned about it, the public might not be convinced of the veracity of the announcement and would be sympathetic with the plotters.[14]

---

10. Some of the officers who had been given death sentences on spying charges, including General Muslih, Brigadier Sirri and five others, were executed on January 21. The total number of executions was 44.

11. The writer's interview (Baghdad, January 11, 1976).

12. According to the account of some who fled the country and arrived in London, the *Manchester Guardian* (January 31, 1970) reported that an officer learned of the plot in December (others said some three months earlier) and reported it to the Government. He continued to work with the conspirators, and brought into the plot both a number of officers loyal to the Government and others whose loyalty the Government wanted to test. Taperecordings of conversations between the conspirators and Persian representatives were made by the loyal officers and given to the Government. Taha al-Jazrawi confirmed this report to the writer and said that the taperecordings were presented to the conspirators during the trial as evidence against them, and they admitted that the conversations were correct.

13. See pp. 148ff., below.

14. After the plot was crushed on January 20, 1970, the Government stated that on April 15, 1969, the third Secretary of the Iranian Embassy in Baghdad had first contacted the plotters; on Sept. 28, 1969, some met an Iranian official at the Iranian Embassy in

On January 20, the day fixed for the projected coup, Salih Mahdi al-Samarra'i headed a group of some 50 persons who had assembled at the Rashid Camp, at the outskirts of Baghdad, and began his march on the Republican Palace. Some were armed, but others were told that weapons had been sent on ahead. When Samarra'i reached the Palace, the gates were thrown open and he entered without resistance. Hardly had he declared the coup than the gates were closed behind him and he and his followers found themselves under arrest by loyal soldiers, as the Government had known the details about his movements and took all the necessary steps to foil the conspiracy. Two loyal soldiers were killed when Samarra'i and his followers tried to break through a group of soldiers who rushed to arrest them.[15] Meantime, the security police arrested others who were hiding in secret places where weapons had been stored. The Special Court, as noted earlier, had no difficulty in exposing the principal conspirators and condemning them to death, as they were caught red-handed. General Rawi, alerted about the arrest before he returned to Iraq, remained out of the country. He was sentenced to death *in absentia,* and a year later escaped an attempt on his life in Iran, where he is still living.

Since the Government suspected Iran's complicity in the Rawi-Samarra'i projected coup, 'Izzat-Allah 'Amili, the Iranian Ambassador to Iraq, and four members of his staff were ordered to leave the country on January 22 within 24 hours. The staff of the Iranian Consulates in Baghdad, Basra and Karbala were expelled at the same time. Iran retaliated a few hours later by ordering the expulsion of the Iraqi Ambassador in Tehran, the Military Attaché and four of his staff.[16]

---

Kuwayt. Following these contacts, the Iranian Government supplied the plotters with 3,000 submachine guns, 650,000 rounds of ammunitions and two mobile radio transmitters. It was also stated that secret correspondence between General Rawi and his collaborators had been transmitted through the Iranian Embassy in Baghdad. The Government also stated that it possessed the letters from General Rawi and other documents seized from the conspirators, photographic copies of which were subsequently published in the press.

15. A state funeral was given to the two soldiers on January 22.

16. There have been accusations and counter-accusations of ill-treatment of staffs in the Iraqi and Iranian Embassies in both countries. It is said that one of the Iranian Embassy staff, 'Abd al-Khaliq Bushehri Zadah, was kidnapped and tortured. After he returned to Tehran on January 26, Zadah claimed that he had been seized at gun-point in the street on January 20, blindfolded and taken to Vice President Tikriti's office, where he was questioned and tortured in the presence of General Taymur Bakhtiari, exiled by the Shah in 1962. Zadah is said to have admitted Iranian complicity in the abortive coup and promised after returning to Iran to form an underground movement to overthrow the Shah. Upon his release, he informed the Iranian Ambassador of his experiences. General Bakhtiari began to recruit volunteers to form an armed underground movement against the Shah.

Tension between the two countries rose so high that war was expected to break out at any moment. The Iraqi Government appealed to the United Nations on February 2 to take measures to prevent the situation from degenerating into actual fighting. The Iraqi appeal was prompted by the concentration of Iranian troops on Iraqi borders. Meantime, Salih Mahdi 'Ammash, Minister of Interior, arrived in the Turkish capital on February 3 requesting Turkish good offices to prevent the crisis from developing into an armed conflict. Informed of the talk between 'Ammash and the Turkish Government, Iran replied that if Iraq attacked, the Iranian troops would fight to defend their country and it proposed that both governments should withdraw their troops from the frontiers. War was averted, but the dispute between the two countries over the Shatt al-Arab continued until 1975.

Nor were the regime's opponents, despite reverses, entirely discouraged from scheming to undermine Ba'thist rule. After self-exile, 'Abd al-Razzaq al-Nayif became restive and seemed to the authorities to have had contacts with other exiles active in seeking to return to power by overthrowing the regime. In 1969 he became involved with the Rawi group and others who were plotting against the regime. Though he realized that the Government had known of the plot and he seems to have withdrawn from active involvement in it, his name was used by the plotters in seeking supporters. For this reason, the Government decided to bring his case to the Special Court on March 1, 1970, but no action was taken against him. Dawud, who served as Ambassador first to Spain in 1968 and then to the Vatican in 1969, was put on the retired list on March 6, 1970. Both Nayif and Dawud remained out of the country, the first in London and the other travelling in Arab lands. An attempt on Nayif's life by unknown persons was made in London in 1973, but he managed to survive and he seems to have now completely dissociated himself from political activities.

Following these repressive measures against opponents, the Government showed remarkable readiness to come to terms with the Kurds and offered self-rule on March 11, 1970, as a measure of autonomy.[17] It also tried to reconcile elements that had been antagonized by previous regimes and opponents who gave up involvement in political activities, including the restoration of Iraqi citizenship to the Mar Shim'un, Patriarch of the Assyrian Community,

---

17. See p. 103, below.

on April 20, 1970, of which he has been deprived because of his involvement in the Assyrian uprising of 1933. These and other measures gave the public a sense of security which was important for progress and stability.

## CIVIL VS. MILITARY LEADERSHIP

Before it came to power, the Ba'th Party had no hesitation in cooperating with the military as a method to effect governmental changes, because parliamentary democracy was so firmly controlled by the Old Regime that no opposition could hope to win in general elections. After it achieved power, however, the Ba'th Party maintained that political decisions should be made by the party in formal meetings and not by the military alone. However, the experiences of both Syria and Iraq in civil-military cooperation have demonstrated that the military often tended to impose their own decisions and run the business of Government in accordance with their own imperatives rather than with party principles and guidelines. Though civilian leaders voiced criticism of military control, the increasing civil-military tension remained unresolved.

There were two schools of thought concerning civil-military relationships. The military, less ideologically inclined than civilian leaders, argued that the Army was the shield of the party; therefore, they should have the final word until the regime was consolidated. The civilian school argued that the party's decisions should be overriding no matter who was in power. No agreement seems to have been reached between the two schools, as the military paid no attention to civilian reproaches as long as power rested in their hands. Only after the top military leaders became engaged in a struggle for power did the civilian leaders begin to assert their leadership and try to bring the military under the Ba'th Party's control. The shift in the balance of power took place step by step, and even after the civilian leaders seemed to have won the battle the struggle for power between civil and military leadership continued.

## HARDAN AL-TIKRITI VS. SALIH MAHDI 'AMMASH

The first phase of the struggle within the military leadership was between two top Army officers who, next to President Bakr, were perhaps the most influential in the country. After achieving power in 1968, they were soon fully rewarded—the first, Major-General

Hardan al-Tikriti, became Chief of Staff and later Minister of Defense; the other, Major-General Mahdi 'Ammash, Minister of Interior. Highly respected in military circles, President Bakr, promoted to Field Marshall of the Army in 1969, was able to hold the balance between these two as well as other rival officers. So long as they worked together, the military enjoyed a preponderant position in the country.

However, as the experience of military rule in the past demonstrated, factionalism among the military was bound to develop, encouraged by rival civilian groups vying for power. Factionalism breeds dissension and competition, which are likely to lead to the rise of one strong man who would assert personal rule, as was the case under the Qasim regime, unless collective leadership can maintain a balance between civil and military leadership to prevent the ascendency of one over the other as the experiences of the Ba'th Party demonstrated since it came to power in 1968.

Of the two officers, Hardan al-Tikriti appeared as the stronger man. He served as Commander of the Iraqi Air Force when the Ba'th Party achieved power in 1963 and then became Chief of Staff and Minister of Defense in 1968. He was reputed for his ruthlessness, dash, and strong personality. Like President Bakr, he came from the small town of Tikrit, the birthplace of a clan which provided a number of civil and military leaders, and he had a strong following in the Army. For these reasons, he aspired to occupy a higher position than that which he held. It was rumored that he had his eyes set on the Presidency of the Republic. The rumor did not fail to reach Bakr's ears, who began to watch his movements.

To counteract Hardan's influence, Salih Mahdi 'Ammash, Minister of Interior, seems to have been tempted to enter into rivalry with his counterpart if he was not actually encouraged to do so. As a military leader, 'Ammash was perhaps no less ambitious than Hardan but was not his equal in moral courage. Though not an early associate with President Bakr, he was very close to him and was able to win his confidence since the time both joined the Ba'th Party in 1956. As Minister of Interior, he had the police under his control and had some following in the Army. At the outset, the rivalry between Hardan and 'Ammash prompted Ba'thist civilian leaders to support 'Ammash, partly because Hardan had defected from the party in 1963 but mainly because Hardan appeared too dangerous and arrogant. Early in 1969, 'Ammash seemed to have come very near to winning the first round of the struggle for power when there was a rumor that President Bakr might relinquish the Premiership in favor of 'Ammash rather than Hardan. To block 'Ammash's possible promotion, Hardan instigated his followers to raise the matter with the President and to dissuade him from relinquishing the Premiership. President Bakr seems to have assured them that he had no intention to give up the Premiership; in 1969 when the Constitution was revised, the two positions were merged under a presidential system. Perhaps as a temporary measure, the competition between the two rival officers gave the Ba'th civilian leaders an opportunity to impress on President Bakr the need to assert his own leadership in the regime's best interest. To put an end to rivalry, Hardan al-Tikriti and 'Ammash were appointed Vice Presidents on April 3, 1970. Outwardly they were promoted, but in reality they were relieved of two highly sensitive positions (i.e. Defense and Interior). Lieut.-General Hammad Shihab, Chief of Staff, was given the portfolio of Defense and Sa'dun Ghaydan, Commander of the Baghdad Garrison, the portfolio of Interior. The two officers, considered personal friends of President Bakr, were given these two important military posts in order to strengthen the Presidency against any other possible rival. 'Abd al-Jabbar Shahshal, a non-political figure, was appointed Chief of Staff—a key military position. Almost equally respected in civil and military circles, the President virtually came into firm control of the country. Though he could assert personal rule through control of the Army, he preferred to govern through collective leadership as head of the RCC, the highest decision-making body in the country, rather than as a military dictator.

Ideological differences between the Iraqi and Syrian leaders, though reflecting essentially parochial feelings, resulted in undermining Hardan's position and his following in the Army. The Syrian leaders reproached Iraq for failure to support the Palestinian Liberation Organization (PLO) in its struggle with King Husayn in 1970 and for partial withdrawal of the Iraqi force from Jordan. The Iraqi civilian leaders, reputed to have been in favor of support for the PLO, blamed the military for inaction though the country was not in a position to go to war with Jordan while threatened by an impending war with the Kurds in the north and by Iran, in a dispute over the Shatt al-Arab, in the east. Demonstrations in the nation's capital, in protest against the Army's failure to support the PLO, prompted the Government to hold the military as solely responsible for inaction. Though Hardan was not the only military man who argued against war, it was convenient to single him out as a scapegoat for the failure of the Army to act.

Before he was officially relieved, Hardan was sent as head of a mission to Spain, unaware of the imminent action against him. On October 9, 1971, an order relieving him of his post as Vice President and placing him on the retired list was issued. While in Madrid, he was appointed Ambassador to Morocco and ordered to proceed to Rabat. Disregarding the order, he returned to Baghdad, confident that his influence in military circles would bring pressure on the authorities to change their mind about the new appointment. When he arrived at the Baghdad Airport a special plane was waiting to take him out of the country. Unable to overrule higher orders, he chose Algiers as a place for self-exile where he spent the next six months before he moved to Kuwayt. His wife and children followed him to Algiers; but the wife, already ill and worried about the fate of her husband, died before the plane arrived in Algiers. In February 1971, he decided to move to Kuwayt, where he would be close to his children as the authorities had allowed them to complete their studies in Baghdad.

Shortly after he arrived in Kuwayt, rumors were afoot in Baghdad that Hardan's following was working for his return and a conspiracy against the regime was in the making. Whether Hardan himself inspired the rumor or whether the initiative was taken by officers friendly to him independently is difficult to determine, but the rumor about Hardan's possible return aroused suspicion which prompted his opponents to take a stand against him.

On March 20, 1970, when Hardan had gone early in the morning to a Government hospital in Kuwayt for a check-up accompanied by Ibrahim Jum'a, Iraq's Ambassador to Kuwayt, four unidentified persons who seemed to have had prior knowledge of his visit to the hospital, were waiting in ambush for him. No sooner did the Ambassador's car arrive at the hospital than one of the four men waiting for him hurriedly rushed to open the car's door while another, standing behind him, fired at once five shots which immediately killed Hardan before he stepped out of the car. The four men escaped in a car before the police arrived. Despite careful search, the Kuwayti Government was unable to arrest the assassins. It was suspected that they were Iraqi citizens, but no evidence has yet come to light as to the identity of the persons who committed the crime.

## Eclipse of 'Ammash and the Ascendancy of Civil Leadership

Even before his assassination, the fall of Hardan from power marked the beginning of decline of the military and the growing influence of civilian leaders. Shortly after Hardan had gone into exile to Algeria, a number of high ranking officers were either transferred or relieved from service on the ground of suspicion that they had been Hardan's supporters. Brigadier Taha al-Shakarchi, Commander of the Second Division, was sent to India as Military Attaché, but later returned to active service in his former position. Colonel Hasan al-Naqib, Deputy Chief of Staff, suspected as a Hardan sympathizer, was also retired from service and appointed as Ambassador to Spain in 1970.[18] These and other officers, removed on the ground of failure to support the PLO in September 1970, were replaced by younger officers prepared to take an increasing responsibility in military affairs. As members of the Ba'th Party, these were in favor of party discipline and the assertion of civil leadership over the Army.

Though he remained as Vice President almost a year after Hardan's fall, 'Ammash began to feel increasing restrictions on his powers. Dissatisfied with a position in which he had become virtually a figurehead, he often made unwarranted critical remarks about other party members which aroused antagonism and tarnished his image. For these and other reasons, personal and otherwise, the civilian leaders demanded his removal from the Vice Presidency.[19] He was appointed Ambassador to the USSR in 1971; three years later, he was transferred in the same capacity, first to France and then, two years later, to Finland.

The only high ranking officer who has continued to command the highest respect in civil and military circles is Ahmad Hasan al-Bakr, President of the Republic. Because he has no ambition to become a military dictator, he has tried to maintain party solidarity and to cooperate with civilian leaders in the governance of the country in accordance with Ba'thist teachings.

18. After the July Revolution of 1958, Hasan al-Naqib was appointed a Military Attaché in the Iraqi Embassy in Washington. He seems to have taken 'Arif's side in the struggle with Qasim and was recalled to Baghdad and thrown into prison in 1960. He returned to service after 'Arif had become President in 1963 and went to Egypt as head of a military mission in 1964–66. He took part in the Arab-Israeli war of 1967 and served first as head of a brigade in the Iraqi force in Jordan and then as Commander of the force till 1969. He served as Acting Chief of Staff during 1970 before he retired from service in October of that year. He was appointed Ambassador to Spain on November 25, 1970 (the writer's interview with Brig. Hasan al-Naqib in Madrid in 1973).

19. Because 'Ammash was engaged in a relatively expensive house, rumors were circulated that the money was not altogether derived from private income. Though not exceeding the expenses allowed to other party members, his action to take over an estate from a neighbor by pressure in order to add it to his own aroused critics to undermine his position in high official circles.

## Struggle for Power Among Ba'th Leaders

While the military were still in a preponderant position, the civilian leaders maintained a high degree of solidarity among themselves; their firm stand against military ascendancy contributed in no small measure to the elimination of one military leader after another.

Civilian solidarity, however, proved difficult to maintain as factionalism within the Ba'th Party was bound to develop in civilian as in military ranks. There seems to have been no disagreement on fundamental principles, but very soon differences on minor issues led to a struggle for power among top leaders. True, each tried to serve the Party's best interests according to his lights, but several often disagreed on personal and procedural matters. Some differences were ironed out by discussion in closed meetings, but others seem to have affected personal relations deeply, leading to purges within the regime.

After achieving power, some party members distinguished themselves in public affairs, like 'Abd al-Khaliq al-Samarra'i, 'Abd al-Karim al-Shaykhli and Salah 'Umar al-'Ali, to mention only three names. Samarra'i, member of both the National and Regional Commands, won a reputation as a dedicated and hardworking leader. He became very popular in party congresses and always stood high up in the list of party candidates for elected positions. But he seems to have become very critical of party leaders in higher echelons. Very soon opposition grew against him; he was finally involved in the Kazzar uprising and thrown into prison.[20] Similarly, Shaykhli and Salah 'Umar al-'Ali, the first holding the portfolio of Foreign Minister and the other Information, were dropped from membership of the RCC and appointed to diplomatic posts abroad. Shaykhli was sent to the United Nations as his country's head of mission in 1971 and 'Ali as Ambassador to Sweden in 1972. 'Abd-Allah Sallum, though he held a junior Cabinet post, was first dropped from membership of the RCC in 1970 and appointed as Iraq's delegate to the Arab League before he was sent as Ambassador to India in 1971. 'Izzat Mustafa, an influential member of the RCC and the Regional Command, was dropped from both in 1977.[21] There were, on the other hand, some party members who maintained solidarity with devotion, and were amply rewarded. 'Izzat Ibrahim al-Duri, Taha al-Jazrawi, Sa'dun Hamadi, Na'im Haddad, 'Adnan al-Hamdani, Ghanim 'Abd al-Jalil, Tayih 'Abd al-Karim, Ja'far Qasim Hammudi,

---

20. See pp. 65–66, below.
21. See p. 69, below.

Tariq 'Aziz and others were but a few examples of those who rose to higher Party positions by dedication and hard work.[22]

Saddam Husayn, who quietly worked up his way in the party's echelons, proved capable of surrounding himself with a number of young men who gave him almost unlimited support to rise to the highest position in the state, next to President Bakr. Championing the cause of civilian leadership, he was able to mobilize the growing civilian power against military ascendancy. After the battle was won, he relied partly on his young protégés and partly on his personal friendship with President Bakr to maintain his grip over the party.

## THE KAZZAR UPRISING

In his drive for leadership, Saddam Husayn encountered a number of opponents who were prepared to challenge him but none proved more determined, by force if necessary, to oppose him than Nazim Kazzar, Chief of the Security Police. Of humble origin and the son of a policeman, he had come to Baghdad from Al-'Amara, a town on the Tigris in the southern part of the country where the Ma'dan, a wretched and poverty-stricken community, inhabit the area.[23] Young Nazim received his primary education in al-'Amara and then, after he went to Baghdad, at the Technological Institute. While still in school, he joined the Ba'th Party early in 1959; very soon he distinguished himself as an effective party member. He took an active part in the massacre of Communists following the first Ba'thist coup in 1963 and was appointed Chief of the Security Police at Saddam's instance in 1969.[24]

Fearless and impulsive, Kazzar carried out security measures with harsh methods. It is alleged that he was responsible for the arrest, torture and secret executions of several hundred opponents, including Communists, Kurds, Nasirites, dissident Ba'thists and others. Despite

---

22. Duri, Jazrawi and Haddad are self-made; Sa'dun Hamadi holds a doctor's degree in economics from the University of Wisconsin and served as President of the Iraqi National Oil Company in 1968 before he rose to a Cabinet position in 1970. 'Izzat Mustafa and Shaykhli studied medicine in Damascus and Baghdad; Hamdani, Ghanim 'Abd al-Jalil, Tayih 'Abd al-Karim and Tariq 'Aziz studied at the University of Baghdad. The last named became editor of the Ba'th Party's organ *al-Thawra* in 1969 before he became Minister of Information in November 1974. In 1977 he was elected a member of both the Regional and National Commands.

23. His father, of obscure origin, was probably a member of the Sabaean community and seems to have become a Shi'i Muslim early in life.

24. Kazzar had not yet completed his course of study at the Technological Institute when he became Chief of the Security Police, but he passed the final examination and received the diploma in 1970, according to Durayd al-Yawir, one of his instructors.

his repulsive methods, which aroused criticism within the Party, Kazzar's influence rose high because he eliminated elements considered dangerous to the party when the position of the Ba'th regime was uncertain.

Though he agreed in principle on major issues, Kazzar came into conflict with other Ba'th leaders on the method of dealing with the Kurdish question and the Communists. Because his harsh measures proved decisive in silencing opponents, Kazzar advocated settlement of the Kurdish question by force and was responsible for the initial clashes between Kurds and security forces and for two unsuccessful attempts on Mulla Mustafa's life in 1971 and 1972. However, most Ba'th Party members felt that violence and ruthlessness would not settle the Kurdish question. They also maintained that cooperation with parties having in common certain basic principles, as defined within the framework of the Progressive National Front, should be pursued. Kazzar, whose reputation rested on the use of violence, would have nothing to do with peaceful methods—he demanded that Communist activities should be suppressed and the Kurdish military force crushed. These measures were opposed by Saddam Husayn who counselled cooperation with the Communists and, at least in the initial stage, peaceful methods to resolve the conflict with the Kurds.

Believing that his services to the Party were not sufficiently recognized, Kazzar tried to realize his ambition by violence. Since he had at his disposal the Security Police, he contended that if Lieut.-General Hammad Shihab, Minister of Defense, who had control over the Army, and Lieut.-General Sa'dun Ghaydan, Minister of Interior, who had control over the police, were to be detained by the Security Police, the combined national forces would enable him to control the regime. It is not clear whether he was able to secure the cooperation of others in high military rank. He seems to have conjectured that if President Bakr and Vice President Saddam Husayn were assassinated, the Ministers of Defense and Interior would be induced to cooperate with him and the regime would fall under his control. The initial step of the plot was to be carried out by a handfull of his Security Police. It was later revealed that Kazzar had planned to assassinate Bakr and Saddam on June 30, 1973, when President Bakr would have arrived at the Airport at 4:00 p.m. on his return from an official visit to Poland.

To secure control over the Army and Police, Kazzar invited the Ministers of Defense and Interior and a few other officers on June 30 to visit an electronic center for espionage and counter-espionage which he had recently established at the outskirts of Baghdad.[25] Upon their arrival, he ordered their arrest and held them as hostages.[26] A squad of Security Police was stationed at the Airport presumably to insure security, but in reality these policemen were instructed to open fire at the President after his arrival and the Vice President, who was expected to be at the Airport, to welcome the President. As the President's arrival was to be televised, Kazzar with his hostages were to watch the assassination on television.

Matters, however, did not proceed in accordance with Kazzar's plan. President Bakr's plane was late in leaving Warsaw and when it stopped at Varna, the Bulgarian Government had prepared an official welcome during his stop. As a result, President Bakr's plane, contrary to Kazzar's expectation, did not reach Baghdad until 7:50 p.m. The head of the security squad, thinking that the delay meant that the plot had been discovered, dispersed the squad without informing Kazzar.

Noticing on television that President Bakr's assassination orders were not carried out, Kazzar concluded that the plot must have been discovered and decided to flee the country. With his hostages, he left Baghdad heading toward Iran in a number of armored cars, presumably on the ground that Iran, then in conflict with Iraq over the Shatt al-Arab, would allow him to cross the frontier without arrest. On his way, he broadcast a message to President Bakr offering to meet him at the house of 'Abd al-Khaliq al-Samarra'i to discuss his differences with the regime and resolve them peacefully. He offered a number of proposals, put forth as an ideological rationale for the uprising rather than as personal demands. These proposals included the active

25. Sa'dun Ghaydan told me that Kazzar called him early on June 30, 1973, inviting him to visit and inspect the recently installed new instruments at the electronic center, though he had visited the center before. Ghaydan left his office with his personal guard at 10:00 a.m. and Kazzar met him outside the center. Trusting him as a party member, Ghaydan followed Kazzar to enter the center without his guard. No sooner had he entered the center with Kazzar than four Security Policemen, with machineguns in hand, told him that he was under arrest. He was taken to an underground prison cell and, handbound, detained till the evening. Next door in another cell, he heard Hammad Shihab, Minister of Defense, who, in reply to his neighbor's inquiry as to what was happening, said that he heard that a military uprising was underway and that they were detained for their own protection. The two Ministers remained in the cells till 6:00 p.m. when they were taken out by the Security Police to accompany Kazzar in his attempt to flee the country (the writer's interview with Sa'dun Ghaydan, Baghdad, January 12, 1977).

26. Kazzar ordered the arrest of some 11 other prominent figures, most of them relatives or friends of the President, whom he suspected were likely to conspire against him during the abortive uprising.

participation of the Iraqi Army in the war against Israel, stronger support for Palestinians in their resistance movement, resumption of hostilities against the Kurds, a purge of "opportunist elements" in the Ba'th Party and the transfer of power into the hands of leaders enjoying the confidence of the National Command.[27] Kazzar threatened to shoot Generals Shihab and Ghaydan if these demands were not conceded. President Bakr, on behalf of the Government, refused to negotiate and ordered the capture of Kazzar dead or alive. Saddam Husayn, proving himself up to the occasion, led the Ba'th militia and took control of key positions in Baghdad. President Bakr, Commander in Chief of the national forces, issued orders to mobilize the Army and air force to stop the fugitives before they fled the country. They were intercepted by planes and helicopters before they reached the Iranian frontier. Before he was arrested, Kazzar's men shot General Shihab dead and wounded General Ghaydan.[28]

A Special Court of four members, headed by 'Izzat Ibrahim al-Duri, Minister of Interior and member of the RCC, was set to try Kazzar and his followers. On July 7, 1973, eight security officials and 13 officers were given summary secret trials and executed on the same day. It was reported that Kazzar would give neither the names of his accomplices nor the motives for his action. On the following day (July 8) some further 36 persons, including 'Abd al-Khaliq al-Samarra'i and Muhammad Fadil, members of the Regional Command, were tried. It was reported that Fadil confessed that Kazzar had informed him of the plot at 5:00 p.m. on June 30 and that he told 'Abd al-Khaliq al-Samarra'i about it an hour later while they were waiting at the Airport, but Samarra'i denied all knowledge of the plot. Because they failed to pass on the information to higher authority, both were found guilty of treason and were condemned to death, with 12 other persons. Two more were given short terms of imprisonment; the other 20 were acquitted. President Bakr, prompted by Samarra'i's clean record, commuted his death sentence to hard labor for life, but Fadil and others, who had been condemned to death, were executed on the same day.[29]

---

27. See *The Observer*, London, July 15, 1973.
28. Ghaydan said that Kazzar ordered his men to kill both Shihab and himself, but the bullets killed Shihab, who fell over him while he, pretending he was killed, kept quiet though seriously wounded until the loyal force that arrived to arrest Kazzar found he was still alive. He was immediately taken to the hospital in Baghdad (the writer's interview with Sa'dun Ghaydan).
29. The writer's interview with 'Izzat Ibrahim al-Duri, Minister of Interior and President of the Special Court (Baghdad, January 7, 1976). See also *The Guardian* (August 11, 1973), pp. 12–13.

It is tempting to conclude that the Kazzar affair was the culmination of a long struggle between the civilian Ba'thist group led by Saddam Husayn and the military led by Hardan al-Tikriti. The latter group, it will be recalled, was weakened first by the liquidation of Hardan in 1970, then by the transfer of 'Ammash to a diplomatic post abroad in 1971, and now by the ill-fated Kazzar's plot. The position of the leaders headed by Saddam had already won, partly by the policy of cooperation with the Soviet Union, but mainly because of the proposed peaceful settlement with the Kurds on the basis of provincial self-rule and cooperation with the Communist Party and other groups within the framework of the Progressive National Front. Needless to say, the rash action of Kazzar was discredited by all who rejected violence as a party method and he had to bear the blame for all acts of violence committed against alleged enemies of the regime.

The Kazzar uprising had far-reaching consequences on the structure of politics. On July 7, 1973, an emergency meeting of the Regional Congress was called which decided to hold new elections within four months for an enlarged Regional Command (the membership was to be raised from 13 to 21), presumably to include members reflecting the enhanced position of Saddam Husayn. Because of the misconduct of some elements in the Security Police under Kazzar, it was decided to purge them and lay down rules restricting security activities. It was also decided to demolish the *Qasr al-Nihaya* (formerly *Qasr al-Rihab*), notorious as a prison in which Kazzar had inflicted torture and death on the regime's political opponents. Meanwhile, the Government began to abolish certain restrictions on the freedom of individuals and concentrate on social and economic development which gradually led to prosperity and a feeling of relaxation and confidence in the Government. Subsequently, settlement of the frontier dispute with Iran and termination of the Kurdish war in 1975 contributed in no small measure to the stability and consolidation of the regime.

## UNREST IN THE MIDDLE EUPHRATES REGION AND THE NAJAF-KARBALA DEMONSTRATIONS IN FEBRUARY 1977

While the Ba'th leaders were preoccupied in social and economic development and pursuing a foreign policy aimed at enhancing Iraq's position in the Arab world, their position was challenged by the counterpart Syrian Ba'th regime with which they have been at loggerheads. The war of words in the press was soon to lead to acts of violence resulting in serious attempts on the lives of men in high authority on both sides. Though these attempts have fortunately been mostly unsuccessful, they did result in the destruction of property and the stirring of suspicion and hard feelings in both countries. On December 1, 1976, 'Abd al-Halim Khaddam, Syrian Foreign Minister, was shot and wounded by unidentified assailants. In mid-December an explosion in the Baghdad Airport occurred (resulting in the death of three persons) for which Syria was held responsible.

More serious indeed were the disturbances in the two principal Shi'i centers of al-Najaf and Karbala, in the Middle Euphrates, on February 5 and 6 which Syria was accused of having instigated. The occasion was the annual religious procession between Najaf and Karbala to celebrate the fortieth day after the death of the Imam Husayn b. 'Ali. The fall of Husayn as a martyr in the struggle to regain authority from the Sunni Caliph in A.D. 680 is a symbolic event which reminds the Shi'i community each year that it is still under Sunni rule though the members of this community form the majority of the population in the country. This does not mean that the Shi'is each year register a protest on the matter; but on this particular occasion verbal abuse against the Ba'th leaders was freely sounded despite police intervention. For two days the riots increased and the situation got out of hand. It was only after the Army intervened that the disturbances were suppressed and a tense calm was restored. A large number of the rioters were rounded up and the principal instigators turned over to a special court for trial.

The disturbances took the Ba'th leaders by surprise as the Middle Euphrates area had been quiet and an increasing number of Shi'is had begun to cooperate with the Ba'th regime. For this reason, it was suspected that the riots were inspired by Syrian Ba'th instigators, on the ground that the Iraqi rulers were a Sunni clan not different in their attitude toward the Shi'is from previous Sunni oppressors. Since some of the top Syrian Ba'th leaders are 'Alawis—a Syrian Shi'i community—they were held by Iraqi Shi'is with high respect, although an increasing number of young Iraqi Shi'is are now members of the Ba'th Party of Iraq.

The Ba'th Government acted harshly with the instigators but prudently avoided Shi'i disaffection by accusing the Syrian Ba'th leaders of exploitation of religious demonstrations. The instigators were referred to a Special Court headed by 'Izzat Mustafa, Minister of Municipalities and member of the Regional Command, and sentences were handed out—eight capital punishment and fifteen for life imprisonment. There seems to have been differences of opinion among top Baʻth leaders on the action of the Special Court—some counselled moderation and others urged sterner punishment. As a result, the Regional Command convened on March 22, 1977, to discuss the matter. There seem to have been recriminations between the advocates of leniency and harshness in the course of which ʻIzzat Mustafa and Falih Jasim were reproached for leniency. In defending themselves, the accused indulged in abuse which compelled the Regional Command to relieve them of their offices and expel them from membership of the Baʻth Party. Though it came as a shock, the disturbances served as a signal to the Baʻth Party that the loyalty of the Shiʻi community has yet to be won by the regime.

Since the Army has supported the regime during the disturbances the position of Baʻth leadership seems to have been enhanced. As a result, Saddam Husayn, the rising star of civil leadership, has emerged as the most influential man in the Baʻth Party. And yet the Army's influence should not be completely ignored, as the man who can swing the Army to his side may still be able to impose his will over the regime. President Bakr, who keeps a vigilant eye over the military, has been able to focus the Army's attention to internal security and defense against foreign attacks. It is in this *modus operandi* between Bakr and Saddam that the stability of the regime has been possible to be maintained. An inquiry into the personality and character of the two leaders should therefore be illuminating.

## President Bakr

The Army's intervention in politics opens an opportunity to officers who aspire to play the role of politicians if they possess the qualities necessary to appreciate the play of political forces. In recent years a number of Iraqi officers have aspired to play a role in politics—Bakr Sidqi, ʻAbd al-Karim Qasim, the ʻArif brothers and others—but none has been able to preside over an enduring regime, either because he lacked the requisite political qualities or because the regime was overthrown by another adventurist officer who could bring the Army under his control. President Bakr, presiding over a relatively stable regime, possesses certain qualities of survival worthy of a close study.

Ahmad Hasan al-Bakr was born in 1914 to a relatively poor family which had long resided in Tikrit, a small town on the River Tigris (about half-way between al-Mawsil and Baghdad). He is by marriage related to the ʻUbayd and Shawi clans, both reputed to have enjoyed some influence under former regimes.[30] Before he went to study in Baghdad, little is known about Bakr's life in Tikrit. After completing his primary school, he entered the Teachers' Training College of Baghdad in 1929. His choice to enter this college (then a three year course), the only one in the country to prepare primary school teachers in a short course, is indicative of his family's poor conditions and the urgent need to earn a living, as young men belonging to families in better condition normally preferred to enter high school in preparation for a career in law, medicine or engineering. Graduating in 1932, Bakr taught for the next six years in several primary schools and began to learn about conditions in the country outside his birthplace. Though outwardly quiet, he was far from being satisfied with his modest income and the limited opportunities that a teaching position in a primary school offered. But he could scarcely change his career unless he had first completed high school education as a step for further study at the college level.[31]

In 1936, when the first military coup took place, General Bakr Sidqi, the new Chief of Staff, began to reorganize and enlarge the country's armed forces. The increasing need for Army officers opened the opportunity for primary school teachers to enter the Military College, to which only high school graduates were eligible. Bakr resigned from teaching and enrolled for military training in February 1938. He found that life in the Military College, where he spent the next four years, more congenial to him. Older and perhaps more mature than most other young men who came directly from high school, he took his military training very seriously and performed his work to the satisfaction of his superiors. His record shows that he was prompt in performing his duties, and he won the respect of both classmates and instructors. Graduating from the college at a time when the Army had just suffered defeat the year before, during the Rashid 'Ali uprising in 1941, he served as a Second Lieutenant in a number of units and kept aloof from political activities as the Army was purged of elements that had taken an active part in politics. Military life proved more stimulating to him and he developed warm and friendly relations with a

30. The 'Ubayds and Shawis used to live in a special quarter in al-Karkh, a section of Baghdad situated on the Western bank of the Tigris, and were renowned for their clannish cooperation.
31. Because the period of study in the Teachers' Training College was much shorter than in high schools, graduates of that institution were employed only as teachers in primary schools and could scarcely pursue further study in higher institutions unless they passed the Government high school examinations.

number of officers who became his staunch supporters after he entered politics.

Bakr's ambition to play a role in politics was aroused when the Free Officers movement began to spread secretly in the Army in 1952. It was then that the Ba'th Party was organized and a number of officers joined it shortly after the abortive coup of 1956 in which Ba'th leaders had participated. Like other officers, Bakr was drawn into the activities of a political party whose ideological outlook he found attractive to him. Because he was essentially a nationalist, he joined the Ba'th rather than other ideological parties.

The July Revolution of 1958, in which Ba'th leaders participated, was an important landmark in Bakr's career. He supported 'Abd al-Salam 'Arif in his struggle for power with Qasim because 'Arif was in favor of Arab unity which the Ba'th Party advocated. He was forced to retire from service (October 19, 1958) when 'Arif fell from power, thus demonstrating that he was committed to a certain group and was prepared to subordinate personal to party interests. It is not our purpose to give an account of Bakr's activities from the July Revolution of 1958 to the July Revolution of 1968, which has already been summed up before,[32] but to assess his character and leadership qualities. Since his career as leader of the Ba'th Party has been so closely linked with Saddam Husayn, it is deemed necessary to give an account first of Saddam's background and qualities before an assessment of the leadership of both is attempted.

## SADDAM HUSAYN

Like Bakr, Saddam Husayn was born in Tikrit on April 28, 1937 to a poor peasant family. Though not closely related to Bakr, he was born in a town where intermarriage among peasants established a special form of kin relationship. Family ties—even among persons remotely related—created a deep sense of personal loyalty and solidarity among young men of the same locality, which was often manifested in their readiness to cooperate and assist one another after they move into big towns or cities. It has been observed that a few young men from Tikrit who made their way up in the Baghdad milieu seem to have worked so closely together that it earned them the label of the Tikriti clan, though such cooperation among people who moved from small to big

---

32. See pp. 16–17, 19–20, above; and *Republican Iraq*, Chap. 8.

communities was not confined to Tikrit alone. Despite his social background, Saddam has shown greater independence than his contemporaries after he went to Baghdad and began his public career.

From the time when he was still in Tikrit, a number of significant events seem to have had an indelible impact on his future career. Khayr-Allah Talfah, a maternal uncle, who was then an officer in the Army, participated in the ill-fated Rashid 'Ali uprising and took part in the military operations against Britain in 1941. After the fall of Rashid 'Ali, Talfah was expelled from service. His detention, along with other officers, grieved all members of his family. Family grievance was only one among other instances which nourished Saddam with hatred of foreign influence, because British intervention in his country's internal affairs resulted in the ruining of his uncle's career and in the reestablishment of foreign influence. This event, as Saddam told me, was humiliating to him and to other young men and created in his mind resentment of foreign influence regardless of what form it may take.[33] The impact of the Rashid 'Ali affair, Saddam went on to say, was one of the principal reasons that prompted him to participate in nationalist activities which have as their goal the elimination of foreign influence not only from his country but also from all Arab lands.

The second important event in Saddam's life was his decision to continue his studies in Baghdad. After he finished primary education in Tikrit, and while he was still in the second year in high school, he began to follow student activities in Baghdad and aspired to be in the midst of those events. He left Tikrit in the fall of 1955 and entered the Secondary School of al-Karkh. While still in school, he became involved in the activities of the Ba'th Party and participated in the abortive coup of 1956. That event was then considered as a significant landmark in nationalist activities and the Ba'th Party played an important role in enlisting students to take part in it. In the following year, Saddam became a member of the Ba'th Party.

The third important event was Saddam's participation in the attempt on 'Abd al-Karim Qasim's life in 1959. He was one of ten young men selected to assassinate Qasim in accordance with a plan laid down by Ba'thist leaders.[34] Though he was wounded and sentenced to death *in*

---

33. The writer's interview with Saddam Husayn (Baghdad, August 6, 1974).

34. The other members of the commando were: Iyad Sa'id Thabit and Khalid al-Dulaymi, who organized and supervised the act, and 'Abd al-Wahhab al-Ghariri, 'Abd al-Karim al-Shaykhli, Salim Zibaq, Samir Najm, Ahmad Taha al-'Azzuz, Hatim al-'Azzawi and Yasin al-Samarra'i, who carried it out. For an account of the plot, see my *Republican Iraq*, pp. 126–32.

*absentia*, he fled the country *via* his native town in disguise and went to Syria.[35] A year later he made his way to Cairo where he completed high school in 1961. Meanwhile, he was drawn into nationalist activities during 1961–62 and became the leader in the Cairo unit of the Ba'th Party. After completing high school, he enrolled in the Cairo University Law College in the fall of 1962 but before he could finish the first year he returned to Baghdad after the Ba'th Party seized power in February 1963. As an activist, he became fully involved in the Ba'th Party and was arrested and thrown into prison in November 1964, after the fall of the Ba'th from power. His star began to rise when he and other Ba'th members supported Bakr in his drive to control the Regional Command leadership. He worked closely with Bakr after the Ba'th seized power in 1968.[36]

Shortly after he returned from Cairo, Saddam was married (May 5, 1963) to his uncle's daughter Sajida Talfah, a teacher in a primary school, whom he had known from childhood. After marriage, he seems to have been quite content with his family life and he has set an example of immunity from social temptations outside the family circle.

Believing higher education to be necessary for a political career, he never stopped attending classes at the Baghdad Law College save when he was in prison; he was able to continue his college work during 1969–70 and graduated with a law degree in 1970. Even after College, he kept his interest in literary works he regarded important for his career. Asked by the writer about books that most interested him, he replied he was interested in historical works as a whole and in works on political thought and ideologies in particular. He went on to say that the Memoirs of Colonel Salah al-Din al-Sabbagh,[37] dealing with contemporary political events in Iraq, was a source of great inspiration to him, because Colonel Sabbagh was in his eyes a great nationalist who tried to achieve Pan-Arab objectives. True, Sabbagh failed in his objectives, but his teachings inspired other young nationalists to achieve them. He, Saddam went on to explain, was inspired by Colonel Sabbagh's memoirs to pursue the same nationalist goals which Colonel Sabbagh and his followers had advocated.

35. For testimony of those arrested and made references to Saddam's role in the attempt on Qasim's life, see Ministry of Defense, *Muhakamat al-Mahkama al-'Askariya al-'Ulya al-Kubra* [Proceedings of the Special Supreme Military Court] (Baghdad, 1962), Vol. XX, pp. 32, 63, 64, 88–89, 95, 122.
36. Details concerning Saddam's activities from 1963–68 have already been noted before (see pp. 16–17, above).
37. *Fursan al-'Uruba Fi al-Mizan* (Damascus, 1956).

Saddam possesses certain qualities—patience, prudence and courage, combined with ambition and single-mindedness—which enabled him to make his way up not only in the Ba'th Party's echelons but also in the country at large. In his twenties, these qualities were negatively expressed in strikes and street demonstrations and in the daring attempt on Qasim's life in 1959. They were partly the manifestation of distrust in a society which failed to afford him the advantages enjoyed by other schoolmates and partly a reaction against foreign domination. Growing up in such an atmosphere, his character was moulded by an aversion to foreign influence and to deprivation in a system under which only privileged schoolmates derived advantages. These conditions may well explain his readiness to become an extreme nationalist and adopt socialist doctrines which the Ba'th Party embodied in its program.

While in Egypt, Saddam keenly observed the working of the Nasirite regime at first hand. Like many other young Ba'th leaders, he was an admirer of Nasir, and he learned how Nasir ruled and conducted foreign policy. He told me that he often heard Nasir reiterating the phrase "trial and error," and he tried to follow this method himself. Possessing a discriminating mind, he could see Nasir's shortcomings and his high-handed methods, and he learned as much from Nasir's failures as from his successes. Though an admirer, he was not a blind follower of Nasir.

In Iraq, Saddam learned much from his own experiences as well as from the experiences of others. He told me once that he was aware that the Iraqi people did not welcome the Revolution of 1968 as they had welcomed the Revolutions of 1958 and 1963, mainly because they have become disenchanted with revolutionary changes that failed to bring about reforms and prosperity which the revolutionary leaders had promised to achieve. For this reason, he went on to explain, the Ba'th Party had to achieve prosperity and progress in order to demonstrate the advantages of Ba'thist rule. Only four or five years after the Ba'th came to power did his countrymen begin to see some of the advantages of the new regime; earlier the majority were still distrustful of the new rulers. Military authoritarianism, he maintained, proved to be a failure; he held that stability and progress would ultimately depend on democratic rule. The present regime, he said, will eventually be transformed into a democratic system. Asked by the writer about the prospect of achieving Ba'thist goals like socialism, Arab unity and freedom, he pointed out that one should not expect these goals to be achieved overnight, especially in the wake of military uprisings. Most difficult of all, he said, is to achieve freedom and democracy. Before these goals could be achieved, social and economic development must be undertaken. As to Arab unity, he maintained that it should take the form of a federal union before all Arab countries could be united. Nor should the Arab countries necessarily have one political system; each must first develop its own local system before they are integrated into a large system.

Today, the two leading personalities who preside over a relatively stable regime and maintain a balance between competing forces are Ahmad Hasan al-Bakr, President of the Republic, and Saddam Husayn, Vice President of the RCC. Few persons who possess so different professional background and outlook are prepared to work so harmoniously as these two top leaders in the Ba'thist hierarchy. Their tacit agreement to collaborate stems partly from their realization that neither one can govern the country without the other and partly from disparity in age and the complimentary qualities of their personality and character.

In a country like Iraq which has been almost continuously ruled by the military since the Revolution of 1958—indeed, the Army had often intervened in politics even before the Revolution of 1958—the military will perhaps always have a say in politics no matter who is in the saddle. However, continuous military intervention has aroused public concern, and the demand that the Army should keep out of politics. But the country's past experience with civil regimes has not been very encouraging and the military's principal reason for intervention was to put an end to the perennial quarrel among parties and politicians which impeded progress and development. Today, no civilian regime is expected to survive unless it receives the blessing of the military, and the military are not likely to keep out of politics if the regime is not legitimized by one form of public consent or another. It is perhaps for this very reason that President Bakr, who enjoys the confidence of the military, is so well suited to preside over a civil regime. For long a loyal member of the Ba'th Party, he has no intention of subordinating civil to military authority. Nor has he the ambition, in his old age, to impose his will or govern as a "sole leader," even if he were called upon to do so by his military peers—Qasim, a predecessor, tried this and met his demise in personal rule. Thus, Bakr is well prepared to share power with a civilian leader who cooperates with him to maintain a balance between competing civil and military authorities.

Saddam Husayn belongs to a different generation. Popular among young members of the Ba'th Party, he has been given support in party congresses and rallies to provide leadership for the new generation. He also enjoys popularity among an increasing number of young officers who are on their way up to higher positions of responsibility.[38] Because of old age and ill health, Bakr has found it quite convenient to leave matters of detail to Saddam and concentrate only on fundamentals.[39] However, he has not closed his eyes to the demands and concerns of his age group who keep in close touch with him and who possess a conservative turn of mind. But all party members are agreed on the need for cooperation against the regime's opponents, because dissension undermines the very regime which all have common interests to protect. As Vice President of the RCC, Saddam is the heir apparent who is expected to step in the country's supreme position of power in accordance with the regime's constitutional framework. More important perhaps are his potentials in prudence, flexibility and resourcefulness which quickly come into operation whenever he has to make an important decision at a time of crisis. These qualities, combined with integrity and high moral courage, are his Party's best promise for the country's future leadership.

38. Saddam's acceptance of an honorary degree from the Military College and a rank in the military hierarchy reflects his desire to obtain support for his leadership in military circles.

39. Saddam has made it almost a habit to attend to all matters of detail both in and outside the Government. He has also made it known that he would directly listen to complaints brought to his attention by the people concerned either in person or by direct telephone calls.

Chapter V

# Struggle Among Ideological Groups

THE OLD REGIME, claiming to be democratic in principle, might have survived had it allowed political parties to operate within the framework of parliamentary system. But the rulers of Iraq, deeply suspicious of liberal no less than of radical groups, did not permit these groups to form political parties, although political parties were necessary for the working of parliamentary democracy. After World War II, when political parties were allowed to be reorganized under pressure of public opinion, only moderate groups were given license to form parties while radical elements were denied permission to exist in any form. In 1946 five political parties were organized.[1] They were all in agreement on fundamental issues and differed but little on political objectives. Very soon only two survived—the National Democratic and the Istiqlal (Independence) parties. These could easily have been merged into one moderate political party to their mutual advantage and formed one center party had they agreed on common leadership.[2] With one center party, there would have been room for a right-wing party, composed of the elder politicians and their followers on the one hand, and a left-wing party, consisting of radical elements of various shades of

---

1. For a brief account of these parties and their programs, see my *Independent Iraq*, (London, 2nd. ed., 1960), pp. 299–342.
2. Kamil al-Chadirchi, leader of the National Democratic Party, preferred to remain the effective leader of a small party than to be the nominal leader of a larger organization which would include the Istiqlal Party, as the latter showed readiness to join the former party (see my *Arab Contemporaries* [Baltimore and London, 1973], Chap. 8.

opinion on the other.³ Unable to form a left-wing party, the radical elements were gradually drawn into Communist circles and gave their ready support to overthrow the regime by violence. Even moderate liberal groups, looked upon with suspicion and disfavor by the ruling oligarchy, were bound to fall under radical influences—when they were finally suppressed in 1953, they joined the opposition and advocated violent change.

The hostility of the Old Regime to the party system was ultimately responsible for encouraging all opposition leaders to engage directly or indirectly in clandestine activities. Before the opposition parties were alienated by the Old Regime, only two radical groups sought change by violent methods—the Communists and the Ba'thists. Both were admittedly revolutionary parties and almost equally opposed to the old oligarchy, though the Communists were identified with an international proletarian movement, while the Ba'thists claimed an association with the Pan-Arab movement and sought to establish a socialist society within the framework of Arab nationalism.

In 1957 the opposition parties met secretly to form a National Union Front with the avowed purpose of overthrowing the Old Regime by violence if necessary. An account of how these parties came to cooperate with young army officers to overthrow the regime has already been given in another volume,⁴ but none seems to have paid attention to the need for future cooperation save the tacit agreement that a multiple party system should be recognized by the new regime.

## Two Ideological Parties

After the Revolution of 1958, all political parties were engaged in a struggle for power in varying degree of intensity, and the two parties that consciously tried to dominate the political scene were not the two moderate parties that had long been in existence—the National Democratic and the Istiqlal parties—but the two relatively small parties whose activities were essentially clandestine and confined to limited circles: the Communists and the Ba'thists.

Because these parties advocated two diametrically opposed viewpoints on Iraq's relations with the outside world—the Ba'thists called for an immediate unity with the United Arab Republic and the

---

3. In 1949 and again in 1951, General Nuri al-Sa'id tried to organize a right-wing political party which attracted only a few old and young politicians but it was sabotaged by conservative leaders (see *Ibid.*, Chap. 3).

4. See my *Republican Iraq* (London, 1969), Chaps. 2–3.

Communists for an association with the international Communist movement—'Abd al-Karim Qasim, who presided over the Revolutionary regime, encouraged the moderate parties to unite against extremist demands and assert Iraqi independence. Unwilling to cooperate with a military dictator, the two moderate parties reluctantly gave Qasim support but failed to unite against the radical parties. Nor did the public find in the programs of moderate parties anything different from the pre-Revolutionary slogans to respond to their appeal. Needless to say, the moderate parties seemed outdated and their reform programs could hardly match the ideological promises of Ba'thists and Communists, though Qasim's support might have given them the opportunity to play a constructive role. Unable to keep a balance between Communists and Ba'thists, Qasim leaned toward the Communists because Ba'thists did not compromise their commitment to Arab unity.

Incited by Communists who desperately tried to save the Qasim regime in the coup of 1963, the Ba'th Party came into a conflict with the Communist Party. Very soon, Ba'thists and Communists began to realize that the beneficiaries of this conflict were none other than the groups opposed to socialist principles with whom they had little in common. After achieving power in 1968, the Ba'th Party finally came to the conclusion that it had to reconcile its differences not only with the Communists but also with the Kurds and other leaders if it were to rule the country in cooperation rather than in rivalry with former opponents. Before we discuss this reconciliation, which led to the establishment of the Progressive National Front, a brief account of the activities of the Communist Party and other groups is in order.

## THE COMMUNIST PARTY

The vicissitude of Communist activities—persecution under the Monarchy, rivalry and competition with Ba'thists following the Revolution of 1958 and reconciliation with them after they achieved power in 1968—has been noted in earlier works;[5] though both suffered losses, it was the Communists who paid the higher price for this vain game. As a result, Ba'thists and Communists began to have second thoughts and concluded that the right-wing groups were the principal beneficiaries of their rivalry. Therefore, they agreed to cooperate in

---

5. See my *Independent Iraq*, pp. 358–64; *Republican Iraq*, pp. 117–26.

their opposition to the 'Arif regime which, in their eyes, represented an obstacle in the country's struggle to achieve progress and development. This was a turning point in Ba'thist-Communist relationship and an end of the cold war between them. It was perhaps the Communist Party that suggested cooperation, either by the establishment of a National Front or a Coalition Government.[6]

Before the Communists were able to resume political activities, they first had to put their own house in order. Ever since Yusuf Salman Yusuf (Fahd), founder of the Iraqi Communist Party, was executed in 1949, leadership of the party became a bone of contention among Fahd's successors with the consequential splits within party ranks. In 1956 splinters were eliminated and Husayn al-Radi (Salam 'Adil), though his leadership was by no means universally acknowledged, was able to control the party in difficult circumstances. 'Adil, however, was killed in the coup of February 1963 which ended the Qasim regime and brought the Ba'th Party to power for the first time. For five years, from 1963 to 1968, the Communists were engaged in resolving the leadership crisis. Before unity was restored, Communist leaders held a number of conferences in which rival leaders were either reconciled or expelled. In December 1967, leadership was entrusted to a Central Committee which assumed control of the party. Comrade 'Aziz Muhammad, who played an important part in mending differences, became the First Secretary of the Central Committee. As spokesman of the Communist Party he conducted the negotiations with the Ba'th Party for reconciliation and future cooperation between the two parties.

Before 'Aziz Muhammad's leadership was finally acknowledged, he had to undergo an ideological struggle with a group led by Comrade 'Aziz al-Hajj, whose claim to leadership rested on the need to follow Peking rather than Moscow. Whether al-Hajj was prompted to oppose 'Aziz Muhammad's leadership on personal or ideological grounds is difficult to determine. According to one informant,[7] Habib Muhammad Karim, Secretary-General of the Kurdish Democratic Party, and spokesman for Mulla Mustafa, was able to influence 'Aziz al-Hajj (a close friend and perhaps distant relative of Karim) to take Mulla

---

6. The writer's interviews with several members of the Political Bureau of the Communist Party in Baghdad in 1974 and 1976. See also the Communist Party, *Documents Relating to the National Convention of the Iraqi Communist Party* (September 1970) (Baghdad 1970), pp. 38-39, 81-82.

7. Interview with Mukarram al-Talabani, Minister of Irrigation and Kurdish member of the Communist Party (Baghdad, January 10, 1976).

Mustafa's side in his conflict with Ibrahim Ahmad and Jalal al-Talabani, the two Kurdish leaders who supported the Ba'th regime against Mulla Mustafa. Because the Soviet Union was considered an ally of the Ba'th regime, al-Hajj began to criticize Soviet support for the Ba'th on ideological grounds and this criticism brought him into conflict with 'Aziz Muhammad and his group who were in favor of Soviet policy.[8] According to another informant,[9] the conflict was purely ideological as there was always a small band within the Communist Party advocating Maoist views and criticizing others for rightist and moderate notions. In 1967, al-Hajj, supported by this group, sought by violence to impose Maoist ideology on the party. Since Maoist followers existed before al-Hajj and 'Aziz Muhammad became rival leaders, there is reason to assume that a personal motive must have prompted al-Hajj to lead the Maoist group, which may or may not necessarily have been the motive of his followers, inspired by Mulla Mustafa who promised support of the al-Hajj movement if the Ba'th regime was eventually overthrown by the Kurdish leader.

Unity having been achieved, the Communist leaders began to focus attention on fundamental objectives and to call for cooperation with other parties to overthrow the 'Arif regime on the ground that it was opposed to the multiple party system. Meanwhile, the Ba'th leaders seem to have realized that after the Six-Day War cooperation with Communists had become a necessity if the Arab position were ever to be strengthened against Israel. Communist activities, as well as the activities of other opposition groups, contributed in no small measure to the downfall of the 'Arif regime; but Communists and Ba'thists, though agreed on cooperation in principle, were unable to come to an understanding until after the Ba'th Party achieved power in 1968.

At the outset the Communists welcomed the coming to power of the Ba'th Party and joined its leaders in their cry against "colonialism" and "feudalism" but they demanded that the Ba'th regime should grant "democratic freedoms" which they considered essential for the working of democratic institutions. On July 27, 1968, the Communist

---

8. Comrade al-Hajj seems to have begun his movement as early as 1967 and tried to liquidate opponents by cold-blooded methods. It is said that he and his followers killed quite a few opponents, and made attempts on the lives of Ibrahim Ahmad and Jalal al-Talabani. After the Ba'th Party achieved power, al-Hajj and his group were captured in 1969. Al-Hajj pleaded guilty and was pardoned, but others who refused were thrown into prison (For al-Hajj's confession and explanation of his position see an interview with him broadcast on television, in *al-Thawra*, Baghdad, April 4, 1969).

9. Comrade 'Amir 'Abd-Allah's letter to the writer (dated July 20, 1976).

Party made public, after a meeting of the Central Committee, what it regarded as the minimum popular demands, summed up as follows:

1. The establishment of a parliamentary system which would put an end to repression and persecution and lead eventually to the emergence of a constitutional structure embodying democratic principles.
2. Settlement of the Kurdish question by peaceful methods on the basis of the principle of self-rule within the country's constitutional framework.
3. Improvement of social and economic conditions.
4. Restoration to Iraq of its oil resources previously granted to foreign concessionary oil companies by former regimes.
5. Suppression of foreign spy networks and the exposure of all individuals who worked for them.
6. Purging the regime of all corrupt and disloyal elements.
7. Intensification of the struggle against feudalism, imperialism and Zionism and cooperation with all socialist countries to achieve these objectives.[10]

In order to demonstrate its readiness for cooperation, the Communist Party called for the establishment of a National Front composed of all parties and the formation of a Coalition Government that would carry out a program agreed upon by all parties. This was not the first time that Communist leaders called for cooperation within the framework of a National Front, but the Ba'th Party, though agreed on cooperation in principle, seems to have preferred to consolidate first its position before entering into an alliance with other parties. The Communists, demonstrating their earnest call for cooperation, avoided any action that might be construed as a negative attitude toward the Ba'th regime. They called the attention of the Ba'th leaders to the narrow popular base on which their regime depended and continued to stress the value of cooperation. Meanwhile the Communist Party paid tribute to the Ba'th leaders whenever they achieved specific national objectives, but reproached them for not granting the other parties freedom to act despite their acceptance of the need for opposition in principle. Specific demands, put forth by Communist leaders on various occasions, were either made public in the press or in circulars distributed among party members. These demands touched various national issues—the Kurdish question, oil negotiations with the IPC and some specific grievances concerning the arrest or imprisonment of members of the Communist Party. For over two years the Communists reiterated in vain the need for recognizing the existence of opposition

10. See *Documents Relating to the Second National Convention of the Iraqi Communist Party*, September 1970 [Baghdad, 1970], pp. 37–38.

parties, especially parties that have in common with the Ba'th Party such principles as democracy and socialism, and opposition to colonialism and foreign influence.

In September 1970, the Second National Convention, considered in Communist circles as an important landmark in the Communist movement, was held.[11] Not only did representatives of the various units meet to review the position of the party in the country but also many leaders and members of various committees attended in person to express and display solidarity and unity with other leaders. Though very few speeches were made in plenary sessions, the key speech was reserved for Comrade 'Aziz Muhammad, First Secretary of the Central Committee, who reviewed the progress achieved by the party and its activities. In the name of the Central Committee, 'Aziz Muhammad submitted proposals for a new program, based on the principles that had already been accepted in the First National Convention. These were submitted for a close examination to two *ad hoc* committees, one to recommend possible changes in the draft and the other changes in the party's internal regulations. The party's program, consisting of long- and short-term objectives, was first discussed as a whole and then in detail before it was approved in a final plenary session.

The program made it clear that the Communist movement in Iraq is part of the larger International Communist movement which aims at enabling the proletariat to achieve power in each country independently, before they unite in a large federation of socialist republics. The Iraqi Communist Party considers the Communist Party of the Soviet Union as the vanguard of the International Communist movement. Any attempt at obstructing the work of the Soviet Communist Party is considered in the eyes of the Iraqi Communist Party contrary to Marxist-Leninist teachings and opposed to the International Proletarian movement as a whole. In the World Conference of Communist Parties held in Moscow in 1969, in which the need for the unity of the International Communist movement was stressed, the Iraqi delegates supported the unity and solidarity of the International Communist movement and were opposed to the Chinese delegates who expressed views considered contrary to Marxist-Leninist principles.

With regard to the Arab world, the Iraqi Communist Party viewed with satisfaction the failure of Western defense plans designed against the Socialist bloc and the success of the Arab liberation movement in

---

11. The First National Convention was held in 1945.

achieving full independence and the elimination of Western influence. It also viewed with satisfaction the overthrow of Arab regimes considered tied up with foreign powers, but regretted that in some parts of the Arabian Peninsula, where Arab rulers were still under foreign and reactionary influences, national goals had yet to be achieved. The Iraqi Communists, their program states, have always supported other Arab countries struggling against Western domination and against Israel which has become an instrument of Western imperialism, both of which are opposed to the Arab liberation movement. The Iraqi Communists welcome the role of the Soviet Union in its support of Arab rights against Zionist and Western claims. Soviet military and economic assistance, the program states, proved invaluable to the Arabs in their struggle against Israeli aggressions and in the implementation of their economic and social reform plans.

With regard to the Arabs of Palestine, the Iraqi Communist Party considers their activities as a "national liberation movement" while other parties have merely demanded Israeli withdrawal from Arab territories occupied in 1967. The Communists do not demand, as some Arab nationalists—like the Ba'th—the recovery of Arab territories occupied by Israel before 1967. (The Communist position toward Israel has been indeed vague, because the Soviet Union, on more than one occasion, has declared that it recognized the existence of Israel as a state but not its continued occupation of Arab lands since 1967. However, the Iraqi Communist Party has consistently supported full Arab rights in Palestine and has pressed upon other Communist parties to adopt the principle of the Palestinian right to self-determination and the establishment of a state in their homeland.)[12]

The Iraqi Communist Party, states its program, applauds the role of the Soviet Union in exposing Israel as an aggressor to world public opinion. Before 1967, the Arabs have often taken a negative attitude toward the Palestine question and committed errors which made them appear as aggressors, but the support given them by the Soviet Union and other socialist countries, especially at the United Nations, proved instrumental in isolating Israel and in mobilizing an increasing number of countries that demanded her withdrawal from the territories occupied in 1967. The program goes on to state that even the United States, which has given an almost unqualified support to Israel by providing her with full military equipment, seems to be quite prepared

12. 'Amir 'Abd-Allah's letter to the writer (Note 9, above).

to reconsider its policy toward the Arabs, because the Soviet Union has supported them to the point of threatening American interests in the region. The ultimate objective of the United States is to destroy any possible alliance that might be achieved between the Arabs and the Soviet Union and to undermine the position of Communist parties in Arab lands with the consequential strengthening of "reactionary" regimes and rulers whose interests coincide with Western interests. For these reasons, the United States has given support to "moderate" elements in the Arab world who would accept a compromise settlement with Israel based on partial withdrawal from occupied territories.

With regard to Iraq, the Communist Program laid down two sets of objectives—a long- and a short-term objective.

The first consists of steps to be undertaken under favorable circumstances to achieve those objectives. True, the Revolution of 1958 has overthrown the Old Regime and achieved the country's independence, but the country has yet to achieve economic independence. Owing to rivalry among competing parties, the Revolution's objectives of wiping out feudalism and achieving agrarian reform were not fulfilled. Nor did the Revolution establish the political democracy which its leaders had promised. Moreover, the Kurds, who supported the Revolution, were denied the autonomy which they had repeatedly been promised.

Socially, Iraq has achieved little progress as its class structure remained virtually unchanged almost as it existed before the Revolution. The condition of workers, socially and economically, is still in need of improvement as their standard of living falls far behind some of the countries whose economic resources are more limited than Iraq. Moreover, the status of women, though seemingly improved in the cities, is still qualified by traditional fetters in rural and tribal communities.

As to short-term measures, the program calls for democratic freedoms and the establishment of a parliamentary system based on the principle of free elections. In order to achieve this objective, all restrictive and repressive measures should be abolished or replaced by others which recognize individual liberty and freedom of expression.

As the spokesman and defender of the rights of the working class, the Communist Program pays high tribute to Iraqi workers and toilers who have demonstrated a class consciousness and an ability to struggle against exploitation and corruption by supporting the national liberation movement whenever they were called upon to do so. Iraqi workers have paid a high price for the disproportionate share they gained to improve the conditions of labor. The laws and regulations that have been issued so far have not yet abolished exploitation because capitalism still controls the country's economy. "Exploitation," the program asserts, "will disappear only if socialism and public ownership of capital were established under the control of the working class itself." This objective can be achieved only when workers are united in well organized trade unions. For this reason, the Communist Party demands that freedom should be given to all workers to organize trade unions and cooperative societies. Workers who have been put out of work should be allowed to return to their jobs and given freedom to exercise their rights to elect their trade union leaders without interference. The state should protect workers from pressures and permit them to exercise their rights of strike as a method to protect themselves against exploitation. The Communnists also demand that workers should be allowed to participate in administrative control of factories and in labor courts and committees that review wages and prepare labor laws and other matters connected with the conditions of the working class. They also demand an increase in wages and a minimum of wages for unskilled workers proportionate to their living conditions. Moreover, working hours should not exceed 42 per week. With regard to social welfare and health conditions, the Communists demand free medical service and social security to all workers and their families. They demand the inspection of workers' dining rooms and reduction of food prices, the improvement of housing conditions of workers, reduction of rents and improvement in transportation facilities as well as other social services. They also call for extending cultural facilities to workers by setting up special public libraries and cultural societies and schools that would help to wipe out illiteracy.

Finally, the Communists demand improvement in the conditions of the Army. In the past, the Old Regime paid attention only to a small coterie of old officers in the hope that they would control the Army; the younger officers and especially the soldiers were either ignored or completely neglected. The morale of the Army was low, because the soldiers were treated harshly and with utter disdain by older officers—they were often insulted, beaten or imprisoned for flimsy reasons without proper legal proceedings. Since most soldiers have been recruited from workers and peasants, the Communist Party urges that the Army as a whole should be well treated and given ample opportunities for free expression of opinion. Moreover, its social, economic and cultural levels should be improved. More specifically, the Party demands that all elements that have been relieved from service be allowed to return to their former positions, especially those who have been purged by former regimes. It also calls for permission of the military to participate in political activities. Finally, the Army should be imbued with democratic and revolutionary principles.[13]

Learning from past experiences how harmful the rivalry with the Ba'th Party proved to be, Communist leaders spared no time to impress on Ba'th leaders the need for cooperation and on almost every public issue they presented their views directly to the Ba'th Party or made them public in the press. For example, the Communist Party expressed its views on the Kurdish question quite clearly and pointed out that the conflict between Kurds and Arabs should be resolved by peaceful methods on the basis of autonomy or self-rule for the Kurds—a principle which had already been accepted by both Kurds and Arabs—and that hostile action, which cost the country millions of Iraqi pounds, led to the devastation of rural areas which should have been developed to increase production and strengthen the country against its enemies.[14] On the question of the nationalization of the oil industry the Communist Party supported with great enthusiasm the action taken by the Ba'th regime in 1972.[15] As a result, the Ba'th leaders showed readiness to come to an understanding with the Communist Party and organized the Progressive National Front to which other parties were later invited.[16] Though negotiations went on for over two years, the Front was finally established after the crushing of the abortive Kazzar coup in 1973.[17]

From 1973 to 1975, cooperation between the Communist and Ba'th parties vacillated from need to convenience but it never reached the

---

13. For full text of the program, see *Documents Relating to the Second National Convention*, Sept. 1970, pp. 61ff.

14. See the Iraqi Communist Party, *Hawl Ittifaq 11 Adhar 1970* [Concerning the March 11 Agreement], (a mimeographed circular); and a petition submitted by five groups, including the Communist Party, to President Ahmad Hasan al-Bakr, dated April 5, 1970 (mimeographed).

15. See the Iraqi Communist Party, *Hawl Mufawadat al-Naft* [Concerning Oil Negotiations], dated January 10, 1972; *Bayan al-Hizb al-Shuyu'i al-'Iraqi* [Proclamation of the Iaaqi Communist Party (concerning Oil Negotiations)] dated May 23, 1972; and *Bayan al-Hizb al-Shuyu'i al-'Iraqi Hawl Ta'mim 'Amal Sharikat Naft al-'Iraq* [Proclamation of the Iraqi Communist Party concerning the Operations of the Iraq Petroleum Company], dated June 1, 1972.

16. The Iraqi Communist Party, *Taqrir al-Ijtima' al-Muwassa, al-Lajna al-Markaziya li al-Hizb al-Shuyu'i al-'Iraqi* [Report of the Enlarged Meeting of the Central Committee of the Iraqi Communist Party] (Baghdad, 1969), pp. 20–22.

17. See pp. 79–101, below.

breaking point. After conclusion of the Iraqi-Soviet Treaty in 1972, the Ba'th regime seems to have been encouraged by the Soviet Union to initiate formal cooperation with the Communist Party. Iraq's feeling of isolation, resulting from the frontier dispute with Iran and misunderstandings with Arab neighbors, must have prompted the Ba'th Government to seek Soviet support in foreign affairs and Communist cooperation in domestic affairs. Following settlement of the frontier dispute with Iran and termination of the war with the Kurds,[18] the Ba'th leaders must have felt less dependent on Communist support and began to show greater independence in their actions than before. Perhaps no less significant is Iraq's need for Western technology and commerce after the launching of ambitious programs for development as Soviet technology proved inadequate in comparison with Western know-how and technology. Despite the weakening of cooperation, the relations between the Ba'th and Communist parties continued to exist as the regime is still dependent on Soviet arms and equipments and the Communist leaders have kept correct relationship with Ba'th leaders both in official and unofficial capacities. The Communist Party has supported the Ba'th Government in all actions on which they have agreed upon within the framework of the Progressive National Front, but not on others concerning which they have expressed different views. For instance, the Communist Party urged greater cooperation with socialist countries and warned against cooperation with countries allied with Western Powers, but, it held, since the Ba'th is the ruling party, it would be responsible only for actions on which both parties have agreed in formal discussion. In the press and in party circulars, the Communist Party expresses its own views on questions of the day.

In 1976, the Communist Party held its Third National Convention in Baghdad. Like the Second National Convention, the party's Central Committee prepared a draft program which Comrade 'Aziz Muhammad, First Secretary of the Central Committee, submitted to the delegates in a plenary session for discussion, and both the program and the party's rules were adopted after scrutiny and some changes.

In the opening meeting (May 6, 1976), the delegates warmly greeted messages received from Central Committees of the Communist Party of the Soviet Union and other socialist countries. In his report to the Convention embodying the party's program, 'Aziz Muhammad

---

18. See pp. 101ff. and 148ff., below.

reviewed developments in the international and domestic affairs.[19] In the report, he pointed out that since the time that the Second Convention held its meetings in 1970, Communists have witnessed a fundamental change in the correlation of forces in the world—greater influence and might of the world's socialist system, consolidation of its alliance with the national liberation movement and all peace-loving and progressive forces, expansion of the revolutionary-democratic and anti-imperialist movements, and intensification of the working class struggle against monopolies. The 25th Congress of the Communist Party of the Soviet Union, the report stated, had become an outstanding event in the life of the Soviet people and the International Communist Movement. As stated in the Second National Convention of 1970, the achievements by the Soviet Union were reiterated and admired by all Communists. "We convey," said Comrade Muhammad, "our congratulations to our Soviet Comrades for their success in all fields." Warning of the power that the International Communist Movement holds, the Iraqi Communit Party stated that it condemned the activities of the Peking leadership. Maoism, the report states, is contrary to Marxist-Leninist teachings and against the interests of the working class all over the world. Therefore, opposition to Maoism is declared to be a duty of all Communist and progressive forces.

In the Arab World today, the report states, there is a fierce struggle between the Arab liberation movement and its allies—the forces of progress and socialism—and imperialism, especially American and its satellite in the region—Israel—and the reactionary regimes. This struggle centers around the elimination of the consequences of Israeli aggression and recognition of the legitimate rights of the Arab people of Palestine. The differences and contradictions within the Arab world, states the report, made it possible for Israel to continue the occupation of Arab lands. The Sinai agreement, signed behind the back of the Arabs, inflicted a blow on the Arab liberation movement. It undermined Egypt's role in the struggle for the liberation of captured Arab lands. The friendly relations of the Soviet Union with Arab countries, the report states, is the main target of the machination of imperialism and reaction, as the Soviet Union is a guarantee and source of strength for the Arab liberation movement and its progressive regimes and their mainstay in the struggle against Israel and

---

19. In his reference to domestic affairs, Comrade 'Aziz paid tribute to the Ba'th Government and extended his party's greetings to the Ba'th Party.

imperialism. Progressive forces, the report adds, are quite aware that alliance with the Soviet Union is a national duty of prime importance. For this reason, the Iraqi Communist Party is opposed to the forces struggling against Soviet support for the Arab liberation movement.

The Persian Gulf, the report states, is turning into a scene of feverish activities by the oil companies and of increasing domination by the imperialists. Attempts are being made to suppress the national liberation movement in 'Uman (Oman) and the People's Republic of Yaman, and to turn the Indian Ocean into a strategic zone in support of imperialist and reactionary influences in that area. To achieve these objectives, the imperialists have reinforced their military bases in the Gulf by supplying reactionary regimes with huge quantities of arms and providing know-how and technological assistance. The United States, operating hand in glove with reaction, aims at setting up a security system in the Gulf area for conducting its aggressive strategy. The Iraqi Communist Party, therefore, deems it necessary to include in its struggle the elimination of foreign military bases and American and British military presence in the Gulf area and the expulsion of Persian and British mercenaries taking part against 'Umani nationalists.

Turning to domestic affairs, the report pays special attention to the further consolidation of the Progressive National Front, whose creation and activities are regarded as one of the greatest achievements of the revolutionary movement. The Iraqi Communist Party will, in cooperation with the Ba'th Party and other progressive elements, strive to prepare the country for the ultimate victory of socialism.[20]

After it was licensed in 1973, the Iraqi Communist Party began to conduct its business in the open and no longer were its activities considered as clandestine, though the legacy of repression and persecution remained like a millstone around its neck.[21] Communist leaders attended official functions on behalf of their party and no longer in a personal capacity; conversely, Communist anniversaries and festivals were attended by high officials and representatives of other groups and shades of opinion.[22] Communist leaders also attended regional and international

20. For text of the report, see *Tariq al-Sha'b*, Baghdad, May 9, 1976.
21. Both in 1974 and 1976, when the present writer visited the party's headquarters, he noticed security measures taken for all who were working inside or frequenting the compound from the outside.
22. On the occasion of the 42nd anniversary of the foundation of the party on March 31, 1976, Saddam Husayn, Vice President of the RCC, and Shibli al-'Aysami, Assistant Secretary of the National Command, and Na'im Haddad, Secretary of the Progressive National Front, attended the celbration. Haddad made a speech on behalf of the Front and congratulated the party on that occasion.

conferences as official delegates of the Iraqi Communist Party, especially the conferences held in the Soviet Union and other socialist countries and expressed their views on world issues and events on behalf of the Iraqi Central Committee.[23]

Despite continuous struggle against the difficulties of spreading the Communist gospel for over forty years, the Communist Party made relatively little progress in Iraq in comparison with the Ba'th Party which began to compete with it some twenty years later. As in other Arab countries, the Communist movement in Iraq began to spread among the minorities and was confined at the beginning to the literate and minority groups. Although Fahd, founder of the movement, worked assiduously to attract workers, his strongest supporters were essentially the literate and students. Until today, the Communist Party has not made much headway, though its leaders speak on behalf of workers and toilers throughout the country. Islam and nationalism have been the principal barriers that deterred Muslims in Arab lands from joining the Communist Party;[24] in Iraq, lack of effective leadership and personal differences have confined its activities to small groups. Out of long suffering from internecine conflicts, the Iraqi Communists seem to have at last learned from bitter experience the need for closing ranks and are prepared to work together under the prudent and benign leadership of 'Aziz Muhammad.

## KURDISH POLITICAL PARTIES

Under the Monarchy, no political party for the Kurds was licensed even when restrictions on political parties were relaxed after World War II, on the ground that a political party representing an ethno-cultural group would undermine solidarity and national unity. Since right and center parties identified themselves with Arab nationalist symbols in varying degree, only in left-wing parties, licensed or unlicensed, could the Kurds participate without necessarily abandoning their national identity, since these parties were essentially ideological and stressed no special nationalist outlook. There were, however, several unlicensed Kurdish parties and groupings, some of which had come into existence long before the war; others developed after the war.

The most important Kurdish nationalist party that developed before the war was the Hiwa Party which, though receiving the support of

23. For a brief account of the participation of the Iraqi Communist Party in these conferences, see Richard F. Staar (ed.) *Yearbook on International Communist Affair*, 1976 (Stanford, 1976), pp. 28-29; Ibid. 1977, pp. 516-19.
24. See my *Political Trends in the Arab World* (Baltimore, 1970, 1972) pp. 122-28.

many leaders, became inactive and split into several groups long before World War II broke out, mainly because it paid little or no attention to young and liberal elements. One of the major groups, calling itself the Ruzkari (Liberation) Party, advocated liberal nationalist views and another, called Sharash (Revolution), adopted Marxist and revolutionary principles. Both, however, merged with other parties after the war. The former joined the Kurdish Democratic Party which came into existence in 1946 and the latter, operating as a Communist unit in Kurdistan, became part of the Iraqi Communist Party.

The Kurdish party which played the most important role after the war was the *Parti Democrati Kurd*—the Kurdish Democratic Party (KDP)—which was originally organized in Mahabad by a group of Iraqi Kurds who had fled Iraq after the collapse of the Kurdish rebellion of 1945, led by Mulla Mustafa of Barzan.[25] Upon the collapse of the Mahabad Republic in 1946, Mulla Mustafa and some of his followers, considered rebels in Iraqi circles, sought asylum in the Soviet Union, where they resided for the next twelve years until they were pardoned and returned to Iraq after the Revolution of 1958. Hamza 'Abd-Allah, Secretary General of the Kurdish Democratic Party, returned to Iraq in 1946 to resume Kurdish nationalist activities. Meanwhile, Ibrahim Ahmad, a young Kurdish lawyer, who was inspired by Kurdish nationalist activities in Mahabad, became active with a group of young liberal Kurds early in 1946. He appealed to Mulla Mustafa for leadership who only reluctantly agreed after Ibrahim Ahmad and Hamza 'Abd-Allah joined hands to coordinate their activities within the scope of the Kurdish Democratic Party (KDP) which became licensed only after the Revolution of 1958.[26] However, Mulla Mustafa, though highly respected by Kurds as a military leader, proved incapable of rallying young men around him as his methods were too authoritarian and he often made political decisions adversely affecting Kurdish inter-

---

25. The founders of the Kurdish Democratic Party were Mulla Mustafa (leader of the rebellion of 1945), Mustafa Khoshnaw, Mir Hajj, Muhammad Mahmud (army officers), Hamza 'Abd-Allah (a lawyer), Anwar 'Abd-Allah (a physician) and others.

26. The writer's interview with Hamza 'Abd-Allah (Baghdad, August 15, 1974 and Mukarram al-Talabani, January 13, 1977). For a brief account of the Kurdish Democratic Party, see my *Republican Iraq*, pp. 144–145, 176–177. In an interview in London (1970), Ibrahim Ahmad told me that the party he had organized in 1946 was an Iraqi chapter of the Kurdish Democratic Party that had been established in Mahabad. Hamza 'Abd-Allah, one of the founders of the Kurdish Democratic Party, was replaced by Ahmad who became its Secretary General. Ahmad was born in 1914 (not in 1920 as I stated in *Republican Iraq*, p. 176); he studied in Baghdad and graduated from the Law College in 1938.

ests against the advice of younger counsellors. When relations between Mulla Mustafa and Qasim became strained and war broke out in 1961, the young leaders supported the Mulla; but when he suddenly made peace with 'Arif in 1963 before he was given an assurance that his demand for Kurdish autonomy was accepted, the younger leaders—Ibrahim Ahmad, Talabani and others—began to question the Mulla's political methods and dissension ensued. The KDP was virtually split into two groups; one followed Ibrahim Ahmad, urged continuation of the war until Kurdish autonomy was acknowledged, and the other, distrustful of younger leaders, remained loyal to Mulla Mustafa.[27]

After the Ba'th Party came to power in 1968, the conflict between Mulla Mustafa and the Ahmad-Talabani group was still going on. The Ba'th Government, seeking a peaceful settlement of the Kurdish question, offered its good offices between the Mulla and his opponents and its efforts bore fruition in the proclamation of the Manifesto of March 11, 1970, which all factions seem to have accepted in principle.[28] However, when war broke out in 1974 following disagreement on the implementation of the March Manifesto, Mulla Mustafa tried in vain to influence other leaders to turn against the Ba'th Government. Except Talabani, all other younger leaders saw no reason to come to a clash with the Government. After the collapse of Mulla Mustafa's regime, the leaders of the KDP, though in disagreement with the Mulla, obviously could not find themselves in the same comfortable position to negotiate with the Ba'th leaders, as the war added to the complexities of the Kurdish question.

When the war broke out in 1974, 'Aziz 'Akrawi declared that the faction of the KDP under his leadership would remain loyal to the Ba'th regime and sought to achieve Kurdish self-rule in accordance with the March Manifesto of 1970. He was supported by a number of Kurdish leaders, including Hashim Hasan, now Chief of the Executive Council of the Kurdish Province, who held that Kurdish interests would be best served by peaceful rather than by violent methods.

There were two other groups which turned against Mulla Mustafa when the war broke out—The Kurdish Revolutionary Party and the

---

27. After disagreement with Mulla Mustafa, the Ahmad-Talabani group (*circa* 200 persons) was chased out of the country and made its way to Iran in 1964. The group returned two years later after an agreement between the Iraq Government and Mulla Mustafa was proclaimed in 1966. Ahmad and Talabani seem to have been satisfied with that agreement though remaining dissatisfied with Mulla Mustafa's leadership.

28. See pp. 103ff, below.

Kurdish Progressive Group. The first, led by ʿAbd al-Sattar Tahir Sharif, claimed that it had long been in existence as the left-wing of the KDP, advocating socialist ideas which the Mulla had repudiated. Like other young Kurdish leaders, Sharif was resentful of the Mulla's traditional methods and sought, by cooperation with the Baʿth Party, to play a more constructive role in the development of the Kurdish provinces along socialist lines. He has been invited by the Baʿth Government to represent his party, considered as the counterpart of the Baʿth Party for the Kurds, in the Progressive National Front.

The other faction is the Kurdish Progressive Group, led by ʿAbd-Allah Ismaʿil. As a moderate Kurdish nationalist, he believed in liberal and democratic principles, but he has not been able to organize a political party. Since there are Kurdish nationalists prepared to cooperate with the Baʿth Government without organizing a political party, Ismaʿil seems to Baʿthists as the suitable person to represent them in the Progressive National Front. Needless to say, he is not the only one who has been disenchanted with Mulla Mustafa's leadership and sought by cooperation with the Baʿth to repair the ruptured relations between Kurds and Arabs.[29]

Finally, there are other Kurdish elements, reluctant to be identified with particular parties and groupings, which preferred to cooperate with the Baʿth Government as independent leaders. ʿUbayd-Allah al-Barzani, eldest son of Mulla Mustafa and for long in conflict with him, has come to terms with the Baʿth regime.[30] Still others—Taha Muhyi al-Din, an independent leader, and Babakr Ashdari, President of the Legislative Assembly of the Kurdish Provinces—have been appointed members of the Progressive National Front. These dozen Kurdish parties and political leaders, unable to work as a team within one political organization, revealed a fundamental weakness in the Kurdish nationalist movement as they failed to subordinate personal to national interests.

Disappointed with traditional leadership, many a young Kurd found an outlet in the activities of ideological parties, especially the Iraqi Communist Party, in which Kurdish leaders play an important part. ʿAziz Muhammad, Karim Ahmad and Mukarram al-Talabani, to mention but three examples, hold high positions in the Communist

29. The writer's interviews with ʿAbd al-Sattar Tahir Sharif, Secretary of the Kurdish Revolutionary Party and ʿAbd-Allah Ismaʿil, Minister of State and Secretary of the Central Committee of the Kurdish Progressive Group (Baghdad, January 8, 1977).
30. In an interview with the writer (Baghdad, January 5, 1977), ʿUbayd-Allah denounced his father's leadership as contrary to Kurdish national interests. He holds a cabinet post as Minister without Portfolio.

Party: the first is leader of the party, the second a member of its Central Committee, and the third is one of its representatives in the Cabinet. Others may be found as active members in national organizations, like the Partisans of Peace, and in various professional unions and academic institutions. The collapse of the tribal and feudal leadership has made room for the emergence of a new leadership; it is the hope of the new generation that this leadership, imbued with a liberal spirit, should be able to repair the havoc wrought by Kurdish wars and reconcile Kurdish with Arab nationalism.

## OTHER POLITICAL PARTIES AND GROUPS

It would be idle to discuss the old political parties that survived the revolutionary changes, like the Istiqlal and the National Democratic parties, as these exist today only in name, though some of their leaders may continue to speak as having a following. The Government did not allow them to operate and did not even recognize their existence. Since they are opposed to the "revolutionary" regime in principle, they are all labelled either as right-wing or reactionary parties.[31]

There are, however, several small but active groups which advocate nationalist and democratic principles and claim to hold progressive and not traditional notions of nationalism and democracy. Some, called the Nasirites, advocate socialism and unity with Egypt in addition to revolutionary methods. But the following of most of these groups are relatively small and have not been able to organize themselves as political parties. In principle, they have much in common with the Ba'th Party and have supported the regime. For this reason, they are considered in official circles as progressive groups and some, like the Progressive Nationalists and the Independent Democrats, have been invited to join the Progressive National Front.[32] But each is formed of only a few individuals who gravitate around a single leader and failed to form a political entity. The most important of these groups are as follows:

First, the Independent Democratic Group, headed by Muzhir al-'Azzawi, President of the Corporation of Barristers (Naqib

---

31. After the death of Kamil al-Chadirchi, leader of the National Democratic Party, the principal leaders who are still in the country are Muhammad Hadid, Husayn Jamil, Yusuf al-Hajj Ilyas and a few others, but they are no longer active in politics. Muhammad Mahdi Kubba, leader of the Istiqlal, is an old man and leadership of the party has passed to Siddiq Shanshal and Fa'iq al-Samarra'i. The latter, opposed to the regime, has left the country, and the former is engaged in business and no longer active in politics.

32. See p. 99, below.

al-Muhamin), who represents the group at the Progressive National Front. 'Azzawi has for long been associated with the defunct National Democratic Party and a member of its Executive Committee. Since this party has failed to reorganize itself, 'Azzawi has been chosen to speak on behalf of all who still regard themselves as Democrats at the meetings of the Progressive National Front. The choice of 'Azzawi seems to have been a happy one as he is on good personal relations with all who claim to be Democrats, owing to his moderate views about nationalism, socialism and democracy and to his congenial character which made him agreeable to both the Ba'th Party and former members of the National Democratic Party. Moreover, his position as President of the Corporation of Barristers placed him in the unique position of keeping in touch with men in the legal profession as some have always been interested directly or indirectly in politics. Asked by the writer about his functions as member of the Progressive National Front, 'Azzawi replied that he has always tried to present the views of Democrats on all relevant questions and has acquainted the Democrats with the decisions of the Front.[33] However, 'Azzawi seems to be reluctant to organize a political party mainly because the old leaders of the National Democratic Party are no longer active and the younger Democrats seem to be interested in radical rather than in moderate political parties.

Another group represented in the Progressive Nationalist Front is the Progressive National Group led by Hisham al-Shawi. This group exists only as independent individuals with no organization, as they represent various shades of "Arab nationalism" and seem to be reluctant to agree on a common platform. Shawi had been once active among young Arab nationalists who organized the Nationalist League in 1958, but the League never really made significant progress and those who advocated unity with Egypt—often called the Nasirites—failed to coordinate their activities under a single organization. Since the Ba'th Party is in favor of Arab unity, it showed readiness to cooperate with all elements that call for unity. Shawi has been chosen to speak on behalf of these elements at the Progressive National Front because he has kept good personal relations with them; but he does not feel that there is a real need for an active political party.[34]

33. The writer's interview with Muzhir al-'Azzawi (Baghdad, January 17, 1977).
34. In 1977 he was appointed Chief of the Office of the Republican Palace.

## The Progressive National Front

The idea of organizing a "front" goes back to the pre-Revolutionary period when political parties and groups, persecuted and outlawed, sought by concerted action to influence rulers to relax their restrictions. In the post-war years, when liberal elements became stronger, the Communist Party suggested cooperation among radical groups within the framework of a National Front to counteract the old oligarchy and their right-wing supporters. Finding the Old Regime increasingly restrictive and unable to be reconciled to the party system, all other parties eventually came to the conclusion that they had to unite not only for their own survival but also to change an oppressive regime in favor of another that would allow freedom for the expression of political opinion. In 1957, one year before the downfall of the Monarchy, the United National Front, composed of half a dozen political parties, including the Ba'th and Communist parties, was set up and began secretly to collaborate with the Free Officers who brought about the downfall of the Monarchy in 1958. For almost a decade, from the July Revolution of 1958 to the July Revolution of 1968, the United National Front existed only in name, because the two radical parties, the Ba'th and the Communist parties, were engaged in rivalry and competition, which rendered cooperation within the Front impossible despite attempts to revive it. Not until the Ba'th Party seized power in 1968, and steps to come first to an understanding between the Ba'th and Communist leaders were undertaken, that the idea of the Front was seriously considered.

The initial talks between the Ba'th and Communist leaders revealed deep differences on the form and substance of cooperation. For this reason the Ba'th took the initiative to prepare a draft Charter for National Action which might become the basis of negotiations for possible future cooperation. On November 15, 1971, the Charter was made public in the press and all parties and groups were invited to discuss it. It called for "joint action" of all the revolutionary forces in the Arab homeland to struggle against imperialism, Zionism and reaction—forces considered to have impeded the progress and development of Arab countries, individually and collectively. For Iraq, the Charter delineated some of the specific steps that should be undertaken to achieve social, political and economic development, like the promulgation of a permanent Constitution, the granting of autonomy for the Kurds, implementation of agricultural and industrial plans designed to improve the conditions of peasants and workers and others. It called for a strong foreign policy which would protect Arab interests, oppose Zionist designs and foreign influence, and cooperate with the Soviet Union and other socialist countries that support Arab rights and interests.

For almost two years, from 1971 to 1972, the Charter was discussed in the press and in public meetings attended by representatives of various shades of opinion. The discussion and specific suggestions made during the two years were taken seriously by the Ba'th leaders and some were incorporated in the final draft submitted for discussion at meetings held by Ba'thist and Communist representatives. In these meetings the Ba'th Party was represented by Saddam Husayn and Tariq 'Aziz, and the Communist Party by 'Aziz Muhammad and 'Amir 'Abd-Allah; but a number of other party members, both Ba'thists and Communists, attended as observers.

In the course of several meetings, the first of which was held on March 3, 1972, the differences between the two parties were narrowed and agreement on fundamental principles was reached.

Saddam Husayn, who presided, opened the first meeting with a short speech in which he welcomed all those who attended. He urged the leaders of Ba'th and Communist parties to be tolerant and flexible and reminded them of the dangers of intransigence and rivalry that undermined their respective positions in the past. "Both parties," he said, "have common objectives which form the basis for cooperation—the more intimately the two parties coordinate their efforts and activities, the greater the advantages for the two parties and the country."[35] He warned that the forces of reaction were still strong in the country and might frustrate cooperation, but he hoped that the establishment of a National Front in Iraq would prove to be a model of cooperation among parties for other countries undergoing similar revolutionary change in their endeavor to achieve progress and prosperity. In reply 'Aziz Muhammad, First Secretary of the Central Committee of the Communist Party, welcomed on behalf of his party cooperation and coexistence of the two parties, and, as he said he had already done on other occasions, admonished that such cooperation should be more meaningful and "strategic," and not merely "formal" and empty in actuality. He said that his party had agreed to cooperate on the basis of the Charter, but suggested that the Charter should be

---

35. The writer's interview with Tariq 'Aziz (Baghdad, Aug. 12, 1974).

*Struggle Among Ideological Groups* 99

considered merely as a set of proposals for discussion and possible changes. It was agreed that the Charter, once revised and approved by all the parties concerned, would become the official statute of the National Front.

In subsequent meetings, the Charter was subjected to a close scrutiny, but the substance remained essentially the same as proposed by the Ba'th Party. The "introductory" section, in which basic principles were embodied, was agreed upon as a full expression of the goals of both parties. With regard to the political system proposed in the Charter, consisting of institutions in which the people would be represented, the Communist delegates enthusiastically declared that they would not only endorse, but also participate in such a system actively.

In their comments on the section on national economy, the Communist delegates stated that, while they approve of the program in principle, they would like to emphasize in particular the country's economic independence, industrialization, and transformation of the economy from a "feudal and capitalist" into a fully collectivist system. It was their hope, they said, that further steps would be undertaken to establish ultimately a socialist society.[36]

The Charter having been approved, the delegates proceeded to draw up a statute for the internal regulations of the Front. The Statute provided that the Front is a form of voluntary union among progressive parties and groups seeking to achieve the objectives agreed upon in the Charter. It also provided to set up a central executive committee called the High Committee of the Progressive National Front, or simply the High Committee (HC), which forms the principal executive organ of the Front. The HC is composed of 16 members; half were reserved for the Ba'th Party, as it is the ruling party which undertakes to carry out the Front's decisions through official channels. The Communist Party was given three seats, the Kurdish Democratic Party three, and the Progressive Nationalists and the Independent Democrats one seat each. The HC, designed to operate as an executive committee, meets regularly once a month and also in extraordinary session, either by an invitation of the President or the Secretariat whenever necessary. In its meetings, it seeks to provide ways and means to achieve the objectives of the Front and to lay down plans which would make possible for public opinion to influence official organizations. It ultimately seeks to strengthen

---

36. For text of the Charter of National Action, see Appendix B.

national unity and bring about harmonious relations among national minorities. The HC is presided over by the Secretary General of the Regional Command or by his deputy. The Statute also provided for the establishment of a Secretariat composed of seven members, four nominated by the Ba'th Party, two by the Communist Party and two by the Kurdish Democratic Party. The Secretariat is headed by a Secretary appointed by the Ba'th Party from among the four members nominated to represent it in the HC. A number of committees and study groups whose work would be under the direction of the Secretariat may be appointed by the HC.[37]

Though the Kurdish Democratic Party was at first invited to join the Front, division of the party in two factions—one under the control of Mulla Mustafa and the other in favor of cooperation with the Ba'th Party—prevented their participation. After the fall of Mulla Mustafa, an invitation to other Kurdish leaders to join the Front was renewed. Since splits continued and there existed more than one group representing the Kurds, membership in the Front was raised from 16 to 18 and five seats were offered to Kurdish representatives. Meanwhile, the Front invited the Progressive Nationalists and Independent Democrats to join, each represented by one member. As a result, the Front today is composed of three parties and two groups—all considered as "progressive" organizations. But the parties and groups considered to hold right-wing views were not invited, as these have failed in their national duties and, therefore, are not worthy of being solicited for their cooperation.[38]

The Front, composed of five shades of opinion, provides a form of indirect popular support to the present regime; however, it is taken for

37. For text of the Statute, see *al-Thawra*, Baghdad, August 26, 1973.
38. The writer's interview with Na'im Haddad, Secretary of the Front (Baghdad, January 7, 1976). The composition of the Front is as follows:

I. The Ba'th Party:
   1. Ahmad Hasan al-Bakr     President of the HC
   2. Sadam Husayn            Vice President of the HC
   3. Na'im Haddad            Secretary of HC
   4. Ghanim 'Abd al-Jalil    Member
   5. Tariq 'Aziz             Member
   6. Hasan al-'Amiri         Member
   7. Hikmat al-'Azzawi       Member
   8. Ja'far al-'Id           Member

II. The Communist Party:
   1. 'Aziz Muhammad          Member
   2. Karim Ahmad             Member
   3. 'Amir 'Abd-Allah        Member

granted that the Ba'th, the ruling party, holds the predominant position and is entrusted with the enforcement of the Front's decision. All decisions having been freely discussed, are taken by unanimous vote; but in circumstances necessitating quick action, decisions were taken by consensus and "persuasive arguments." Since the Ba'th is the ruling party, it is taken for granted that it is solely responsible for all actions, irrespective of the views of other members of the HC, because the regime is not, strictly speaking, a "coalition government," but a Ba'thist regime supported by other parties and groupings.[39]

## THE KURDISH QUESTION: THE POLITICAL AND IDEOLOGICAL ASPECTS[40]

Divided in the main among four countries—Turkey, Iran, Iraq and Syria—the Kurds of Iraq hoped that in a country under British influence they might enjoy greater freedom and their national life develop into maturity. The Iraqi Government agreed to recognize the Kurds as a people having their own cultural identity and granted them full status as Iraqi citizens. Upon the termination of British tutelage, it was hoped that in time the Kurds would be integrated with Arabs and other ethno-cultural groups to form the Iraqi nation.

But after independence neither the Kurds nor the Arabs were prepared to give up their national identity and failure to create a new national identity for Iraq was the root cause of Kurdish reluctance to give up their Kurdish identity. As the Arabs always asserted the Arab

---

   III. The Kurdish parties and groups:
   1. Hashim 'Akrawi (Secretary of the Central Committee, KDP, and President of the Executive Council of the Kurdish Provinces).
   2. 'Abd al-Sattar Tahir Sharif (Secretary of the Central Committee of the Kurdish Revolutionary Party).
   3. 'Abd-Allah Isma'il (Secretary of the Central Committee, Kurdish Progressive groups and Minister of State).
   4. Babakr Ashdari (President of the Legislative Assembly of the Kurdish Provinces).
   5. Taha Muhyi al-Din (Independent Kurd).
   6. 'Aziz 'Akrawi (Independent Kurd), Minister of State.

   IV. Independent Democrats: Muzhir al-'Azzawi

   V. Progressive Nationalist Group: Hisham al-Shawi

39. The writer's interviews with Na'im Haddad, 'Amir 'Abd-Allah and others.
40. A full account of the Kurdish question is deemed outside the scope of this study, but its political and ideological aspects may well fall in the category of other groups and movements dealt with in this chapter.

character of the country and the new generation identified itself with Pan-Arabism, the Kurds feared that their dependence on an Iraqi identity might be merely a step toward their ultimate assimilation by the advocates of Arab nationalism. The Kurdish nationalism that had been in the making before independence began to grow and was given impetus by the corresponding growth of Arab nationalism after World War II, without a serious attempt to discourage either trend or to impress on both Kurds and Arabs the necessity of stressing the supremacy of the Iraqi national identity.

We have already had occasion to discuss in previous studies the steps taken under the Monarchy and the Republic to deal with the rising tide of Kurdish nationalism by negative methods.[41] Since Kurdish nationalism took the form of tribal uprisings led by tribal chiefs—Mulla Mustafa and others—it was suppressed by force on the ground that they were rebellions challenging the authority of the central Government. Nothing constructive was done to win the confidence of the Kurds and the root cause of dissatisfaction remained virtually untouched.

Long before it came to power in 1968, the Ba'th Party was perhaps the first political party to tackle the Kurdish question with a positive and constructive approach. The party's attempt to deal with the Kurdish question in 1963 came to an unsuccessful end as the party fell from power within eight months and was quite unprepared to deal with the problem. For the next five years, from 1963 to 1968, the Ba'th leaders gradually came to realize that if Iraq was ever to be strong and united Kurds and Arabs must coexist and cooperate rather than remain in conflict. In both the National and Regional Command congresses, the Kurdish question was discussed and resolutions were adopted in favor of the recognition of the Kurdish national rights as an ethnic group within the framework of the Arab homeland. More specifically, the need for a settlement of the Kurdish problem was stressed in the resolutions of the ninth and tenth congresses of the National Command. It was stated that cooperation between Kurds and Arabs was essential in order to achieve unity and mobilize the Iraqi national forces to defend the Arab homeland against foreign threats.[42]

41. See my *Republican Iraq*, pp. 144–45, 173–81, 268–78.
42. For the platform of the ninth National Command Congress held in Bayrut in 1968, see the Ba'th Party, *Istratijiyat al-Marhala al-Rahina* [Strategy of the Present Transitional Period] (Bayrut, 1968), p. 48. See also platform of the tenth National Command Congress held in Baghdad in 1970, in *al-Taqrir al-Siyasi* [Political Report], p. 81.

After achieving power, the Ba'th leaders began to take practical steps to settle the Kurdish question. First, the Ba'th Party and the Kurdish Democratic Party (KDP) initiated negotiations with a view to arriving at a set of proposals embodying essential Kurdish national demands. Second, the proposals were reformulated as a manifesto, came to be known as the March Manifesto, acceptable to the two parties on behalf of Kurds and Arabs and issued by the Revolutionary Command Council (RCC) as an official proclamation on March 11, 1970. Third, the March Manifesto was endorsed by the Progressive National Front and the Government was committed to settle the Kurdish question on the basis of that Manifesto. Negotiations between the Ba'th leaders and Mulla Mustafa began a year after the Ba'th Party seized power in 1968. It took almost two years, in the course of which private emissaries went back and forth to narrow the differences between the Mulla and the Ba'th leaders, before a final agreement on essential Kurdish national demands was reached. Before it was issued as an official proclamation, the March Manifesto was submitted to a number of leaders concerned with Kurdish affairs for scrutiny. On March 11, 1970, the Manifesto was approved and issued by the RCC as an official statement of the Iraqi Government. The principal points may be summed up as follows:

1. Recognition of the legitimate existence of the Kurdish nationality as it had already been stated in previous Ba'th pronouncements. This recognition will be given official expression in the temporary Constitution and eventually in the permanent Constitution.

2. The RCC approved the establishment of a university in Sulaymaniya and a Kurdish Academy of letters. The RCC has also approved recognition of all the Kurdish cultural and linguistic rights and of the teaching of the Kurdish language in all schools, institutes, teachers colleges and universities and in the military and police colleges. It also provided for the distribution of Kurdish literary, scientific and political publications which express the national aspirations of the Kurdish people and to enable Kurdish writers and poets to organize a union which would publish their works and offer opportunities to develop their scientific and artistic talents. It also approved the establishment of a printing and publishing house for the publication of a weekly newspaper and a monthly magazine and for the inclusion of a Kurdish broadcasting program in the Kirkuk TV Station, pending the construction of a special Kurdish TV Station.

3. In recognition of Kurdish rights to revive their national traditions and holidays, the RCC decided to regard the Nawruz—a Kurdish National Day—to be a National Day for the Iraqi Republic.

4. The RCC has issued a Provincial law in which the principle of decentralization of local administration is embodied and created the new province of Duhok.

5. The RCC has proclaimed a general amnesty for all civil and military personnel who had taken part in "violent acts" (i.e., military operations) in order to restore order and security in the northern part of the country.

In order to give expression to the foregoing provisions, which have been accepted by Mulla Mustafa, leader of the KDP, the RCC has decided that:

1. The Kurdish language, together with the Arabic language, will become an official language in the areas inhabited by a majority of Kurds and will be the language of instruction in the schools of those areas. The Arabic language will be taught in the schools where Kurdish is the language of instruction and Kurdish will be taught as a second language throughout the country in accordance with the limits set by law.

2. The Kurds will participate in all public offices, civil and military, without discrimination.

3. Because of the lag in the cultural and educational levels in the Kurdish area, the following plan has been laid down:

(a) In order to speed up the implementation of the RCC decisions relating to Kurdish cultural and linguistic rights, it has been decided to establish a Directorate-General of Kurdish Culture and Information to be entrusted with these functions.

(b) The number of schools in the Kurdish area will be increased and an attention be given to raising the standard of instruction and increasing the number of Kurdish students in the colleges and universities at a fair rate.

4. In the administrative units inhabited by a majority of Kurds Government officials will be Kurds, or persons well versed in Kurdish; but all high posts, official and unofficial, will be held by Kurds.

5. The Government recognizes the rights of the Kurds to organize unions for students, teachers and others; these will be represented in similar national organizations of the country.

6. The decree concerning the general amnesty issued in 1968 will be applied to civil and military in the northern part of the country and all those who had been in civil and military service before the operations will be allowed to return to service.

7. A committee will be appointed to speed up the development of the Kurdish area and repair past injustices. A special plan for development will be laid down to ensure implementation of the general development relating to the Kurdish area.

8. Displaced Kurds and Arabs will be allowed to return to their places of residence (or to the nearest place of residence) and compensated for losses incurred by displacement.

9. Steps will be taken to speed up the implementation of the Agrarian Reform Law in the Kurdish area.

10. The Temporary Constitution will be amended to include the principle that Iraq is composed of two principal nationalities—Arabs and Kurds. The Constitution will also recognize the national rights of other nationalities within the framework of Iraqi unity.

11. The heavy arms and broadcasting station in possession of Kurds in the northern provinces should be returned to the Government (this item will be included in the implementation of the final stages of the agreement).

12. One of the Vice Presidents of the Republic will be a Kurd.

13. A Provincial Law will be enacted in accordance with the tenets of this Manifesto.

14. Necessary steps will be undertaken to reorganize and unify the provinces inhabited by Kurdish majority in consultation with a High Committee set up to supervise the provincial reorganization. Pending the achievement of administrative unity, Kurdish national affairs will be handled jointly by the High Committee and the provincial governors. As self-rule is to be exercised within the framework of the Iraqi unity, the exploitation of natural resources in the area will be carried under the jurisdiction of the central authority.

15. The Kurds will be represented in the Legislative Assembly in proportion to their percentage of the population of the country.[43]

The implementation of the March Manifesto was expected to lead eventually to "self-rule" in the Kurdish area within the framework of the new Provincial Law in which the principle of administrative decentralization was enshrined. As an administrative measure, decentralization was no innovation, as it had already been introduced into the provincial system with Mulla Mustafa's approval. It was a compromise between the Mulla's demand for autonomy and direct control of the Kurdish area by the central authority. In the new Provincial Law, self-rule for the Kurdish area was a form of decentralization which the law has provided for the rest of the provinces in order to preserve the country's unity within the new decentralized system. The Ba'th leaders naturally took it for granted that under the new administrative system the central authority was supreme while Mulla Mustafa contended that certain residuary powers were to be exercised by him through the mechanism of self-rule. The Kurds might have accommodated to the new compromise and might have even derived some social and economic advantages under the Five-Year development plans, but Mulla Mustafa was not fully convinced that the Ba'th conception of self-rule would ultimately achieve his cherished ideal of autonomy.

43. For full text, see Appendix C.

Having spent almost all his career as a military leader and enjoying almost unlimited power over his followers, it was exceedingly difficult for the Mulla to surrender or limit his personal rule over a people for whom he had worked so assiduously to achieve national identity. In the Mulla's eyes, national identity was summed up in the word "autonomy." When he accepted "self-rule" as a compromise, it was but a step that would eventually lead to autonomy. The Ba'th leaders looked at the matter from a different perspective. They realized that the Kurdish people, who are different in language and culture from the Arabs, are entitled to preserve and cultivate their national heritage but to have a separate political existence is an entirely different matter. Only within the framework of the Iraqi political system was the Ba'th Party prepared to recognize Kurdish national rights but such recognition should not eventually lead to the separation of Kurds from Arabs. These divergent views as to what would be the ultimate outcome of self-rule led Mulla Mustafa and the Ba'th to find themselves going in different directions when the principles of the March Manifesto were put to the test.

Three points might be singled out as the most important differences in the interpretation of the principle of "self-rule" as envisioned in the March Manifesto. First, Mulla Mustafa demanded that four of the provinces specified in the new Provincial Law—Sulaymaniya, Kirkuk, Arbil, Sinjar and Duhok—should be considered Kurdish even though some of the towns and localities within them may not be inhabited by a majority of Kurds, like the cities of Kirkuk and Khanaqin. Moreover, the towns of Sinjar and al-Shaykhan in the Nineva province, where the Kurds are intermingled with other ethnic groups were also claimed by the Mulla to be considered part of the Kurdish area on the ground that these ethnic groups are non-Arab and are closely associated with Kurds. Second, he demanded the retention of certain powers to conduct Kurdish foreign relations which he had exercised during the *de facto* regime over which he presided when he was at war with the central Government. Third, he demanded the retention of control over the Pesh Merga—the Kurdish militia—though he agreed that this force should become part of the national Army.

The Ba'th leaders rejected the Mulla's three demands because they considered them inconsistent with the principle of sovereignty, though they agreed to establish a joint Kurdish-Turkoman administration for the city of Kirkuk on the ground that the inhabitants of the city itself are made up of a mixture of Kurds and Turkomans. To the Mulla, however,

Kirkuk was an important center in the midst of the Kurdish area and would not accept its exclusion though he offered to accept a mixed administration for the city itself. Although he continued his contacts with Iran and other countries (including indirect contacts with American and Soviet messengers), the Mulla agreed to give up his demands for direct negotiations with foreign powers in principle but demanded Iraqi support for Kurdish national rights in Iran and Turkey.

From 1970 to 1972 negotiations between the Ba'th and Mulla Mustafa were continued with a view to narrowing the differences, but suspicion seems to have often been deepened by indirect threats to resort to armed conflict or by attempts to gain certain tactical steps in protracted negotiations. Most dangerous of all were the two attempts on Mulla Mustafa's life in 1971 and 1972 and the arrests and shootings on both sides which created deep suspicion that the March Manifesto was but a temporizing measure to gain time for a final resort to force to settle the problem once and for all.

The Ba'th leaders, realizing that Mulla Mustafa was not prepared to accept "self-rule" within the country's political system, came to the conclusion that confrontation with his forces was perhaps inevitable. Since the Mulla's leadership was by no means uncontested in the Kurdish area—he was opposed by some tribal chiefs (Zibaris and others) and by younger leaders (Ibrahim Ahmad, Talabani and others)—the Ba'th decided to cooperate with the younger leaders who might be more interested in social and economic development of the area than with autonomy. The Ba'th Party was able to persuade these leaders that their cooperation was in the interest of both Kurds and Arabs. The Mulla, suspecting that his authority and prestige might slip from his hands, denounced the young Kurdish leaders as traitors and gave up the hope that Kurdish national demands would be conceded under the Ba'th regime.

From the time he went to war with the central authority in September 1961, Mulla Mustafa's prestige and influence had been widely increasing, especially when his army fought successfully against the Iraqi Army. By 1972, the Mulla had become virtually the *de facto* ruler over the entire Kurdish area, even though the civil administration in the cities remained operating nominally under control of the central authority. He kept in touch with foreign governments through official or semi-official emissaries, and was receiving foreign military and economic aid despite warnings from the central authority against his foreign ventures. From a position of strength, he felt that he should press for an interpretation of the March Manifesto which would virtually guarantee not only self-rule as he understood it, but also his own personal rule, which to him symbolized legitimate Kurdish claims to autonomy. In personal conversations he often denounced the Ba'th regime as repressive and undemocratic, and he called upon opponents of the regime to replace it with his support by a democratic system which would be acceptable to both Kurds and Arabs. Attempts by conciliatory missions to prevail over the Mulla to change his mind were unsuccessful, as he was fully convinced that the Ba'th leaders were determined to get rid of him and impose the March Manifesto as they understood it.[44]

In 1973 the Ba'th Government tried to enlist the support of other political parties in an effort to influence the KDP to reconcile the differences between Kurdish and Arab demands. During the negotiations for the establishment of the Progressive National Front, a special meeting was held (January 3, 1973) in which the Kurdish question was thoroughly re-examined. The Ba'th leaders seem to have been quite prepared to concede certain Kurdish demands such as the distribution of civil and military posts, the application of the agrarian reform law, return of displaced persons and others; but the larger political issues—the deeper causes of conflict—were not discussed. By the end of 1973 it became clear that Mulla Mustafa could not be prevailed upon to come to terms with the Ba'th. On the contrary, it was suspected that he was working with opponents to overthrow the regime by force.

On March 11, 1974, the fourth anniversary of the Proclamation of the March Manifesto, the Government declared that it would enforce the law governing self-rule and invited the Kurds to whom the principles of the law were acceptable to cooperate in its enforcement. Appointments to administrative posts in the Kurdish area under Government control were made, but Mulla Mustafa denounced the Government's action and warned his followers against collaborators with the Ba'th regime.[45]

---

44. The Ba'th Party submitted a detailed Memorandum to the KDP on Sept. 23, 1972, reviewing all the points of differences and tried to impress on Kurdish leaders the need for cooperation in the interest of both Kurds and Arabs, but to no avail. For text of the Ba'th Memorandum and the KDP reply, see al-Thawra, *Likay Yusan al-Salam Wa Tu-'azzaz al-Wihda al-Wataniya* [In order that Peace be Protected and Unity Strengthened.] (Baghdad, 1973), pp. 183–186, 189–233.

45. See pp. 105–106, above. Self-Rule Law for Kurdistan, issued on March 11, 1974 provided for separate Legislation and Executive Councils for the Kurdish area as well as a

Since the Kurdish leaders were divided and an increasing number of younger elements were prepared to compromise with the regime on the basis of the proposed self-rule law, Mulla Mustafa's leadership necessarily became dependent on the tribal sections and he appeared to represent an old generation struggling to perpetuate tribal and feudal traditions rather than the enlightened sections of his people. To the younger Kurdish and Ba'th leaders the removal of Mulla Mustafa became necessary if negotiations were to be resumed between Kurds and Arabs.

Early in 1974 the Ba'th Government finally decided to crush Mulla Mustafa by force. During the spring and early summer the Iraqi Army concentrated on relieving besieged garrisons and opening roads and moving slowly into the Kurdish area. In July and August the Pesh Merga were forced into the mountains along the Turkish and Iranian borders after an intensive offensive launched by the Iraqi Military Command. From this time the Pesh Merga had to rely on Iranian reinforcements without which they could not resist the heavy Iraqi offensive, including the bombing of Kurdish towns and villages. For the next six months, the advance of the Iraqi Army into the mountain area slowed down, especially during the winter of 1974. In 1975 the offensive was resumed in the spring and the agreement between Iraq and Iran on the frontier dispute in March, 1975, left the Pesh Merga at the mercy of the Iraqi Army bombing. Iran agreed to encourage Mulla Mustafa to accept a cease-fire announced on March 13 by both sides. The RCC declared that an amnesty would be granted to all Kurds, including deserters from the Iraqi Army, who surrendered by April 1.

The KDP, even before Mulla Mustafa's departure for Iran, offered to negotiate a settlement with the Ba'th leaders, but the offer was rejected and President Bakr declared that the only way to "avoid further bloodshed" was to accept the terms of the general amnesty which was to expire on April 1. Meanwhile, the Iranian Government called on the Kurdish refugees in Iran to decide by April 1 whether they

---

decentralized administrative system. These were designed to allow the Kurds to use the Kurdish language as official and have a separate budget for social and economic development of the region. The Legislative Council, composed of 80 members, is to be freely elected by the people; the Executive Council, composed of a President, Vice President and a number of other members, is to be organized by a member of the Legislative Council appointed by the President of the Republic. For text of the Self-Rule Law, see the *Official Gazette*, Baghdad, March 26, 1974. See also Ministry of Information, *Qanun al-Hukm al-Dhati Li-Mantaqat Kurdistan* [Law of Self-Rule for Kurdistan] (Baghdad, 1974).

wanted to remain or to return to Iraq, as the frontier between the two countries would be closed on that date. Several thousands returned late in March but when the amnesty was extended to the end of April a few thousand more returned, as both the Iranian and Turkish borders were closed to Kurdish infiltration. The Iraqi Army took complete control of the Kurdish area by the end of March.

It is not our purpose to give a narrative of the military aspect of the Kurdish conflict, as this belongs to military history, but it is significant to note that tribal warfare in the mountainous area, which was difficult to end in the past, is no longer possible to continue without support of a neighboring regular army in the face of full scale war waged by a well-equipped army of the Iraqi Government. Consequently, when Iraq came to an understanding with Iran to cease its support for the Kurds, Mulla Mustafa's fate was sealed.[46] He surrendered to the Iranian authorities, and the Kurdish leaders prepared to cooperate with Arabs were bound to accept an accomodation with the Ba'th regime on its own terms. The Kurdish rebellion seemed to have been suppressed by the removal of Mulla Mustafa, but integration of the Kurdish area with Iraq would depend on the mutual acknowledgement of Kurdish legitimate demands and the need for repairing the ravages of war and past injustices. These, the Ba'th Government declared, it is prepared to carry out within the means which are now at its disposal.[47]

46. Apart from settlement of the border dispute with Iraq, the Shah of Iran declared that he ceased support for the Kurds because "they were making no progress in the war" (see Joseph Kraft, "What Restrains the Shah," *The Washington Post*, April 27, 1975).
47. For policy statements made by the Ba'th Government on the Kurdish question, see *al-Thawra*, Baghdad, Aug. 27, 1976.

Chapter VI

# Social and Economic Development

THE OLD REGIME, considered to have been the bulwark of vested interests, followed an agricultural policy whose beneficiaries were tribal shaykhs and landowners and paid little or no attention to the poorer classes. The Revolution of 1958, presumably to repair the injustices of the Old Regime, promised to carry out social reforms and achieve progress and economic prosperity. Rejecting the advice of foreign experts who had discouraged industrialization and urged agricultural development, the Revolutionary leaders consciously sought to launch industrialization and economic development, including an emphasis on agricultural policy. However, most of the reform measures promised by the July Revolution (1958) were not carried out because the struggle for power among rival leaders and groups for almost a decade, from 1958 to 1968, left little or no time for constructive work.

Following the Revolution of 1968, when the country was spared changes of regimes and rulers, grandiose schemes of development were initiated which marked a significant departure from the social and economic policies of previous regimes. Not only did the new rulers seek to transform the economic system from free enterprise to collectivism, but also to achieve the country's economic independence without which political independence cannot be long sustained. True, the Revolution of 1958 asserted the country's political independence and achieved some measures of economic independence, but social and economic developments were neither correlated nor pursued to their logical conclusions. Only after 1968, when the political system became fairly stabilized, did the government lay down a consistent policy correlating political, economic and social affairs and take steps to carry them out. The immediate objective of this policy was to increase production and raise the standard of living, but the ultimate objective was to establish a socialist society in which all injustices would be wiped out and all citizens enjoy the benefits of progress and prosperity.[1] Six major steps, laid down to achieve these goals, may be singled out as the most important for discussion: First, planning and research; second, agrarian reform; third, nationalization of the oil industry; fourth, industrialization; fifth, irrigation; sixth, social and cultural development.[2]

## PLANNING AND RESEARCH

Planning as a method to achieve development began in 1950 when a considerable increase in oil revenues was made possible on the basis of 50-50 profit sharing between Iraq and the oil companies. A Development Board was established in 1950 to formulate and implement various projects for reconstruction, especially those relating to irrigation and flood control. Before 1950 no organization had yet existed for planning, although a number of specific projects were laid down and carried out by such departments as irrigation, transportation and communication, and others, whenever funds were earmarked for reconstruction. These projects, especially those laid down by the Development Board, were then criticized on the ground that they were essentially focussed to increase agricultural production and paid little or no attention to rural or urban reform. More important, the projects were not adequately correllated nor were they worked out within an overall development plan.

After the Revolution of 1958, a certain awareness that planning should be oriented toward a more balanced development and social goals became noticeable. During the decade from the July Revolution of 1958 to the July Revolution of 1968, development plans stressed agrarian reform, slum clearance (especially in the Baghdad area), the improvement of working conditions, education and health services. The Development Board of the Old Regime was abolished; a Planning

---

1. For a general statement of the Ba'th economic policy, see Regional Command, *al Taqrir al-Siyasi al-Sadir 'An al-Mu'tamar al-Qatri al-Thamin* [The Political Report of the Eighth Congress of the Regional Command] (Baghdad, 1974), pp. 66–80, 114–40.

2. These steps are listed roughly in the order in which the Government has tried to carry them out.

Board and a Ministry of Planning were established in 1959. A growing feeling that some attention to industry must begin to be paid was noticeable; but only a modest beginning was attempted. A Four Year Provisional Economic Plan (1959–63), in which a number of industrial projects were included, was laid down, but its implementation was tediously slow. A detailed Economic Plan (fiscal year 1961/1962–1965/1966),[3] designed to supersede the provisional plan and to emphasize industrial development, was launched. For the first time, it was noticed, the aim of economic development was to double the level of national income in ten years. Although the plan failed to achieve its objectives (owing to inadequate funds and technical shortcomings), it was a step in the right direction for economic development.

In 1965, a new economic plan, called the Five Year National Economic Plan (1965–1970) was laid down. By far more detailed, the plan concentrated on raising the level of production, both agricultural and industrial, and it aimed at reducing dependence on oil revenues as the primary financial source for development. The implementation, however, did not measure up to expectations, because agricultural development lagged far behind the target and industrial development was very slow. Nor was dependence on income from oil as the primary source for development reduced, as the progress in agriculture and industry proved far below expectations for a number of reasons, technical and otherwise.

At the outset, the Ba'th Government was bound to concentrate first on the projects that had already been laid down under the former regime. By the time the first Five Year National Development Plan of 1971–1975 was launched, there was a definite qualitative departure from the plans of previous regimes. First, the Ba'th Party was committed to socialism in principle and sought to formulate the first five year development plan along socialist lines. To achieve this objective, an increase in agricultural and industrial production was considered a primary step in the process of development. In this respect, the Ba'th Government possessed a clearer understanding of what development meant and sought by an increase in production to achieve social and cultural development, and a higher standard of living. The ultimate aim of development, according to the Ba'thist platform,

3. The fiscal year in Iraq begins in April. For this reason the development plans have been officially dated to begin on 1961/1962, 1964/1965, 1969/1970, 1974/1975 and 1975/1976. In this study the dates in accordance with the calendar rather than the fiscal years would be used for the sake of simplicity.

was to achieve social justice for all and not merely for a particular group or class.

Second, the plan sought to balance the structure of economy and diversify production; it also sought to reduce dependence on oil exports and introduce other domestic resources. It was realized from the beginning that at the initial stage there would be even greater dependence on oil income to improve agricultural production and expand industry, but that in the long run the country would ultimately depend on domestic resources and capital to carry out social and economic programs. This initial or transitional stage was stressed in the First Five Year Plan (1971–75), but the long-term objective is made clear in the Second Five Year Plan of 1976–80.

As the concept and functions of planning boards changed from limited to broader aims, so did the machinery and procedure begin to change to meet new demands and expectations. It is a healthy approach to development that the machinery should undergo changes and the whole system was and still is under review as the process of development continues.

After the Revolution of 1958, when the concept of planning was adopted, the Development Board of the Old Regime was only slightly changed in structure to include the Ministers of Finance, Economics, Agriculture, Social Affairs, and Communications and Works. The full time membership was abolished. A Steering Committee, headed by the Development Minister, was established, composed of the directors general of the departments concerned and a few experts selected for their professional experience. The Development Board and the Development Ministry were abolished a year later (1959), replaced by an Economic Planning Board and a Ministry of Planning: the latter was entrusted with the formulation of plans, taking into consideration the recommendations of the former. Although membership was twice changed in 1964 and 1966, the structure remained essentially the same.

The radical departure in the planning system began to take place after 1968, partly under the influence of Ba'thist ideas and partly under the influence of planning experts who had drawn on Iraq's experiences in planning during the past ten years. "It became very clear now," says Jawad Hashim, a former Minister of Planning, "that the formulation of a plan was a sequentially linked process, and hence had to be put on a firm ground from the very first stage of plan formulation."[4] To achieve its

---

4. Jawad Hashim, *Development Planning in Iraq* (Baghdad, 1975), p. 89 (mimeographed). For a discussion of economic planning within the framework of the Ba'th Party's ideology, see a lecture by 'Adnan al-Hamdani in *al-Thawra*, Baghdad, February 2, 1975 (Hamdani is Minister of Planning).

purposes, the Iraqi experts state, the planning system must have two prerequisites. First, data and statistics; and second, technical cadres and expertise (technical know-how). These prerequisites were gradually met; data were meticulously accumulated and young experts, trained in Western institutions, were given responsibility to serve and in time they have shown readiness to learn from experience and contribute to development under an effective leadership.

In 1968 the Planning Board was reorganized to include the President of the Republic and the Ministers of Planning, Finance, Economics, Industry, Agriculture, Agrarian Reform, Irrigation, Works and Housing, Education, Higher Education and Scientific Research, and the Governor of the Central Bank. The Board also included five experts as part-time members. Heads of technical departments in the Ministry of Planning were allowed to attend meetings as non-voting members. Although alterations were often made, the structure remained essentially unchanged. As it stands today, the Planning Board is composed as follows:

First, the permanent members, representing the various departments concerned with planning, are as follows: Vice President of the Revolutionary Command Council (Saddam Husayn), Minister of Planning, President of the Higher Agricultural Council, Minister of Economics (now subdivided into the Ministries of Foreign and Domestic Trade), Minister of Industry and Minerals, Minister of Agriculture and Agrarian Reform, Minister of Irrigation, Minister of Education, Minister of Works and Housing, Minister of Higher Education and Scientific Research, Governor of the Central Bank, and President of the Organization for Scientific Research.

Second, seven permanent members, drawn from various national organizations, were appointed for their expert advice.[5]

The Planning Board's executive organ is the Steering Committee, composed of 12 members, which serves as a body of experts and prepares projects for approval by the Planning Board on the one hand and directs and supervises the work of various technical committees on the other. The members of the Steering Committee are as follows: Minister of Planning, Chairman; the five part-time members of the Planning Board; and the Director Generals of the technical departments of the Ministry of Planning (Agriculture, Industry, Economics,

---

5. They are as follows: Zayd Haidar, member of the National Command; Fakhri Qadduri, Governor of the Central Bank; Jawad Hashim and Kazim al-Sa'idi, advisers in the RCC Office of Economic Affairs, Sari al-Hardan, member of the Supreme Agricultural Council; 'Arif al-Rawi, Deputy Minister of Irrigation; and Salah al-Shaykhli, President of the Iraqi Fund for External Development.

Transportation and Communication, Education, Building and Services) as ex-officio members.

Apart from committees for formulating and coordinating development plans, a number of units were created to conduct research and deal with technical problems relating to planning and development. The principal units are as follows:

1. National Center for Consultancy and Management Development
2. Iraqi Specifications and Standards Organization
3. National Center for Engineering and Architectural Consultancy
4. National Computer Center

These centers were designed to give advice to all departments upon request, organize training courses for executive personnel and lay down technical standards and conduct specific research projects. Moreover, in almost all Ministries there are planning units, each designed to examine the projects proposed by each department and coordinate them within the general framework of the central planning authority before they were scrutinized and approved by the Ministry of Planning and the Planning Board.[6]

Apart from the ideological framework and general guidelines provided by the National and Regional Commands, the projects are usually formulated on the basis of the specific proposals submitted by the various Ministries which take part in the formulation of plans, such as the Ministries of Agriculture and Industry. These proposals are then submitted to the Steering Committee of the Planning Board and, before scrutinizing them, they are first referred to the various units and technical departments' committees of the Ministry of Planning which correlate and fit them together within a general plan for development. It may take a long time before the general plan is ready for scrutiny, but it is always the Steering Committee, composed of experienced and highly technical men, which lays down the framework and the specific projects of the plan. When final formulation is completed, the plan would be taken up by the Planning Board for final scrutiny and approval. For a formal action, the Revolutionary Command Council, presided over by the President of the Republic, enacts a law for implementation. Upon becoming a law, the plan would be entrusted to

---

6. See Subhi al-Kachachi, *al-Takhtit Fi Al-Iraq: Islubuh wa Ajhizatuh* [Planning in Iraq: Its Methods and Machinery] (Baghdad, 1976); and Sabri Z. al-Sa'di, *A General Evaluation of Approach and Performance of Building Investment Planning* (Baghdad, 1974) (mimeographed).

the Planning Board for distribution of the projects among the departments concerned for implementation. The Ministry of Planning undertakes the supervision of implementation.[7]

## AGRARIAN REFORMS

The deplorable conditions of the peasantry, stricken with poverty, disease and illiteracy, have long been the theme of reformers and writers—before and after the Revolution of 1958—who warned that those conditions could not be long neglected without adversely affecting the country as a whole. It was held that the root cause of the peasantry's misery lay in the land tenure system, often referred to as "the feudal system," which enabled a large number of landowners—many of them were absentee landlords—to hold lands which they secured from the state on easy terms and forced a large number of peasants to work for remuneration so small that it left them barely on a subsistence level. The landowners took the lion's share of the crops on the ground that they owned the land and provided the capital necessary for cultivation. Presumably to improve the peasantry's conditions, the Old Regime embarked on large schemes of irrigation and flood control which were considered necessary to increase agricultural production and improve the methods of cultivation. While landowners expanded their landholdings and agricultural production became an attractive business, the condition of peasantry hardly improved as was expected. On the contrary, the rich landowners became richer and most peasants virtually became poorer, mainly because of the increase in prices and other demands which were not matched by a corresponding increase in the peasantry's income.

After the Revolution of 1958, reformers demanded the abolition of the nefarious "feudal system" and called for immediate agrarian reforms. The revolutionary leaders were bound to respond to public pressures and an Agrarian Reform Law was issued on December 30, 1958. This law, hailed as one of the great achievements of the Revolution of 1958, empowered the Government to take away lands

---

7. The writer's interviews with several members of the Planning Board and economic advisers, including Fakhri Qadduri, Jawad Hashim, Kazim al-Sa'idi, 'Abd al-Amir al-Anbari, Subhi al-Kachachi and others, during his visits to Baghdad in 1974, 1976 and 1977. For a compilation of the laws and regulations relating to the Planning Board and the Ministry of Planning, see Hadi Sa'id Khalifa, *al-Majmu'a al-Kamila Li al-Qawanin wa al-Anzima, etc. Relating to the Planning Board and the Ministry of Planning* (Baghdad, 2nd. ed., 1975).

from landlords in excess to a certain minimum ownership and distributed to peasants who were to cultivate their newly acquired lands and enjoy the fruits of their work.[8]

However, the general effects of the law, presumably intended to relieve peasants of feudal fetters and raise their standard of living, led to an immediate drop in agricultural production and to an initial worsening in their conditions. Of the 3,839,300 *dunams*[9] taken away from landowners, only 2,580,947 *dunams* were distributed among peasants within a decade after the law came into force, because of the negative attitude of landowners toward agrarian reform (as reflected in the administrative difficulties raised in the course of dispossession and distribution) and the inability of peasants to take responsibility and make use of the land that came into their possession. Because of the relatively high annual payments to the Government for the newly acquired lands (including interest) and the need for capital which was not always accessible, many peasants left the land and migrated to big towns and cities where there was an increasing demand for workers following the launching of new industrial enterprises. Despite attempts to lower the annual payments and encourage peasants to stay on the land, agricultural production did not much improve and the country began to import crops it used to export in previous years.[10]

For this reason, the Ba'th Government tried first to correct the consequences of agrarian reforms. In 1969 the Agrarian Reform Law of 1958 was revised with a view to abolishing compensation for the lands taken over from landowners on the ground that these lands were originally state lands and that the dispossessed tribal shaykhs and landlords had obtained their landownerships by political influence with little or no payment to the state. Thereupon the lands taken over from them in excess of the minimum landholdings were distributed among peasants without charge. Owing to a number of defects in the agrarian law of 1958 as well as to administrative difficulties in its implementation, the revisions of the law proved inadequate to correct the situation.[11]

---

8. For a background of the Agrarian Reform Law of 1958, see my *Republican Iraq* (London, 1969), pp. 150ff.

9. The *dunam* is equal to one fourth of a hectare or 2500 square meters.

10. Dar al-Thawra, *Al-Tatawwur al-Iqtisadi Fi al-Iraq Ba'd al-Sabi' 'Ashar Min Tammuz* [Economic Development in Iraq After July 17, 1968] (Baghdad, 2nd. ed., Dar al-Thawra Press, 1974), pp. 34ff; Sa'dun Hamadi, *Nahwa Islah Zira'i Ishtiraki* [Toward a Socialist Agricultural Reform] (Bayrut: Dar al-Tali'a, 1964), pp. 9–11, 14–29.

11. See 'Amir al-Khashshali, *Fi al-Mas'ala al-Zira'iya* [On the Agrarian Problem] (Baghdad, 1975), pp. 12–13.

In order to deal with the agrarian problem as a whole a comprehensive law for agrarian reform, called the Agrarian Reform Law of 1970, superseding all earlier laws dealing with land tenure, was issued on May 21, 1970. The new law, based on socialist principles, was designed to improve the peasantry's condition, increase agricultural production, and correlate development in the countryside with urban areas. Even before it achieved power, the Ba'th Party had envisioned extensive reforms in rural areas as part of a broad social reform framework for Arab society.

The new law provided a number of innovations designed to overcome the difficulties encountered before and to achieve justice in accordance with Ba'thist teachings. Since almost all peasants did not own any land and had long been oppressed by landowners, it was deemed necessary to enable every peasant—indeed every citizen prepared to engage in agriculture[12]—to have the right to acquire land for cultivation. A maximum limit of ownership was established—200 *dunams*—and every landowner in possession of lands in excess of that limit had to give it up on the ground that all lands belonged originally to the state and that most of them had obtained it by political influence.[13] However, the dispossessed lands, though given to peasants free of charge (thus abolishing the compensation specified in accordance with the earlier law), the area of land given to each peasant varied from one place to another as the value of the land depended on certain qualities such as fertility, the method of irrigation (whether by rainfall or artificial irrigation), the kind of crops cultivated, and proximity to markets.[14] The peasants were also provided with such facilities as seeds for cultivation, irrigation water (if it were artificially irrigated), fertilizers, insecticides, and others. These facilities were considered as an advance to be repaid in kind or in cash roughly estimated by the authorities. However, the law made an exception in the case of gardens and fruit trees whose owners were to retain title on the ground that such farms were still relatively small and are in need of technical knowledge beyond the ability of farmers to control.[15]

---

12. Article 18 (c) states that any Arab citizen of other countries as well as graduates of agricultural colleges, institutes and schools and any other Iraqi citizens not occupied in other professions but agriculture may be included.
13. See the official justification for dispossession in the *Official Gazette,* Baghdad, May 30, 1970.
14. A maximum of 200 dunams of land, if irrigated by rainfall, was given free to peasants but a maximum of only 60 dunams, if it were artificially irrigated (Article 16).
15. Article 31.

No less significant was the stress the new law laid on the immediate need to set up cooperative societies. It was noticed that reluctance to establish cooperatives after the enforcement of the Agrarian Law of 1958 was one of the important reasons for failure to improve agrarian conditions. The new law provided not only the establishment of cooperatives to help peasants individually but also to help them in collective farms. The functions of these cooperatives may be summed up as follows:

1. To organize the various kinds of agricultural production and utilize the lands intensively.
2. To assist farmers in the implementation of agricultural plans and to increase agricultural production.
3. To provide farmers with the requisite technical material and equipment for the development and increase of agricultural production.
4. To assist farmers in acquiring or hiring agricultural machinery, tools and means of transportation as well as to help them in the method of utilizing chemical fertilizers and insecticides, and the reclamation of land and its improvement.
5. To assist in the marketing of agricultural products generally and in the steps to be undertaken before marketing such as gathering the crops, classifying, storing, dehydrating, canning, shipping and others.
6. To improve housing and living conditions and to raise the social, cultural and hygienic standards with a view to narrowing the great disparity between rural and urban standards of living.
7. To assist in obtaining loans for farmers and render any other services needed to speed up agricultural development.[16]

It is significant to note that three types of farms have been organized—cooperative, collective and state farms. In the first, ownership of the land belongs to the cooperative and the peasants who participate in cultivation receive remuneration, each in accordance with the amount of work contributed. In the second, ownership is collective and farmers share the product roughly on the basis of their active participation in cultivation. In both types, the farmers are given crops and machinery by cooperative societies in lieu of a certain percentage of the product amounting to roughly about 10 per cent. The products are normally sold through cooperatives to Government agencies which in turn distribute and sell to private shops. In the third type, the state owns the land and controls production and marketing. Peasants are employed as wage earners. In all three categories, the Government supervises the

16. See Articles 39–40 and 42–43.

operation and all activities in order to ensure that peasants will equitably be treated and derive the utmost benefit from their work.

A Higher Agricultural Council, directed by a Cabinet Committee, was set up in 1970. It was headed by the President of the Republic and composed of the Ministers of Agriculture, Agrarian Reform, Irrigation, President of the Union of Farmers and five technical experts. The functions of the Council are mainly to formulate agricultural policy and planning, and to coordinate and supervise all operations connected with agricultural production. It is designed to inspire efficiency and increase agricultural production.[17]

The Ba'th Government was prompted to improve conditions in rural areas not only on the ground of justice but also because the country was, and still is, essentially agricultural and the peasantry forms the majority of the people (about 70 per cent). Before nationalization of the oil industry, agricultural production provided more than 25 per cent of the national income. Industrialization is a policy to which the Government is still committed, but agricultural production will always be an important part of the country's economy; if the oil industry suffers a setback, agricultural production would be the principal source of national income. Before the Ba'th Party achieved power, its leaders committed themselves to improve conditions in the countryside on ideological grounds. The peasants, they declared, were still living in relatively primitive conditions, which were desperately in need of improvement. The agrarian reform law and other measures were but a step to repair these conditions and put the rural areas on the path of progress and development.

In 1970, after the Agrarian Reform Law was issued, the Ba'th Government laid down a Five Year Development Plan in which agrarian development was given a primary consideration.[18] More specifically, the plan called for real reforms in the agricultural sector on the ground that more than two-thirds of the population of the country still live in the countryside. The plan provided for an increase in agricultural production, improvement of irrigation methods, and an increase in the facilities and benefits for the peasantry.[19]

The Government's stress on agrarian reform as one of the primary

17. For texts of the Agrarian Reform Law and the Higher Agricultural Council Law, see *Official Gazette,* Baghdad, May 30, 1970.
18. For text of Law of National Development for the years 1970–1974, see *Official Gazette* (Baghdad, 1970), pp. 1–4.
19. See Planning Council, *Development Planning for the Years, 1970–74* (Baghdad, 1974), pp. 131–133 (mimeographed).

objectives of the Five Year Development Plan is reflected in the increasing amount of expenditure after the projects were underway. When the plan was first laid down, only ID 180,000,000* were earmarked for agricultural projects. In the fiscal year of 1974–75, the estimated expenditure had been raised to ID 420,000,000, more than double the original figure set for agricultural development.

By the end of the five year period, the Government declared that feudal relations had been liquidated when it took over the rest of the lands from landowners in accordance with the Agrarian Law of 1970. Under the law of 1958, only 4,200,000 *dunams* had been dispossessed. In accordance with the new law, another 5,800,000 *dunams* were dispossessed, bringing the total of lands taken over from landlords to about 10 million *dunams*. Of these some 7.5 million have already been distributed and perhaps over another half a million are in the process of distribution bringing the total to more than 8 million *dunams* which the peasantry can claim to have possessed (approximately some 411,000 families).

Side by side with the distribution of lands, the Government encouraged the establishment of cooperative societies to assist farmers and provide means for cultivation and marketing of agricultural products. Before 1968, there existed only a few cooperatives— estimated at 433 consisting of some 58,000 families—but after the Agrarian Law of 1970 came into effect the number had increased to 1330 in 1974, the terminal year of the 1970–74 development plan. In 1975 the number was estimated to have reached 1600 cooperatives, consisting of over 200,000 families.[20] Moreover, the Government has provided all possible means to encourage farmers to develop and increase the quality and quantity of production. However, despite considerable improvements, the increase in agricultural production has not yet kept pace with the increasing demands of a rapidly growing population and the migration from rural to urban areas is still continuing despite measures to encourage farmers to stay on their farms.[21]

---

20. The writer's interviews with a number of experts at the Ministry of Agricultural Reform (Baghdad, 1974 and 1976).

21. For a survey of agricultural development from 1968 to 1974, see Hasan Fahmi Jum'a, entitled *Munjazat Wazarat al-Zira'a wa al-Islah al-Zira'i* [Achievements of the Ministry of Agriculture and Agricultural Reform] (Baghdad, 1974). For earlier development, see 'Abd al-Wahhab Mutar al-Dahiri, *al-Tahlil al-Iqtisadi Li 'Amaliyat al-Intaj al-Zira'i* [Economic Analysis of the Process of Agricultural Production] (Baghdad, 2nd. ed., 1969).

*ID = $3.37 at this writing. Previous to the devaluation of the dollar, it was $2.80.

Under the current Five Year Development Plan, 1976–1980, the Government promises to increase agricultural production not only to meet domestic needs but also to export surplus crops to neighboring markets. Doubt has been cast on the prospect of rapid increase, mainly because of the difficulty of persuading the peasantry to stay on the farms and their inability to improve the quality and quantity of agricultural production. For this reason, the Government has decided to increase all kinds of facilities—easy credit, machinery, water for irrigation, etc.—in order to encourage peasants to remain on the farms and enjoy a higher standard of living. What militates against efforts to keep farmers in the countryside is the Government's own plans for industrialization which call for more workers; the farmer often finds that his income from industrial employment is higher than from his work on the farm, especially when other members of his family derive additional income from work in industry.[22]

## NATIONALIZATION OF THE OIL INDUSTRY

Ever since Law 80, expropriating 99.50 per cent of the unexploited concessionary areas of the IPC (the Iraq Petroleum Co.) and its associated companies was issued in 1961, the Iraqi oil industry suffered a setback from which it did not recover for almost a decade. Income from oil, on which Iraq has long depended for expenditure and development did not come up to expectations, mainly because the Iraqi National Oil Company (INOC), despite an agreement with ERAP, a French company, to render assistance, could not develop and exploit the areas assigned to it. Since negotiations with other foreign companies to conduct exploration and exploitation of the oil fields failed, the 'Arif regime tried to come to an understanding with the IPC in order to raise production and increase Iraq's income from oil.[23]

Before it came to power in 1968, the Ba'th Party had called for nationalization of the oil industry, epitomized in the slogan "Arab oil for the Arabs." Once in the saddle, the Ba'th began to appreciate the difficulties involved in nationalization and decided to proceed step by step toward the ultimate goal of nationalization. From 1969 to 1972, a

22. The use of agricultural machinery has been very helpful to reduce the impact of migration on rural population, but this may be a temporary measure with the increasing demand for farmers. The Government has invited peasants from other Arab countries and gave them land for cultivation, but only a few have migrated from Egypt, though others might be tempted to come in the future.

23. For a brief account of the negotiations with these companies, see my *Republican Iraq*, pp. 291–292.

number of agreements with foreign countries were concluded to provide the INOC with capital and technical know-how to exploit the oil fields, and a portion of the income was earmarked to pay for the credit extended to the INOC. The first of these agreements, signed between the INOC and the Soviet Machinoexport Organization, stipulated that the Soviet Union would provide equipment and technical assistance with which Iraq would start its own national oil industry. Another agreement, signed between the INOC and the Hungarian Chemokomplex Establishment, promised to provide Iraq with technical assistance and a credit to start drilling in four oil wells in the North Rumayla field. On April 7, 1972, the oil operation of the North Rumayla field started and the ceremony for the inauguration was attended by Soviet Premier Kosygin and by a number of other foreign dignitaries. In 1972, the Iraqi Oil Tankers Company (IOTC) was established in Basra to deliver oil to countries that entered into agreements to purchase oil from Iraq. The initial number of the IOTC's fleet consisted of seven tankers (35,000 d.w.t.) which Spain (the Astilleros Españoles shipyard) provided in 1972 and 1973. These and other arrangements, relieving Iraq from dependence on foreign companies, made it possible for foreign countries to purchase oil directly from the Iraqi authorities.

Despite success in these initial steps, the Iraqi Government was hesitant to proceed toward outright nationalization. At the outset, it preferred to reopen negotiations with the IPC and put forth a set of demands, designed to protect national interests, such as payment of the royalty expensing and increase in oil production and equity participation. Negotiations went on for a while without satisfaction to either side though some payments were made to Iraq, but the way was not cleared for a final settlement as the IPC was reluctant to concede some of the Iraqi demands and there were deeper causes of misunderstanding.

One of the longstanding Iraqi grievances was the slow steps undertaken by the IPC to conduct exploration in the vast concessionary area and to relinquish the unexploited fields which would enable Iraq to enter into arrangements with other companies to exploit them.[24] Failure of the IPC to relinquish these fields was one of the important reasons which prompted the Iraqi Government to issue Law 80, resulting in the expropriation of 99.50 per cent of concessionary rights. Dissatisfied with Law 80 and unable to come to an understanding with

24. Over 250 wells were unsuccessfully exploited before and after World War II.

successive regimes, the IPC found it exceedingly difficult to invest further in order to increase oil production despite repeated protests. The Iraqi Government considered the IPC refusal to increase production as a form of pressure upon itself to comply with previous IPC requests to compensate its losses from the effects of Law 80, which it regarded as contrary to the Oil Agreement. The Iraqi Government complained that the increase of oil production in Saudi Arabia was rising annually on an average of 11 per cent and in Iran over 14 per cent while the increase in Iraq hardly exceeded 4.7 per cent. To Iraq, this meant a loss of some ID 550 millions to its income during the ten years period following the enactment of Law 80. Moreover, the Iraqi Government demanded the payment of an accumulated amount of royalty expensing since 1964, when the principle of expensing was agreed on at a meeting of OPEC in Jakarta in 1964, the amount of which was estimated to be ID 82 millions. Though the IPC agreed to pay the royalty from 1971, when the subject was brought up for negotiations, it withheld retroactive payments pending settlement of the IPC demands relating to Law 80.[25]

Though negotiations continued during 1970 and 1971, the Ba'th Government seems to have come to the conclusion that since negotiations failed to materialize, the time had come to take the first step in the nationalization of the IPC. What prompted the Ba'th leaders to take this step were the repeated attempts to overthrow the Ba'th regime by opponents who were suspected to have been encouraged by foreign companies. It was felt in Ba'thist circles that nationalization would not only enable Iraq to control the oil industry, but also to put an end to political adventurers who would seek the support of foreign interests. Nationalization of oil had become a popular demand in the Arab world ever since Nasir had nationalized the Suez Canal in 1956 and the Ba'th Party had committed itself to it in several party congresses. Before the drastic step was undertaken, the Ba'th leaders had put up the question of nationalization before both the Regional and National Commands and a decision to proceed with nationalization was taken.[26]

Saddam Husayn, Vice President of the RCC, seems to have taken the lead in implementation of the nationalization of IPC. In a conversation

25. The IPC held that such a settlement was part of the 1964 OPEC agreement.
26. The writer's interviews with 'Aflaq, Secretary General of the Ba'th Party, and 'Aysami, Assistant Secretary General of the Party, in 1974 and 1975.

with the writer,[27] Saddam said that the matter was of great importance to him and he was responsible for several preliminary steps taken to insure success of the action as he was concerned about possible foreign retaliations. Despite preparedness to cut expenditures and postpone some development projects, he was afraid that the Iraqi Government might not be able to meet its basic financial needs, if the major oil companies should boycott Iraqi oil. The Soviet Union was consulted on the matter, but, though tacitly agreed on nationalization in principle, seems to have given Iraq no encouragement in the drive to nationalize Western oil operations. Saddam said that he instructed the Ministry of Finance to arrange the transfer of Iraqi assets (small as they may have been) from British to Swiss banks long before the first step was taken in order to avoid the possibility of freezing these assets by the British Government in retaliation. Moreover, the Iraqi Government sounded out some of the Arab oil companies about the possibility of borrowing funds in case of need before it could market its crude oil. Shortly after nationalization, Kuwayt, Saudi Arabia and Libya offered short-term loans which Iraq utilized before the nationalized industry began to operate and yield income.

The steps taken to nationalize the oil industry were as follows: Sa'dun Hamadi, Minister of Oil and Minerals, was instructed to deal firmly and quickly with the IPC. When the negotiations began early in 1972, the Iraqi Minister stated at the outset that Law 80 and all its legal effects would not be a subject for negotiation. He also stated that arbitration would not be acceptable in any dispute with the IPC, as arbitration is a method of settlement between sovereign states and not between the state and a private company operating under its national laws. The IPC, the Iraqi Minister went on to say, should accept Law 80 as an attribute of sovereignty.

Negotiations did not proceed smoothly as the IPC delegates tried time and again to put forth legal claims relating to the effects of Law 80 and refused to meet Iraqi demands for the royalty expensing. Production of oil dropped again to almost half of the production capacity; this may or may not have been related to negotiations, but the Iraqi Government construed the action, in the light of similar past experiences, as a form of pressure to influence the Iraqi negotiators. On May 17, 1972, the Iraqi Minister warned the IPC that negotiations would be discontinued if the Iraqi demands were not accepted within a

27. Interview with Saddam Husayn (Baghdad, August 6, 1974).

two-week period. Although it was rumored that the Iraqi Government might nationalize the oil industry, the IPC negotiators were not quite convinced that the Iraqi Government could operate the oil fields or market its crude oil, if nationalization was carried out.[28]

On June 1, 1972, the RCC passed a resolution to nationalize the IPC operations and a law, called Law 69, was issued to compensate the company for its assets as redefined under Law 80 (1961). A national company called the Iraqi Company for Oil Operations was established to operate the fields taken over from the IPC and to be responsible for all the rights and assets transferred to it in accordance with Law 69.[29] Having nationalized the IPC, the Iraqi Government passed an act, later put into a form of an agreement with the French Government on June 18, 1972, allowing the French partner in IPC to receive its share from the nationalized oil under the same conditions prevailing before nationalization for a period of 10 years.[30] The Government also left intact the Basra Petroleum Company (BPC), because it did not think it was in the national interest to nationalize all foreign oil interests at once. It preferred to proceed toward full nationalization piecemeal. Nor was the country prepared to operate all nationalized fields; indeed it needed the income from the BPC before it could run its own oil industry.

Faced with a *fait accompli,* the IPC and the other related companies finally came to an understanding with Iraq and settled all pending issues on February 28, 1972, on the basis of the principle of nationalization as embodied in the nationalization laws of 1961 and 1972. It was agreed that £141 million would be paid to Iraq to meet all her claims; £30 million to be paid immediately after the agreement came into effect and the balance to be paid monthly by installments. On its part, the Iraqi Government agreed to compensate the companies by promising to deliver 15 million tons of crude oil from the Kirkuk fields. These were

28. In interviews with some of the high IPC personnel in London (in 1974 and 1977) the question of the fall in oil production was explained to the writer by the coincidental fall of freight rate in the Mediterranean oil and the company had to rely on oil shipment from the Gulf. As to nationalization, the IPC personnel pointed out that they realized that Iraqi experts could operate the oil fields, but they were doubtful that Iraq could successfully market its oil. However, they said, circumstances unexpectedly helped Iraq as there was a sudden demand for Iraqi oil within six months from nationalization.

29. For text of Law 69, see *The Official Gazette*, Baghdad, (June 1, 1972), pp. 3–4.

30. The French company negotiated further oil purchases, which Iraq produced after nationalization. Iraq promised to continue its agreement with ERAP, a French company, for the exploration of oil. France promised to extend technical and financial assistance which would help Iraq to develop its own projects for the oil industry. The reasons for giving France preferential treatment were partly political and partly financial. France supported the Arabs in the Arab-Israeli conflict of 1967 and was prepared to deal with Iraq in a purely businesslike manner as demonstrated in the ERAP agreements.

delivered in an average of one million tons per month. The concessionary rights of the MPC were regarded as terminated and the company agreed to transfer all its assets, including the crude oil stored in Iraq, without charge. The BPC agreed "to use its best endeavors to accelerate its expansion to meet target capacities as follows: 35 million tons in 1973, 45 million tons in 1974, 65 million tons in 1975 and 80 million tons in 1976 subject to good oilfield practice and the Law of Conservation."

In 1973 Iraq took another step to nationalize foreign oil interests when the fourth Arab-Israeli war broke out. Since the United States was considered the greatest supporter of Israel in weapons and financial assistance, Iraq passed a law on October 7, 1973, to nationalize the concessionary rights of two American companies in BPC—the Standard Oil of New Jersey (Exxon) and Mobil Oil Corporation—and the Royal Dutch Oil Company which possessed 60 per cent of Shell Oil Company in the BPC. Iraq also nationalized the Gulbenkian five per cent interests in the BPC.[31] In its official announcement, the Iraqi Government declared that the nationalization of these companies was undertaken in retaliation for the hostile attitude of the American and Dutch Governments in their support of Israel against the Arabs.[32]

The final step to nationalize foreign oil interests was undertaken in 1975. Having felt fully confident that its oil was now in demand in world markets and itself competent to explore and operate the oil industry, Iraq nationalized the remaining foreign interests in the BPC and promised to pay compensation in accordance with its net book value. This step made Iraq master of her oil industry.[33]

From the time it nationalized the IPC in 1972, Iraq began to grant service contracts to foreign state-owned oil companies to perform oil operations in various areas of the country. The first was a contract with Petroleo Brasileiro of Brazil which was entrusted with the functions of general contractor to perform petroleum operations in three areas (totalling 7900 sq. km.) in central and southern Iraq. Purchase agreements for crude oil were signed with a number of countries considered friendly to Iraq—France, the Soviet Union, Spain, Poland, India and others—in 1972 and 1973. Very soon Iraq was able to market her oil in world markets without difficulty.

31. For texts of the nationalization laws, see the *Official Gazette,* Baghdad (October 21, 1973).
32. See the *Official Gazette,* Baghdad (October 21, 1973), p. 1.
33. For text of the law, see the *Official Gazette,* Baghdad (December 8, 1975), pp. 7–8.

During 1974 and 1975, the oil production was increased considerably and new fields were explored. In 1975, following the conflict with Syria over the Euphrates water, Iraq began to construct the so-called strategic pipe lines connecting the pumping station at Haditha, west of the Euphrates, with the newly constructed Port-of-Bakr situated on the Iraqi coast of the Gulf.[34] These pipe lines, begun early in 1975 and completed toward the end of that year, were designed to pump oil not only from the northern fields to Iraqi ports in the south but also from southern fields to Haditha, thereby relieving Iraq from pressures to increase transit duties on oil pumped through the Mediterranean pipe lines. In 1976 Iraq completed the construction of a pipeline to the Mediterranean through Turkish territory. This, as well as the Gulf strategic pipelines, were designed to afford Iraq the opportunity to choose the area for oil delivery on the basis of world prices, to give her greater freedom of action without political pressure.[35]

## INDUSTRIALIZATION

After 1958, as noted earlier, Iraq embarked on a new economic policy which aimed at both agrarian reform and industrial expansion. Neither of the two policies proved fully successful, because the first resulted in an immediate drop in agricultural production and the other, except in the oil industry, failed to measure up to expectations.

After 1969, the Ba'th Government decided to implement the industrial program of previous regimes before it would lay down new programs. Perhaps more important, the Ba'th regime realized that the country's economic development, though stressing industrialization, would be inadequate if it did not take into consideration the need to increase agricultural production and improve conditions in the countryside, because the nation's potentials, apart from oil, are essentially agricultural and the majority of the people still live in rural areas. For this reason, the Government has, in the two five-year development plans of 1971–75 and 1976–80, stressed almost equally the projects for industrial and agricultural reconstruction.

As a socialist party, the Ba'th sought to transform the country from a capitalist, or rather a semi-capitalist (as certain steps toward socialism

---

34. Two large pipes for oil and a small one for gas.
35. For a compilation of the laws and other relevant documents relating to the oil industry, see Qasim Ahmad al-'Abbas (ed.), *Watha'iq al-Naft Fi al-Iraq* [Documents Relating to Iraqi Oil] (Baghdad, 1975), 2 vols.

had already been undertaken in the mid-sixties), to an essentially socialist economy. But it was not unaware that a rapid transformation to full socialism was neither possible nor in the country's best interest, despite extremist calls for a complete transformation into a socialist society. For this reason a private sector, though a relatively small one, has been provided for private investors. Though some hold that this sector might be considerably reduced and perhaps eventually disappear, official reports indicate that investment in this sector is increasing.[36] Moreover, if the role of the private sector proves to be healthy for the economy, Iraq's rulers might well allow it to expand so as to keep a balance between the two sectors. A third, mixed sector, was provided in which the private and public sectors could cooperate and serve as a link between private and public ownerships.[37]

The Ba'th Government did not embark at once on new projects; it first tried to implement the five-year plan of the former regime. "It is a gross mistake," said President Bakr, "to concentrate our attention on the execution of new projects, as it is essential to look meticulously to better exploitation of the existing projects and raising their productive capacity."[38] In order to implement these projects effectively, the Government stressed planning as a method to achieve development. Planning, it was rightly held, became the point of departure in the country's development which distinguished the Ba'th programs from the programs of former regimes.[39]

In order to carry out the industrial projects rapidly and efficiently, the Ministry of Industry was reorganized in 1970 and the Organization for Public Industries, already in existence since 1964, was divided into six units, each designed to formulate and supervise the implementation

---

36. See Ministry of Industry and Minerals, *Istratijiat al-Tanmiya al-Sina'iya Fi al-Iraq* [Strategy of Industrial Development in Iraq] (Baghdad, 1976), pp. 43–44. (This study was prepared by Farhank Jalal, Ja'far 'Abd al-Ghani and 'Abd al-Wahhab Hamdi al-Najjar). It will be referred to as *Strategy of Industrial Development*.

37. The idea of establishing a public sector parallel to a private sector was first discussed by Qasim's experts after the Revolution of 1958 and a modest beginning was made after an agreement of economic cooperation was signed with the Soviet Union in 1959. In 1964, after a set of socialist decrees were issued by 'Arif, the public sector was considerably enlarged but the private sector remained a very important one in the country's economy. The parallel existence of two sectors reflected a struggle between two groups, each tried to assert one school of thought or another about the economic system—free enterprise and socialism. Upon the assumption of power by the Ba'th Party, socialism triumphed and the public sector became the foundation of the country's economy. See *al-Taqrir al-Siyasi, op. cit.*, pp. 113ff.

38. Ministry of Planning, *Progress Under Planning* (Baghdad, 1971), p. 2.

39. *Ibid.*, p. 7.

of the industries under its control. These units were organized as follows:

1. Public Organization for Food Industries
2. Public Organization for Spinning and Weaving
3. Public Organization for Petrochemical Industries
4. Public Organization for Engineering Industries
5. Public Organization for Construction Material Industries
6. Public Organization for Chemical, Leather and Tobacco Industries.

Later, two other units were added, one to deal with research and the other for consultation on projects under study and preparation for possible implementation. A Ministry for National Planning, noted above, was established to formulate and coordinate projects initiated by various departments for implementation. Before these projects were adopted by the RCC as part of the National Plan, they were carefully scrutinized by various committees (including an Advisory Committee of the Ministry of Industry and Minerals), composed of experts well-known for their technical competence and professional experience.[40]

The industrial program of the former regime which the Ba'th Government decided to carry out consisted of a dozen projects. Some were designed to improve agricultural production, such as the factory for agricultural machinery; others, to establish new factories for the manufacturing of glass, paper and textiles, and to expand factories that have already been in existence. The plan for the glass and textile factories were laid down under the Qasim regime and the Soviet Union, in accordance with the agreement for economic and technological cooperation of 1960, agreed to provide the necessary technological equipments for their establishment, but work was not completed until additional funds were earmarked either to complete or extend these projects. The paper mill, designed in 1966 under the 'Arif regime, was only partially completed before 1968; in 1974 it was expanded and completed because of the increasing need of paper for domestic consumption. No less important was the expansion and completion of industries that had just begun to operate in 1968 such as the factory for chemical and fertilizer materials and the factories for the manufacture of rayon textiles. Other factories, such as those for the production of

40. For a summary of the industrial achievements during 1973–74 under the various public organizations, see Ministry of Industry, *Munjazatuna Fi 'Am 1973–74* [Our Achievements in the Year 1973–74] (Baghdad, 1975).

steel, sulfur and sugar, though plans for their establishment had been laid down under former regimes, were launched and completed after 1968.

The Five Year National Development Plan of 1971–75, in which the industrial program was formulated, though ranking second to agrarian reforms, marked an important step in the country's industrial development. Projects that have not yet been completed, such as the petrochemical, textile and sugar industries, were greatly expanded and efforts were made to complete them at the earliest possible moment. New projects to implement the industrialization plans were laid down, including projects for the increase of electrical power, construction of bridges and improvement and reconstruction of an elaborate transportation and communication systems. It was deemed necessary that, before the industrial projects were completed, the various industrial centers should be linked with domestic and foreign markets by an efficient system of transportation.

The primary objective of industrialization is not merely to speed up industrial development but, perhaps more important, to correlate industrial with agricultural development and to concentrate on industries considered important for domestic markets. Only in such industries as cement, vegetable oils and petrochemicals, which Iraq might be able to export to its neighbors, did the plan stress possible expansion. The ultimate objective of industrialization is to achieve self-sufficiency and insure the country's economic independence.[41]

An overall development plan necessarily calls for a review of the country's foreign and domestic trade. Before the Revolution of 1958, no significant restrictions on foreign trade were ever made, save the heavy duties on imports to provide an income for public expenditure. Indeed, rarely were tariffs raised to protect national industries, as the country's chief products, except crude oil, were essentially agricultural. The cement and vegetable oil industries, though proved very successful, were in no need of protective tariffs as they were far from meeting domestic demands.

Restrictions on foreign trade to limit imports on certain commodities were first laid down in 1964 under the 'Arif regime. After 1968, when socialism became the goal of the country's economic development, foreign trade was placed under complete control and no one was

---

41. Ministry of Industry and Minerals, *Strategy of Industrial Development in Iraq*, pp. 24–36.

permitted to import or export goods without a license. Upon the launching of the Five Year Development Plan of 1971-75, a set of guidelines were laid down to regulate trade. Since the implementation of the development plan required a heavy dependence on foreign technology, an increasing percentage of imports was assigned to capital goods and a relatively small percentage to consumers goods. Upon the launching of the second Five Year Development Plan of 1976-80, the percentage of imported capital goods was raised to 80 per cent and only 20 per cent confined to consumers goods. The latter was to include mainly essential material such as flour, sugar and tea and only limited luxury items.[42]

In 1975 the Ministry of Trade was divided into two separate Ministries (though remaining temporarily under one Minister), one for Foreign and the other for Internal Trade. The former, entrusted with the task of regulating the flow of imports and exports, issues permits to individuals who will have the right to import capital goods for the private sector. The other, the Ministry of Internal Trade, is charged with the distribution of imported goods among shopkeepers and owners of private industry.

In the second Five Year Plan of 1976-80, industrialization is stressed as a means to complete the transformation of the country's economy from free enterprise to socialism. The immediate objectives of the plan are to increase and intensify productivity, increase foreign trade and expand and diversify industry along the lines of projects that have already been outlined in the previous plan. "Since the structure of the Iraqi economy," states the Ministry of Planning's Report on Industry, "depends essentially on two pillars—oil and agriculture—industrialization must by necessity proceed to correlate the development of the two together . . . the aim of national industry should maintain a balance between productive and consumptive goods, the former should at first be stressed at the expense of the other in order to insure a self-sufficient and independent national economy."[43] The

42. For a survey of Iraq's foreign trade, see Jawad Hashim, Husayn 'Umar and 'Ali al-Manufi, *Lamahat Fi Tatawwur al-Iqtisad al-Iraqi: Qita' al-Tijara al-Kharijiya* [Aspects of Economic Development of Iraq: Sector of Foreign Trade] (Bayrut, 1973). See also Sahib Dhahab, "Dawr al-Sadirat Fi Khittat al-Tanmiya" [Role of Exports in the Development Plans], *al-Thawra*, Baghdad, March 20, 1975.

43. Ministry of Planning, *Working Papers for the National Development Plan of 1975-80: Report on Industry* (Baghdad, 1976). See also Badr Ghaylan al-Ghazzawi, "al-Tabdhir Fi al-Infaq al-Istihlaki wa al-Istithmari Fi al-Iraq" [Extravagance in Consumption and Investment in Iraq], *al-Thawra*, Baghdad, May 25, 1976.

ultimate objectives of the plan are to achieve full employment, increase wages and narrow the disparity of income between rural and urban areas, and raise the standard of living. It is hoped that greater prosperity and welfare would be achieved and Iraq would become a truly socialist state among the "developed" countries of the world.[44]

If world conditions prove to be again favorable for Iraq, the prospects for the achievements of the Second Five Year Plan should at least be as promising as the first plan. But the Government is under no illusion that increase in production, both in industry and agriculture, is an easy task and that a sudden increase is not expected. The need for greater efficiency and coordination among the various public sectors to increase productivity has been keenly felt as the discussion of the problem by leading Ba'th Party members indicated in 1976. Saddam Husayn, in a public statement, appealed to all—to his party and the public—to be fully responsible, efficient and dedicated if the crisis of productivity were to be resolved. The task is difficult, he said, but it is the only way to achieve the objectives of economic development— prosperity and welfare for all.[45]

## IRRIGATION

The construction of dams and bridges for the control of floods and storage of water for irrigation were the primary objectives of reconstruction under the Monarchy, but the work was necessarily slow and tedious as these ambitious projects required greater efficiency and resources than the country had at its disposal. Because the Old Regime was attacked for its stress on the construction of large dams and bridges, the revolutionary leaders have embarked on a policy of industrialization and agrarian reform at the expense of irrigation projects. As a result, the momentum for the construction of dams and bridges slowed down considerably after 1958 and the irrigation plans suffered a setback from which it did not recover until 1970.

The new policy, spelled out in the First Five Year Development Plan, stemmed from the realization that agricultural production and agrarian reform should be the primary objective of economic planning as the majority of the population still live in the countryside and agriculture is

---

44. Ministry of Industry and Minerals, *Strategy of Industrial Development in Iraq*, pp. 57ff.

45. For full text of Saddam Husayn's statement, see *al-Thawra*, Baghdad, September 10, 1976. See also a statement to this effect by Taha al-Jazrawi, Minister of Industry, *Baghdad Observer*, March 3, 1976.

a permanent source for national income. To improve agricultural production, the Tigris and Euphrates and their tributaries should be brought under complete control and their abundant waters made available for cultivation. Since periodic floods still threaten the big towns and cities on both sides of the rivers, it was keenly felt that new dams should be built and some of the older ones extended to provide adequate safety for urban areas as well as to use the stored water for irrigation. Needless to say, flood control was rightly considered not only as a means to increase agricultural production but also to improve river navigation and fishing and produce hydroelectric energy and other benefits.

In the Five Year Development Plan of 1971–75, it was deemed necessary to complete first the dams which had already been under construction before embarking on new projects. It was rightly held that some of these dams might help to store water which could be used for irrigation in areas where water is likely to become scarce in the summer.[46] Since most of these dams were in the northern part of the country—in the Mawsil (Mosul) and Kurdish provinces in particular—funds were provided for the exploration and construction of dams in the north and elsewhere, such as the projects at al-Haditha and al-Razaza over the River Euphrates.

In the Five Year Plan of 1976–80, funds were earmarked to complete the dams that have already been under construction such as the Haditha and Falluja dams (River Euphrates), the Mawsil Dam (River Tigris), the Humrin Dam (River Diyala) and the Najma Dam (The Upper Zab). In addition funds were earmarked for the Tharthar lake to divert a portion of its water to the Euphrates in seasons when its water would either be too low or in greater demand in Turkey or Syria as was the case in 1974–75. For this reason, it has been decided to store enough water in the Tharthar lake in order to divert it to the Euphrates for irrigation as well as to provide water for the Tigris in seasons when its water is too low. The Tharthar and other water supplies are expected to provide water for irrigation where the rainfall is scarce and irregular. It is hoped that these projects might also improve the environment of areas likely to suffer from drought.

Finally, as salinization has become a real threat to agricultural

---

46. The dams for flood control that have already been completed are the following: The Dukan Dam (the River Upper Zab), the Darbandikhan Dam (River Diyala), the Samarra Dam (River Tigris), the Ramadi Dam (River Euphrates). Other dams, like the Hindiya and Kut dams, were designed for the distribution of water for irrigation.

production, resulting in almost complete abandonment of some agricultural areas, projects to improve the methods of drainage and desalinization have been laid down to save agricultural areas from a scourge that has become widespread in recent years. However, it is realized that salinization is a very complex problem; to solve it locally by cleansing one area while the salt has been accumulating in neighboring areas is not very helpful. A broad plan of drainage is deemed necessary to cleanse all agricultural areas by canals which should carry the salt to the Gulf or to places where the salt would be removed for use in industry.[47]

In an essentially agricultural country, irrigation plans have long been considered a high priority, but implementation of these plans has been complicated and very slow. By their very nature, grandiose projects of flood control and water storage dams require highly technical skills and long experience which were not always available. After the work has started on some of these projects, often certain technical difficulties have arisen such as inadequate means of transportation, scarcity of building material and so forth which contributed in no small measure to slow down the work for which officials in the irrigation department had to bear the blame. Given the difficult conditions in which they worked, the irrigation experts are to be congratulated for the quality of their achievements.[48]

## SOCIAL REFORMS

Before the Revolution of 1958, there was widespread criticism that the Monarchy paid attention only to vested interests and ignored the masses who were in desperate condition, despite growing prosperity in the country as a whole. After 1958 the new rulers consciously began to extend health and social services to workers and peasants which considerably mitigated long felt hardships by the poor and the oppressed. For over a decade, social reform projects suffered from inconsistency and lack of coordination, because their implementation depended almost entirely on the whims of rulers.

47. See Mahdi al-Sahhaf, *al-Mawarid al-Ma'iya Fi al-Iraq wa Siyanatuha Min al-Talawwuth* [Water Resources in Iraq and Pollution Control] (Baghdad, 1976), pp. 132–54, 258–64; Malik Mansur, "al-Masab al-'Am Bidayat al-Hal al-Shamil Li Miluhat al-Ard" [A General Outlet is the Ultimate Solution for Land Salinization], *al-Thawra*, Baghdad, March 12, 1975.

48. The writer's interviews with the Minister and other high officials and experts at the Ministry of Irrigation (Baghdad, 1976 and 1977).

After 1968, the Ba'th Government viewed social reform from a different perspective and sought to transform society as a whole so that workers, peasants and other poorer classes would enjoy the benefits of development. In their early public statements, the Ba'th leaders called for improvement of the conditions of workers and peasants, as these constitute the majority of the people and provide the labor necessary to make the future Arab socialist society viable and healthy.[49] More specifically, the Ba'th leaders addressed themselves to reforms in the countryside and called for the free distribution of lands among the peasants and for making available to them such facilities as free social and health services. To improve the conditions of workers, new laws regulating labor relationship and extending the benefits of social security were issued during 1970-71. The principles enshrined in these laws were derived from Ba'thist teachings and from the general guidelines embodied in the Charter of National Action which the Ba'th and the Communist parties had adopted in 1970. These principles may be summed up as follows:

1. Labor is considered as a right to which every able bodied citizen is entitled and unemployment should disappear as society develops toward the ultimate goals of prosperity and progress.
2. Social security and insurance should be made available to all citizens.
3. A minimum wage level should be established based on the price movement and living costs in order to maintain a higher standard of living.
4. The State should provide a free health and medical care consistent with the development of the country's resources.
5. Free education on all levels should be made available in conformity with the general plan of the country's development. The ultimate aim is to wipe out illiteracy and prepare a new generation imbued with the principles of the Revolution of 1968.
6. The State should provide health and adequate housing facilities to all consistent with the country's development and national resources. The immediate aims should be to fix a minimum level of rents consistent with the individual's income, but the ultimate aim should be to provide large housing units all over the country equipped with the general requirements of health, security, communications, and education.
7. Women, who have suffered discrimination and restrictions in the past, should be emancipated. They should be given equal opportunities so that they could share equal responsibility with men.[50]

49. For a compilation of statements relating to the role of workers and peasants by Ba'thist leaders, see *al-Ba'th wa Nidal al-Tabaqa al-'Amila* [the Ba'th and the Struggle of the Working Class] (Bayrut: Dar al-Tali'a, 1974).
50. Ministry of Information, *Charter of National Action* (Baghdad, 1974), pp. 50-53.

In 1970–71, three major laws were enacted designed to translate some of these basic principles into reality. The first, issued on October 14, 1970, dealt with labor problems. It provided protection for workers against discrimination, maltreatment or dismissal during employment and limited working hours to eight a day and a maximum of 48 hours a week. It also provided that wages should be based on the qualification of the worker, the nature of his work, and fixed by a committee set up especially to fulfill this function in which trade unions are represented. The law extended protection to women who want to work and prohibited child labor (the minimum age limit for a worker is set at 18); it also prohibited strenuous jobs to workers below 18 and above 16 (if they were employed by official permission). Disputes between employers and employees should be first settled by negotiations in which union representatives take part but if a basis for settlement was not found workers would be entitled to strike. Finally, the law permitted workers to form trade unions to deal with labor problems. In cooperation with these unions, an employment committee is set up in the Ministry of Labor to help unemployed workers to find jobs.[51]

The second law, issued on October 26, 1970, provided general guidelines and regulations for cooperatives and unions. The law prohibited any person from owning more than 10 per cent in a cooperative or to exercise an influence beyond the function assigned to him if he were to fulfill a certain executive post. All accounts and records of cooperatives and unions were made subject to Government supervision, and the members who violate the laws and regulations of the organization would be subject to penalties.[52]

The third law, relating to retirement and insurance for workers, was issued on March 9, 1971. The law provided that employees contribute five per cent to the general fund, the employers 12 to 15 per cent and the Government up to 30 per cent, out of which workers would be paid for their insurances and eventual retirement. The law also provides payment to workers if they were incapacitated or injured while at work.[53]

These laws and the support given to workers by trade unions have greatly strengthened the position of workers and provided them with security which they have never enjoyed before. On the other hand, since workers have not yet been fully rehabilitated—and most workers

51. For the text of the Labor Law, see *The Official Gazette,* Baghdad, (August 10, 1970), pp. 1–55.
52. For the text of the law, see *The Official Gazette,* Baghdad, (November 10, 1970), pp. 1–14.
53. For text of the law, see *The Official Gazette,* Baghdad, (March 22, 1971), pp. 1–28.

are still illiterate—these protective measures have often been exploited against the employer's interest and tended to encourage tardiness and inefficiency. Perhaps a transitional period of adjustment is necessary before a satisfactory relationship is established between employers and employees.

No less significant are the health facilities the cost of which has been increased from ID 4.9 millions in 1958 to over ID 12 millions since the Ba'th regime has been established. These funds have been mainly devoted to increase the number of hospitals and clinics and enable the poorer classes to avail themselves of free medical services. Since health services have been more available in urban areas than in the countryside, the government is now trying to encourage young medical students to serve in rural areas, as most of them prefer service in the cities. But the villagers are often given free medical care in urban communities, though travel difficulties discourage many from availing themselves of urban health services. The increase in health facilities has been necessarily slow mainly because of the difficulty in preparing a larger medical staff, despite the Government's readiness to provide funds in increasing amounts for medical training.

## EDUCATIONAL AND CULTURAL DEVELOPMENT

No educational policy was ever formulated before the Revolution of 1958 though some experts in the Ministry of Education often offered their views about the aims of educational policy. After the Revolution of 1958, critics of the Old Regime called for greater attention to educational problems and demanded greater freedom for teachers and students to express their views about education and participate in politics on the ground that educational institutions should not be isolated from society. There was an initial favorable response to public demand for educational expansion and funds were earmarked for new schools and educational facilities. Though the budget was doubled within two years, the expansion slowed down after 1960 and the quality of education declined owing partly to participation of teachers and students in politics and partly because students were often promoted from class to class without examinations.[54]

After achieving power, the Ba'th leaders paid increasing attention to educational institutions and tried for the first time to correlate educational plans with the overall national development plans. It was noticed that while the number of students continued to increase, no corresponding increase was made in the number of schools and other

---

54. See my *Republican Iraq*, pp. 155–56.

facilities. Consequently the quality of education tended to decline and the percentage of illiteracy remained high. Inadequate facilities in the primary and high school levels necessarily affected the quality of college education, despite efforts made to improve the quality of training on the college level. Since technical colleges, especially medicine and engineering, admitted a relatively small number of students (owing to inadequate facilities), most college students took either to law or the humanities in excess of the country's needs. This has indeed not only made it more difficult for the colleges in the humanities to improve the quality of training but also aggravated the perennial problem of finding jobs for university graduates.

The Ba'th Government, though appreciating the difficulty of dealing with these problems, has proceeded slowly to cope with them. In the two five-year development plans of 1971 and 1976, it was envisioned that illiteracy should be eliminated in two stages; it should be considerably reduced among the young generation in the first stage and then wiped out within a decade after the second five-year plan has been launched. In quantity, educational facilities have been increased, as reflected in the number of schools, teachers, laboratories and other facilities; but in quality, they have not yet been able to improve much on previous standards. Tuition in all educational institutions was abolished in 1974, and all students' needs—text books, stationery, etc.—are being met today free of charge in all schools at all levels.[55]

In rural areas, the educational facilities have not been correspondingly increased as in urban areas, nor are children in the countryside inclined to enter school, though the majority of the population live in rural areas. The government has keenly felt the need to reduce the disparity of educational levels between urban and rural areas and to encourage children in the countryside to receive a minimum level of education necessary to raise their standard of living.

As an ideological party, the Ba'th seems to be quite concerned about the failure of educational institutions to adopt socialist teachings as most students are indifferent to ideological orientation, especially in colleges and universities. Since the ultimate goal of the Ba'th Party is to construct a socialist society, the Ba'th regime insists that educational institutions should prepare a new generation which would be imbued with socialist ideals.[56]

55. See Ministry of Planning, *al-Itar al-Tafsili al-Mabda'i li-Khittat al-Tanmiya al-Qawmiya 1970–74* [The Detailed Framework of the National Development Plan, 1970–74] (Baghdad, 1970), pp. 62–87.
56. Planning Board, *Hawl Waqi' al-Tatawwur al-Iqtisadi fi al Iraq Mundh 'Am 1969 Hatta al-Waqt al-Hadir*, pp. 44–45, 118–125. See also *al-Taqrir al-Siyasi*, op. cit., pp. 155–173.

Chapter VII

# Foreign Policy

THE FOREIGN policy of the Old Regime, reputed to have been largely shaped by General Nuri al-Sa'id, who often served as Foreign Minister whenever he relinquished the Premiership, consisted in the main in asserting Iraq's independence and pursuing a policy of alliances which would protect that independence. As an Arab state, Iraq naturally supported other Arab countries in their struggle to achieve independence and unity and entered into treaty relations with some of them without compromising its relationship with non-Arab neighbors—Turkey and Iran in particular—with whom it has no less common interests than with some Arab neighbors. After winning independence (1932), Iraq not only preferred to have an alliance with Great Britain thus siding with one major Power against other rival Powers, but also entered into regional pacts with almost all her neighbors. This policy proved so successful that Iraq's position in the world seemed quite secure.

After World War II, however, when almost all Arab countries achieved independence, Iraq appeared to lag behind them in exercising full freedom because of her pre-war commitments to Great Britain. When General Nuri moved to rid his country of the objectionable treaty obligations to Britain in 1955, he entered into a new regional defense arrangement—the Baghdad Pact—in which Britain rejoined as a partner, keeping Iraq not only committed to her former ally but also to the Western bloc as a whole against alleged Soviet threats to the Middle East. This was done at a time when Arab public opinion had reached a high pitch of nationalist excitement and was calling for Arab solidarity against Western support for Israel's claims to Arab lands. Nuri's plausible argument that his policy would strengthen Iraq's position (and, consequently, the position of the Arabs as a whole) against Israel by providing Iraq with weapons and technical know-how was denied by other Arab leaders who maintained that Iraq's need for weapons and technical assistance could be obtained from other Powers and not only from the West, and that Iraq's participation in Arab solidarity would provide the necessary strength to achieve national objectives which Nuri had unwittingly undermined by heavy dependence on Western defense plans. Consequently Arab leaders urged their countrymen to remain uncommitted in the cold war and the ideological cry for neutralism was spreading fast in the Arab world—indeed the whole Arab-Asian bloc—in which Iraq remained the committed oasis in a vast neutralist desert. Thus Nuri's principal miscalculation was in overstressing Iraq's common interests with her non-Arab neighbors at the expense of Arab solidarity on the one hand, and in entering into an alliance with the West which, by its support for Israel, presented in Arab eyes a greater danger to Arab interests than the Soviet threat on the other. Iraq gained some immediate advantages from Nuri's policy, but it was unacceptable to other Arab leaders because Iraq's adherence to a Western alliance could neither convince them that their participation in a Western defense plan would lead to their strength and unity against Israel nor influence the Western Powers to resolve the Arab-Israeli conflict in the Arabs' favor. Though opposition to Nuri originated essentially from domestic issues, as we have pointed out elsewhere,[1] his opponents concentrated on foreign policy because it conflicted with an ideology that had become predominant in Arab lands.

Iraq's foreign policy after the Revolution of 1958, though seemingly oriented by ideological influences, was governed by essentially the same forces that shaped the foreign policy of the Old Regime. The revolutionary leaders tried to change certain foreign policy objectives but could not effect a radical departure from Iraq's traditional foreign policy. Under the Old Regime, the opposition leaders demanded Arab solidarity and neutralism in the cold war, but after the fall of the Monarchy the cause of Arab solidarity was not much better off—indeed, there were occasions when the relations between Iraq and Egypt reached the breaking point; today, despite the fact that Iraq and

---

1. See my *Republican Iraq* (London, 1969), pp. 181ff; and *Arab Contemporaries* (Baltimore and London, 1973), pp. 34ff.

Syria are governed by branches of the same party, the relations between the two countries are highly strained. As to neutralism, which was the reason given for opposition to General Nuri's policy, it was but momentarily upheld, as the revolutionary leaders learned very soon that an alliance with a Great Power has always been indispensable if Iraq's independence were to be adequately protected. They also realized that cooperation—indeed even friendly relationship—with Iraq's non-Arab neighbors was necessary if the stability of the country and its internal unity were to be maintained. It did not take very long for the revolutionary leaders to learn that Iraq's foreign policy objectives have not changed notwithstanding changes of Iraq's rulers—the need for an alliance with a Great Power and cooperation with Iraq's non-Arab neighbors. Some form of unity with one or more Arab countries, though a cherished aspiration of revolutionary leaders, remained a mirage and often invited interference in Iraq's internal affairs whenever attempts were made to bring the country into close relationship with one Arab country or another. Although Iraq's former rulers maintained that an alliance with Great Britain or the West would be more advantageous to their country, the revolutionary leaders preferred an alliance with the Soviet Union because of sharp differences with the West on the Arab-Israeli conflict and other related issues.

## IRAQI-SOVIET RELATIONS

Upon the collapse of the Monarchy the new revolutionary regime turned its back to Iraq's former allies and sought by cooperation with the Soviet Union to assert the country's independence which they held was compromised by commitments to Western Powers. In another work, I have already discussed the initial steps taken by the new regime to seek cooperation with the Soviet Union and the difficulties that had arisen to prevent the implementation of Soviet-Iraqi cooperation. There were two schools of thought concerning such relationship: one urged full cooperation and the other warned against it and sought resumption of relations with the West. The ensuing struggle between the two schools culminated in an almost complete repudiation of Soviet-Iraqi cooperation by the anti-Soviet group and came very near to restoring full cooperation with the West under the second 'Arif regime.[2]

2. See my *Republican Iraq*, Chap. 7 (especially pp. 156–160); and Chap. 10, pp. 264ff.

The coming of the Ba'th Party to power in 1968 marked a significant change from cooperation with the West to the resumption of Soviet-Iraqi cooperation, partly because the Ba'th leaders were opposed to American policy toward the Middle East and partly because they were committed to certain ideological goals that ran contrary to American foreign policy objectives as a whole. Apart from the fact that Ba'th leaders resented the support given to their rivals—the Nayif-Dawud group—by Western Powers, they were committed to support the Palestinians who were, and still are, opposed to American peace plans for a settlement of the Arab-Israeli conflict. The Soviet Union, though not opposed to a peaceful settlement of the Arab-Israeli conflict in principle, has supported Iraq's foreign policy objectives as a whole and provided Iraq with her essential defense requirements.

The purchase of weapons was the first step taken by the Ba'th Government to resume cooperation with the Soviet Union. Negotiations were opened in Baghdad early in 1969 and an Iraqi military delegation, led by General Hardan al-Tikriti, Minister of Defense, visited Moscow in May. It was then announced that the Soviet Union agreed to supply Iraq with fighter planes and weapons in accordance with a previous agreement that had been signed in 1959. Iraq declared that the weapons were needed partly for defense and partly to assist other Arab countries (i.e. Jordan and Syria) against Israeli threats as there was an Iraqi force of some 12,000 troops in Jordan and another smaller force in Syria.

Apart from arms and armaments, agreements were also signed dealing with economic and technical cooperation. Soviet economic cooperation was pursued not merely for ideological but also for practical purposes. Since the Ba'th leaders sought to limit Western interests in the oil industry, they naturally needed Soviet economic assistance. They entered into a number of agreements to achieve that objective. The first, signed on July 4, 1969, dealt with Soviet technical assistance to enable Iraq to speed up the development of the oil industry;[3] another dealt with technical cooperation, especially the use of nuclear power for peace;[4] still another (March 3, 1970) provided for the establishment of a permanent Soviet-Iraqi committee to supervise economic cooperation between the two countries.[5] More than a dozen

---

3. For text, see *The Official Gazette*, August 13, 1969. An earlier agreement (June 21, 1969) dealt specifically with technical assistance (*Ibid.*, Sept. 22, 1969).
4. For text, see *Ibid.*, Dec. 17, 1969.
5. For text, see *Ibid.*, Aug. 15, 1970.

other agreements dealt with a variety of technological, cultural and other matters.⁶

Cooperation on the technical level, bringing the two countries closer to cooperating on other levels, culminated in the signing of a general treaty of friendship and cooperation modelled on other treaties signed first with Egypt and then with Syria. Premier Kosygin, while on an official visit to Baghdad, signed a 15-year Treaty of Friendship and Cooperation on April 9, 1972. Preliminary negotiations for this treaty had already been undertaken between Baghdad and Moscow, including a visit by Saddam Husayn to the Soviet Union in February 1972. In that visit the Iraqi leader stated that his country and the Soviet Union were prompted to cooperate because they have certain common objectives—opposition to Western imperialism, Zionism and American designs for peace in the Middle East—stressing in particular the ideological grounds for cooperation. These grounds, he went on to explain, have already been the subject of discussion for possible collaboration between the Iraqi Communist and Ba'th parties as both parties profess to follow a revolutionary method in achieving social change and both advocate the adoption of a collectivist economic system. Ba'thist socialist ideas were not unknown to Soviet leaders, but when the Iraqi leader referred to them as common grounds for cooperation, the Soviet leaders urged the Iraqi leaders to collaborate with their Communist compatriots to achieve common goals. Collaboration between the Ba'th and Communist leaders bore fruition in the establishment of the Progressive National Front after the Iraqi-Soviet Treaty of 1972 came into force. Soviet support in foreign affairs, and the cooperation between the Communist and the Ba'th parties in domestic affairs, enabled the Ba'th regime to pursue an independent policy in such matters as nationalization of the oil industry, settlement of the Kurdish question and other matters.⁷

The treaty provided for an "inviolable" friendship between Iraq and the Soviet Union; the two countries agreed that they would develop all around cooperation, economic, trade, scientific, technical and other fields on the basis of "respect for the sovereignty, territorial integrity and non-interference in one another's internal affairs" (Article 1). The

---

6. See *Ibid.*, May 23, 1971; and Aug. 16, 1971.

7. See pp. 101 & 123, above. See also the Progressive Nationalist Front, *Hizb al-Ba'th al-'Arabi al-Ishtiraki wa Mafhum al-Tahaluf al-Istratiji Ma'al-Ma'askar al-Ishtiraki* [The Ba'th Arab Socialist Party and the Meaning of the Strategic Alliance with the Socialist Bloc] (Baghdad, n.d.) (Mimeograph).

two countries also agreed to cooperate in "ensuring conditions for preserving and further developing the social and economic gains of their people and respect for the sovereignty of each of them over all their natural resources" (Article 2). Iraq and the Soviet Union stand for "peace throughout the world, for the easing of international tensions, and for the attainment of general and complete disarmament, encompassing both nuclear and conventional weapons under effective international control" (Article 3). Both countries condemn "imperialism and colonialism in all their forms and manifestations;" they would continue "to wage an undeviating struggle against imperialism and Zionism [and] for the complete . . . abolition of colonialism and neocolonialism, racialism and apartheid" (Article 4). Iraq and the Soviet Union would "expand and deepen" their cooperation in the economic, technical and scientific fields; would exchange experience in industry, agriculture, irrigation, water conservation, and the utilization of oil and other natural resources, and would expand trade and shipping between the two countries on the basis of "the principles of equality, mutual benefit and most-favored-nation treatment" (Article 5). Moreover, the two countries agreed to develop mutual contacts in the fields of science, art, literature, education, public health, the press, radio, cinematography, television, tourism, sports, etc. (Article 6). In foreign affairs, Iraq and the Soviet Union agreed to consult each other regularly on all important questions affecting their bilateral and multilateral relations (Article 7). "In the event of situations developing which threaten the peace of either of the sides or create a threat of peace or the danger of a violation of peace," Iraq and the Soviet Union would immediately contact each other to coordinate their positions with a view to removing the threat and restoring peace (Article 8). As to security and defense matters, the two countries agreed to cooperate "in the strengthening of their defense capabilities" (Article 9). Each of the two parties "declares that it will not enter into alliances or take part in any groupings of states or in actions or undertakings directed against the other party." Each also "undertakes not to permit the use of its territory for any act capable of doing military harm to the other side" (Article 10). Iraq and the Soviet Union agreed that their commitments under existing international treaties were not in contradiction with the provision of their treaty of friendship and cooperation; they also agreed not to conclude any agreement incompatible with it (Article 11).[8]

8. For text in English, see Appendix D; for the Arabic text, see *The Official Gazette*, April 25, 1972.

The Iraqi leaders were prompted to enter into an alliance with the Soviet Union partly because of their need for Soviet arms and partly to seek Soviet support in regional security plans as well as in domestic projects in accordance with their party's platforms and promises. Moreover, the Kurdish uprisings, supported by Iran as a means to settle the Shatt al-Arab frontier dispute in its favor, were always looked upon by the Ba'th leaders as a threat to their party, to internal unity, and to security of the country. Though the Soviet Union had always supported Kurdish leadership in the past, after the conclusion of the Soviet-Iraqi Treaty of 1972 the Soviet leaders were bound to make a choice between their support of Kurdish and Ba'thist leaderships. When the Ba'th Government went to war with the Kurds in 1974, there was no question as to which side the Soviet leaders should support.

As a *quid pro quo*, Iraq had no hesitation in following certain foreign policy objectives—opposition to imperialism, neo-colonialism and other forms of capitalist exploitations—considered to be against Western interests, though she was mainly prompted to do so because they coincided with her own foreign policy objectives, such as opposition to Zionism and American support of Israel against Arab interests. No less significant was readiness to come to an understanding with the Iraqi Communist leaders and to cooperate with them within the framework of a National Front. More specifically, the Soviet Union and other socialist countries were given certain advantages, economic and otherwise, denied to the West, such as the right to exploit the North Rumayla oil fields, the use of Umm Qasr as an outlet to the Gulf and some other commercial advantages.

But in all these dealings Iraq has not become a satelite of the Soviet Union nor even committed to follow a policy inconsistent with Iraq's national interests. True, Iraq may have appeared to follow an isolationist policy with its neighbors and a policy more friendly to the Communist bloc for at least two or three years after the coming into force of the treaty with the Soviet Union. But today it has become quite clear that Iraq, following the termination of the Kurdish war and the settlement of the frontier dispute with Iran, prefers to remain independent in all her actions and to conduct her foreign policy in accordance with what she considers her own national interests rather than the interests of the power or powers with whom she has entered into an alliance. Nor has the Soviet Union shown readiness to meet all Iraqi demands, for on several matters, political and otherwise, Iraqi and Soviet leaders did not see eye to eye.

## THE DISPUTE OVER SHATT AL-ARAB

The boundary dispute between Iraq and Iran, a legacy which Iraq had inherited from the Ottoman Empire, has become more complicated by political conflicts ever since Iraq achieved independence. In another work,[9] the origins and the temporary settlement of the dispute in 1937 were discussed. The Iraqi-Persian Treaty of 1937 fixed the frontier between the two countries at the low-water mark on the eastern side of Shatt al-Arab. It gave Iraq control of the waterway except the area near 'Abadan and Khurramshahr where the frontier was fixed at the median line in mid-channel or the *thalweg*. On all matters concerning navigation on the Shatt, the treaty stipulated that the two countries should conclude an agreement following the coming into force of the treaty but this had never been done. The treaty also provided that ships using the Shatt should have Iraqi pilots and fly the Iraqi flag except in the area where the frontier was fixed at the *thalweg*. Although relations between Iraq and Iran became friendly, disagreements in the post-war years have arisen mainly because of failure to implement the Treaty of 1937 concerning navigation and other riparian rights. Iran's participation in the Baghdad Pact (1955), in which Iraq played a leading role, induced both countries to subordinate the frontier dispute to larger defense plans because these were then considered necessary to oppose an impending Soviet threat to the two Royal Houses of Iraq and Iran.

After the fall of the Monarchy in 1958, Iraq withdrew from the Baghdad Pact and relations between Iran and Iraq began to deteriorate. Iran charged Iraq with unilateral administration of navigation in violation of the Treaty of 1937 and the Shah of Iran, following an exchange of harsh words with Iraq, declared that the Treaty of 1937 was "intolerable" and "unprecedented" and demanded that the mid-stream in the Shatt (the *thalweg*) should be the frontier between the two countries in accordance with the principles of international law. Iraq retorted by declaring the whole area on the eastern bank of the Shatt, called Arabistan, to have always been an Arab land inhabited by Arabic speaking people and should be returned to Iraq. Very soon, however, friendly relations were restored by direct negotiations; but occasional frontier incidents were by no means brought under control.[10]

---

9. See my *Independent Iraq* (London, 2nd., ed., 1960), pp. 324-30.
10. For a chronological account of the frontier disputes between Iraq and Iran, see Shakir Sabir al-Dabit, *al-'Alaqat al-Dawliya wa Mu'ahadat al-Hudud Bayn al-'Iraq wa Iran* [International Relations and Boundary Treaties between Iraq and Iran] (Baghdad, 1966).

These disputes were intensified after the Baʻth Party came to power in 1968 as Iraq's new rulers have shown deeper differences with Iran both in regional and international affairs. The Baʻth leaders, stressing Arab ideological goals, were determined to assert Iraqi rights and referred to the Shatt as the eastern border of the Arab homeland. Iran's hostility to Iraq's new regime was reflected in her support to opposition leaders involved in a power struggle with Baʻthist leaders. Complaints from one side to the other were not heeded; Iran demanded that the frontier issues should be considered as a whole and Iraq insisted that these should be settled in accordance with the judicial process specified in the Treaty of 1937. Since a settlement in accordance with that treaty was considered unsatisfactory to Iran, the treaty was denounced on April 19, 1969, on the ground that its provisions had been violated by Iraq for many years.[11] Because Iraq had for years unilaterally collected river tolls on the Shatt without giving Iran its share in accordance with the 1937 Treaty, Iran declared that her ships would neither pay tolls to Iraq nor would they comply with the Iraqi requirement that all vessels using the Shatt fly the Iraqi flag. In abrogating the treaty, Iran asserted that the 1937 Treaty was concluded for the convenience of Great Britain and that Iraq permitted British naval vessels to use the waterway first to attack Iran in 1941 and then to threaten her in 1951. Moreover, Iran maintained that the frontier, in accordance with the 1937 Treaty, meant a line that varied with the rise and fall of the tide, whereas the actual frontier should be a median line in mid-stream, as in the case of the Rhine, the Danube and the rivers which form international boundaries for part of their length. Invoking the principle *rebus sic stantibus*, Iran declared the treaty to be null and void.[12]

Iraq, considering the treaty as still binding, declared (Arpil 29, 1969) that Iran's unilateral abrogation as contrary to the principles of international law. She held that the entire Shatt was part of her territory and threatened to prevent Iranian vessels from using the Shatt unless

---

11. ʻAbd al-Husayn al-Qatifi, Dean of the Baghdad Law College, who acted as an adviser to the Iraqi Foreign Office on the Shatt's affairs, told me that Iran's denounciation of the treaty was prompted by the advice given to Iran by a number of lawyers who opined that a judicial settlement on the basis of the 1937 treaty would be unfavorable to Iran. For an exposition of the Iraqi legal position on the dispute, see ʻAbd al-Husayn al-Qatifi, "Hukm al-Qanun al-Dawli fi al-Iʻtidaʼ at al-Iraniya ʻAla al-Watan al-ʻArabi [The Rule of International Law concerning Iranian Aggressions on the Arab Homeland"], *al-Jumhuriya*, Baghdad (February 2, 1975), pp. 4–5.

12. For an exposition of the Iranian point of view, see Ramesh Sanghri, *Shatt al-Arab, The Facts Behind the Issue* (London, 1969). See also R. K. Ramazani, *The Persian Gulf: Iran's Role* (Charlottesville, 1972), pp. 42–45.

they flew the Iraqi flag. To counteract Iraqi measures, Iran placed her naval and air forces on full alert with orders to take immediate actions if Iraq tried to prevent Iranian vessels from entering the Shatt. As a test case, an Iranian vessel left Khurramshahr on April 22 escorted by an Iranian force, and she sailed safely toward the Gulf without any Iraqi action. Perhaps as a reprisal, a large number of Iranians, estimated at over 10,000, were expelled from Iraq on short notice. Iran protested Iraq's action and the matter was discussed at a meeting of the UN Security Council on May 12. Following the abortive coup of 1970, Iraq broke off diplomatic relations on the ground that Iran supported subversive activities in Iraq and the two countries seemed almost on the verge of war.

A series of border clashes between Iraq and Iranian troops took place in 1972 and 1973, especially near the Mandali area (about 60 miles northeast of Baghdad), causing casualties on both sides. Each alleged that the other was the aggressor and the troops of one country violated the territory of the other. Because of Iraq's participation in the October war of 1973, Iran agreed to resume diplomatic relations at Iraq's request and gave an assurance that she would not take advantage of the absence of Iraqi forces to threaten Iraq's security. Following the war, Iraqi troops were redeployed along the Iranian frontier.

In January 1974, border incidents recurred resulting in further casualties on both sides. On February 10 a serious incident took place resulting in the killing of 23 Iraqis and 30 Iranians. Iraq alleged that Iranian forces provoked the fighting by shelling the town of Badra and that Iranian jets entered the Iraqi airspace. Iran, however, claimed that Iraqi tanks and infantry supported by artillery attacked the Mehran frontier post, shelled a dam in an attempt to destroy it, and killed 41 guards and wounded 81. Iraq left behind 14 killed and several wounded. The dispute was taken up by the UN Security Council on February 12 at Iraq's request, but though clashes continued on both sides of the border, resort to peace was initiated at Iran's request. Accepting the good offices of a UN representative, both countries agreed to settle the dispute by direct negotiations and "a normal situation" was declared to have been restored in March.

On May 21, 1974, the Secretary General of the United Nations reported to the Security Council that Iraq and Iran had agreed to a simultaneous withdrawal of their troops along their entire border and to an early resumption of negotiations for settlement of all pending issues. He stated that the border dispute arose in part from the use of different maps, and that Iraq and Iran had indicated that they would accept the findings of a joint delimitation commission. The Secretary General's report, approved by the Security Council, became the basis for an agreement to settle the border incidents.

While direct negotiations were taking place between Iraqi and Iranian representatives, who met in Istanbul from August 13 to September 1, 1974, a new series of frontier incidents recurred which delayed the negotiations but did not interrupt them.[13] Turkey again offered her good offices and the Iraqi and Iranian Foreign Ministers met in Istanbul to resume negotiations. Differences seem to have been reduced and the two Ministers, agreed to meet again for further talks, returned home for consultation. Meanwhile, King Husayn of Jordan offered his good offices during the visit of the Shah of Iran to 'Amman and paved the way for direct negotiations. It was, however, at a meeting of the Organization of Petroleum Exporting Countries (OPEC) in Algiers (March 1975) that Iraq and Iran finally reached an agreement. Bumidian (Boumedienne), President of Algeria, and Butafliqa (Boutaflika), his Foreign Minister, offered Algeria's good offices and the Shah of Iran and Saddam Husayn, Vice President of the RCC, met there to iron out the differences that have remained in earlier meetings between their Foreign Ministers. In direct talks, the Shah and Saddam Husayn seem to have found ample grounds for future cooperation and they quickly came to an understanding. On March 6, 1975, it was announced that an agreement designed to reach a final settlement of all issues between Iraq and Iran had been concluded. A communiqué, announced by Algeria's Foreign Minister, stated that the agreement provided:

1. To make a definitive demarcation of their land borders in accordance with the Constantinople Protocol of 1913 and the minutes of the Committee for the demarcation of borders of 1914.

2. To define their maritime borders in accordance with the *thalweg* line, i.e. the median line in mid-channel.

13. Iran alleged that early in August Iraqi troops had shelled border villages on a number of occasions, killing four civilians. On August 24, Iran and Iraq accused each other of moving forces to their borders and engaging in hostile acts, including attacks on border posts and violations of air space. These incidents continued intermittently to the end of the year. On December 16, Iraq announced that two Iraqi airplanes had been shot down by Hawk ground-to-air missiles in the previous two days while flying in Iraqi air space. Iran asserted on the following day that Iraqi airplanes have been repeatedly intruding into Iranian air space and bombed Iranian villages, and that Iranian forces had been ordered to fire on Iraqi military airplanes which crossed the border. On December 31, Iraq alleged that Iranian artillery shelled Qal'at Diza, a town on the lower Zab (a tributary of the Tigris) near the Iranian border.

3. To restore security and mutual confidence along their common frontiers and to establish control which would put an end to "all infiltrations of a subversive character from either side."

4. The two countries decided to restore the traditional ties of good neighborly relations and friendship so as to insure that the region would remain secure from foreign intervention.

The Foreign Ministers of Iraq and Iran met in Tehran on March 15; a protocol was signed two days later which provided for setting up three committees—the first to examine the demarcation line of Shatt al-Arab; the second, the land boundaries between the two countries; and the third the ways and means of preventing infiltrations across the borders. The committees were to report to another meeting of the two Foreign Ministers within two months. The Prime Minister of Iran, Amir 'Abbas Huwayda (Hoveida), in an official visit to Baghdad (March 26–29), carried on further talks which confirmed the Algiers Communiqué and laid down steps for the implementation.

In June 1975, the Foreign Ministers of Iraq and Iran met in Baghdad to sign a "reconciliation" treaty designed to settle all outstanding differences between the two countries. The Baghdad Treaty, based on the Algiers Communiqué, was finally signed on June 13, 1975. In this treaty all frontier and other differences were settled. The Algerian Foreign Minister, who played a constructive role in previous negotiations, also signed the Baghdad Treaty. The occasion marked the culmination of the steps taken to settle all disputes, to establish "a new era of friendly relations," and to promote economic and cultural relations between the two countries.

Four protocols were attached to the treaty. The first provided that the Shatt al-Arab waterway border between the two countries should be the *thalweg* line rather than the eastern bank. The second delineated some 670 positions on the land border between the two countries on the basis of the Constantinople Protocol of 1913. The third provided for the establishment of border security arrangements to prevent the infiltration of undesirable elements from one side of the border to the other (i.e. all individuals regarded as *personae non gratae* to either regime). The fourth provided to establish two commissions—the first, a commission set up by Iraq to consider the granting of compensation for the property of some 65,000 Iranians expelled from Iraq under the present regime; the second, a commission set up by Iran to help Kurdish refugees from Iraq who chose to settle in Iran.[14]

14. The text was done in French; for text in English, see Appendix E; for Arabic text, see *al-Thawra* Baghdad, June 23, 1975.

The Baghdad Treaty did not merely settle border disputes; it is a landmark which ended longstanding issues between two neighbors whose cooperation was necessary for internal unity as well as for regional peace and security. Retaliatory actions have often resulted in hurting the interests of the citizens of each side domiciled in the other, and each often became involved in encouraging subversive elements against the other's regime. The massive support which the Kurds had received from Iran proved not only a danger to the Ba'th regime but also a threat to national unity. If Mulla Mustafa had won the war, he probably would have pushed Kurdish claims far beyond autonomy. To counter Mulla Mustafa's demands, Iraq was bound to seek Soviet support in the war against the Kurds with the consequential increase of Soviet influence in the Middle East.

The agreement to settle their differences by peaceful methods reflected the readiness of the two countries to subordinate ideological to national interests. It also demonstrated that they preferred to maintain peace and security by mutual cooperation than by dependence on the rivalry among the Great Powers. For these and other reasons—political, strategic and economic—the Baghdad Treeaty may be regarded as the most significant milestone in Iraqi-Iranian relations since the turn of the century.

## RELATIONS BETWEEN IRAQ AND KUWAYT

Ever since 'Abd al-Karim Qasim put forth Iraq's claim to the sovereignty of Kuwayt after the declaration of Kuwayt's independence in June 1961, relations between Iraq and Kuwayt have often been strained over a variety of issues.[15] In 1963, after Qasim's fall from power, friendly relations between Iraq and Kuwayt were restored following a formal visit to Iraq by Shaykh Sabah Salim al-Sabah, then Crown Prince and Premier of Kuwayt. The Crown Prince and the Prime Minister of Iraq, Ahmad Hasan al-Bakr, met to affirm the existing borders between the two countries that were established in 1932. In that year General Nuri al-Sa'id, Prime Minister of Iraq, sent a note to the British Political Agent in Kuwayt—Kuwayt was then under British protection—in which he acknowledged the line that was proposed by the Shaykh of Kuwayt to form the frontier between the two countries. The Shaykh of Kuwayt accepted General Nuri's affirmation of the frontier as defined in earlier correspondence between

---

15. For Iraq's claim to the sovereignty of Kuwayt in 1961 and subsequent developments up to 1968, see my *Republican Iraq*, pp. 166–73.

the two countries in 1920 and 1923. In that correspondence (consisting of an exchange of letters between the Shaykh of Kuwayt and the British Political Agent), it was agreed that the frontiers between Iraq and Kuwayt were recognized as defined in the Anglo-Turkish agreement of 1913 in which it was stated that the islands of Warba and Bubyan were to be included within Kuwayt's borders. However, owing to physical difficulties, the delimitation of frontiers in a desert area was temporarily postponed. After World War II, when the question of delimitation was raised by Kuwayt early in 1951, the Iraqi Government replied that it was prepared to do so if the Island of Warba were included within the Iraqi territory because it was deemed essential to protect Umm Qasr, the newly built port on Iraq's seabord across from the Island of Warba. Kuwayt was prepared to cooperate with Iraq, but she refused to accept modification of her frontiers as defined in earlier agreements. In 1954, in the course of negotiations concerning plans to provide Kuwayt with water from Shatt al-Arab, Iraq put forth the additional claim to include some four kilometers of Khawr al-Sabiya, the Kuwayti coastline west of the islands of Warba and Bubyan, within Iraqi territory. Kuwayt's refusal to accept the Iraqi demand prompted the British Government to propose that perhaps the Island of Warba might be leased to Iraq as a *quid pro quo* for Iraq's agreement to provide Kuwayt with water from the Shatt al-Arab. After protracted negotiations, Kuwayt rejected the proposal in 1956.

Because it has a short seabord, Iraq seems to have felt keenly the need for a deep seaport that would enable her fleet to move out freely into the sea. Faw (Fao), though situated on the entrance of Shatt al-Arab, is an unsuitable port for navigation as the entire coastline on both sides of the Shatt is very swampy and alluvial. Basra, Iraq's port on the Shatt, is within less than one hundred kilometers from the Gulf and its strategic significance has been diminished by Iraq's acceptance of the median line (*thalweg*) of the Shatt to form the new border between her and Iran. Umm Qasr, the new port, is located on an estuary dominated by the two islands of Warba and Bubyan across the Iraqi borders. For these reasons—commercial, strategic and otherwise—Iraq has put forth the claim to modify her frontiers with Kuwayt not only to have a free access to the Gulf but also to be able to defend her narrow coastline and to play her role as a Gulf state.

Iraq's recognition of Kuwayt as an independent state in 1963, though originally intended to disclaim Qasim's territorial demands, was later construed not to imply acceptance of existing borders. For, as subsequent negotiations to delimit the frontier indicated, Iraq has not completely given up territorial aspirations. From 1964 to 1967, when a joint commission, composed of Iraqi and Kuwayti delegates, met to discuss ways and means of delimitation, it often found itself engaged not in a discussion on delimitation but on the legality of the frontier agreements. When the Iraqi delegates were reminded that they met to discuss the implementation and not the validity of the agreements, the Iraqi delegates replied that they were not empowered to accept the validity of the agreements. They maintained that these instruments were concluded at a time when Iraq was still under foreign domination and, therefore, they were not freely negotiated and that modification of the frontiers in favor of Iraq was necessary if they were ever to be accepted. The Kuwayti delegates rejected the Iraqi demands on the grounds that they exceeded the powers of the joint commission which met to discuss the implementation and not the legality of the agreements. In 1967, the meetings of the commission were prorogued *sine die*.

Upon the coming of the Ba'th Party to power in 1968, which had repudiated Qasim's territorial claims and recognized Kuwayt's independence in 1963, there were high hopes in both countries that the border dispute might at last be settled. Because of Iraq's conflict with Iran over the Shatt al-Arab and Kuwayt's readiness to support Iraq, the circumstances were considered favorable to resume negotiations over the frontiers for a final settlement.

However, a year later a new factor entered into the situation which rendered the dispute more difficult to resolve. In 1969, it will be recalled, Iraqi-Iranian relations had so deteriorated that war between the two countries was imminent. In April 1969, Iraq requested Kuwayt to permit Iraqi troops to be stationed on Kuwayti territory as part of a military force on both sides of the border to protect Umm Qasr from an impending Iranian attack. Though Kuwayt was hesitant to allow the entry of Iraqi troops across the border, Iraq pressed her demand and both Hardan al-Tikriti and Salih Mahdi 'Ammash, the Iraqi Ministers of Defense and Interior, proceeded to Kuwayt to request permission for the Iraqi force to be stationed on her territory. Shaykh Sa'd al-'Abd-Allah Salim al-Sabah, the Kuwayti Minister of Defense and Interior, seems to have tacitly acquiesced under pressure, as the two Iraqi Ministers warned that an outbreak of hostilities with Iran was impending. If she wanted, they argued, Kuwayt would be allowed to dispatch a force to be stationed near Basra or elsewhere in Iraq. It was this conversation between the Kuwayti and Iraqi Ministers, later referred to as the unwritten agreement, which formed the basis of the permission given to the Iraqi force to be stationed on both sides of the frontier in an area roughly about two square kilometers in size—the Kuwayti side forming two-thirds of the area of operations. In an interview with the present writer, Shaykh Sa'd, the Minister of Defense and Interior, said that the Iraqi force began to cross the Kuwayti border before the conversation started and that his tacit approval was considered as an agreement by the Iraqi Ministers.[16] Though Shaykh Sa'd would not call the conversation an "agreement," the green light seems to have been given and the permission to station the Iraqi force was a form of *modus operandi*.[17]

Though conflict between Iraq and Iran never really reached the breaking point, Iraq kept her force on Kuwayti territory on the ground that Umm Qasr was still in need of defense as long as the Iraqi-Iranian dispute over the Shatt al-Arab remained unresolved. Indeed Iraq even sought to reinforce her garrison on the Kuwayti side; in 1973 she erected a defense outpost at al-Samita, a point at the end of the area of operations where Kuwayti soldiers were stationed close to the Iraqi force. Despite Kuwayt's objection, the Iraqi commander demanded withdrawal of the Kuwayti garrison when it made an attempt to stop the setting up of the post; upon refusal, the Iraqi commander ordered his troops to open fire on the Kuwayti garrison and forced it to withdraw. Though war between the two countries was avoided, the exchange of fire (March 20, 1973) resulted in the death of two Kuwayti soldiers and one Iraqi.

This incident signalled the occasion for the reopening of negotiations over the frontier dispute. On March 22, 1973, two days following the attack on al-Samita, Kuwayt sent a note of protest to the Iraqi Government demanding the withdrawal of the Iraqi force beyond the Kuwayti border. The Iraqi Government let the Kuwayti Foreign Office know that the borders between the two countries had not yet been formally agreed upon. This prompted Kuwayt to dispatch another note in which it invited Iraq to discuss the dispute and warned that if Iraq were not prepared to do so, the matter would be put to other Arab states for an inter-Arab discussion. Mahmud Riyad, the Secretary

---

16. The writer's interview with Shaykh Sa'd in Kuwayt (June 13, 1976).
17. Cf. The "Ihlen Declaration" in Eastern Greenland Case, see Permanent Court of International Justice, 1933, P.C.I.J., ser. A/B, No. 53, 3 Hudson, *World Court Reports*, 148 (1938).

General of the Arab League, joined by Saudi and Syrian representatives, went to Baghdad and Kuwayt in April 1973 and offered their good offices to resolve the issue peacefully. While the Iraq Government agreed to withdraw its troops from al-Samita it stated that the frontier dispute was a matter of direct negotiations between the two countries and none of the concern of other states.[18]

On April 28, 1973, the Iraqi Government sent a note to Kuwayt, in which it proposed to discuss the frontier dispute on the basis of previous correspondence, referring to them as "indications" rather than as "agreements." Settlement of the dispute, the note added, should serve not only Iraqi and Kuwayti interests but also the interests and the national goals of the Arab world as a whole to which the Ba'th Party and the Iraqi Government have committed themselves. In its reply on May 5, 1973, the Kuwayti Government ignored the ideological goals to which the Iraqi note referred and accepted to negotiate a settlement on the basis of previous correspondence which it regarded as binding international agreements and not merely as "indications."

Iraq rejected the validity of the agreements (in a note dated May 17, 1973) on the ground that they have never been ratified in accordance with Iraqi constitutional procedure. Moreover, the Iraqi note stated, Kuwayt should bear in mind the radical change of circumstances— Iraq's rise to full international status and the elimination of foreign influence—and the Arab national goals to which the Ba'th and the Iraqi people have committed themselves. As Kuwayt continued to regard the frontier agreements as still binding, Iraq proposed to postpone negotiations to more auspicious circumstances.

In 1973 Kuwayt made another attempt to negotiate a settlement but failed. Shaykh Jabir al-Ahmad al-Sabah, Heir Apparent and Prime Minister of Kuwayt, in an official visit to Iraq (August 20–22), tried to impress the Iraqi rulers with the need for a final settlement of the dispute as a step to promote political and economic cooperation between the two countries. The Iraqi leaders insisted that they would accept the *de facto* frontiers only if the islands of Warba and Bubyan were either included within Iraqi territory or leased to her. The Kuwayti Government refused to consider any change in the *status quo*.

---

18. In the press, it was then reported that Iraq was prompted to demand the islands of Warba and Bubyan under pressure from the Soviet Union in order to allow the Soviet fleet to use them as bases for possible penetration into the Gulf area (see Jalal Kushk, al-'Iraq Yutalib Bi al-Juzur al-Kuwaytiya Li al-Sufun al-Sovietiya [Iraq Demands Kuwayti Island for their use by the Soviets], *al-Hawadith*, Bayrut, March 20, 1973, pp. 20–26). These reports, as the writer was informed later in Iraq and Kuwayt, were unfounded.

As a result, a deadlock ensued despite subsequent efforts to keep negotiations uninterrupted.

Following the termination of the Kurdish war and the settlement of the frontier dispute with Iran (1975), Iraq's claim to the islands of Warba and Bubyan and the stationing of a force on Kuwayti territory for defense purposes began to lose weight in Kuwayti quarters. Kuwayt argued that before 1975 there was reason for the Iraqi troops to remain on Kuwayti territory. As the settlement of the Shatt al-Arab dispute ensued into a detente between the two countries, the Kuwayti Government held, Iraq should no longer need a force for defense on Kuwayti territory and she should withdraw it at the earliest possible moment.

In formal and informal talks between the two countries the Iraqi Government admitted that the threat of war was no longer imminent, but held that Umm Qasr was still in need of defense against possible future attacks. For this reason, Iraq pointed out that she was prepared to accept the *status quo* as defined in previous agreements if she were permitted to use the island of Warba and the northern half of the Island of Bubyan for defense purposes under a long-term lease, as these islands were uninhabited and virtually of no use to Kuwayt. "Such an arrangement," Sa'dun Hamadi, Iraq's Foreign Minister, told me, "is a reasonable demand in view of Iraq's security needs and is not unprecedented in the relationship between two neighbors."[19] Kuwayt has rejected the Iraqi offer, though it implied recognition of Kuwayti sovereignty which has been contested in earlier conversations, and began to set up certain outposts and buildings as symbols of Kuwayti authority over the islands. These islands, many a Kuwayti argues, are not a small part of Kuwayt; they form nearly a quarter of her territory, and they lie so close to the coast that their control by a foreign country would not only compromise Kuwayti sovereignty but also might involve Kuwayt in conflicts with neighbors to which she would not like to be drawn. Kuwayt's relations with Iraq became the subject of discussion in the Kuwayti Parliament and a resolution was adopted on July 12, 1975, in which Parliament supported "The positive steps taken to reach a mutual understanding with Iraq and asserted Kuwayt's sovereignty over all the islands within her borders as specified in international agreements."

In conversations with a number of responsible Kuwayti officials, the

---

19. Interview with Sa'dun Hamadi (Baghdad, January 11, 1976).

writer was reminded time and again that Kuwayt has always maintained a policy of peace and neutrality with her neighbors and that Iraq's demand to use the islands of Warba and Bubyan for military purposes would necessarily affect her policy of neutrality.[20] If Iraq were in need of Kuwayti ports for commercial purposes Kuwayt would be prepared to offer all possible facilities to Iraq including economic assistance to develop the area on both sides of the frontier for the mutual advantages of both countries. But failure to settle the border issue, many Kuwaytis have warned, is likely to arouse suspicion about Iraq's motives and has created deep resentment toward a neighbor with whom Kuwayt wishes to be in harmony and peace. These and other arguments have induced the rulers of the two countries to keep the doors of negotiations open and there seems to be today readiness to reach a final settlement. As this book went to press, the Iraqi government agreed in July 1977 to withdraw its forces from Kuwayti territory, as an indication of its willingness to settle the frontier dispute.

## RELATIONS BETWEEN IRAQ AND SAUDI ARABIA

From the time when the Iraqi Government was established, relations between Iraq and Saudi Arabia were by no means friendly, owing partly to the rivalry between the two ruling dynasties but mainly to some other more permanent factors. The majority of the people of southern Iraq belong to the Shi'i creed to whom the people of Saudi Arabia, who advocate the conservative Wahhabi creed, look with disfavor and suspicion. No less significant is the fact that some of the Shammar tribes of Ha'il, rivals to the Unayza tribes (to whom the ruling dynasty belongs) have often crossed the Iraqi frontier and have for long taken residence in the country. These two social situations which both the Iraqi and Saudi authorities have inherited from the past have clouded the atmosphere between the two countries despite attempts to improve relationships between them.[21]

---

20. The writer's interviews with 'Abd al-'Aziz Husayn, Minister of State for the Cabinet Affairs, Shaykh Sa'd al-'Abd-Allah Salim al-Sabah, Minister of Defense and Interior, Rashid 'Abd al-'Aziz al-Rashid, Under Secretary of the Ministry of Foreign Affairs, Tariq Razzuqi, head of the Foreign Office legal division, and others during his visit to Kuwayt in June 1976.

21. To stop the migratory tribes from crossing frontiers a neutral zone of about 2500 square miles was established in 1922 which separated the two countries for some 250 miles, situated to the Western tip of the frontier with Kuwayt. In 1938 an agreement was signed providing for a joint Iraqi-Saudi administration of the neutral zone created in 1922. For a background of this arrangement, see my *Independent Iraq*, pp. 321–24.

The Revolution of 1958, removing one cause of friction by the overthrow of the rival Hashimi dynasty, has created other causes which rendered the tense relationship more difficult to resolve. Not only did the republican system itself become a threat to the Saudi Monarchy, but also the adoption of socialism and other radical doctrines by the present Ba'th regime, to say nothing about Iraq's alliance with the Soviet Union, have aroused even a greater concern in high Saudi circles than under the Monarchy. Moreover, the Ba'th regime has shown a greater interest in Gulf affairs than former Iraqi rulers—a matter which has aroused the concern not only of Saudi Arabia but of all other Gulf states.

In an attempt to improve relations with their southern neighbors, the Ba'th leaders have assured Saudi rulers that they have no intention of interfering in their domestic affairs, least of all to undermine the Saudi dynasty. They tried in vain to impress on Saudi Arabia and other Arab states the need to follow an Arab policy aimed in the main at opposing foreign intervention and limiting immigration of non-Arab elements to the Arabian coast of the Gulf. While the Arab states shared Iraq's concern in principle, they pointed out that an understanding between Iraq and Saudi Arabia is necessary before embarking on such a policy.

In taking up the matter with Saudi Arabia, the Iraqi leaders were told that there were a number of pending issues which should be resolved before embarking on an Arab Gulf policy. Saudi Arabia pointed out that the delimitation of the frontiers, the dispute over the neutral zone and other related matters—tribal migration, smuggling and others—should be settled before tackling the larger political issues. Iraq readily agreed and visits were exchanged by Crown Prince Fahd to Baghdad and Saddam Husayn to Riyad in 1974 and 1975 to prepare the way for formal negotiations.

The most urgent question was the dispute over the neutral zone and the delimitation of the frontier that had been laid down in earlier agreements. Following direct negotiations between Baghdad and Riyad, it was announced on July 2, 1975, that an agreement had been reached providing for an equal division of the neutral zone by a line drawn as straight as possible to replace the existing line. This straight line, Saudi Arabia suggested, should be extended to be the frontier between the two countries without loss of territory by one to the other. Upon completion of the delimitation, the whole arrangement would be embodied in a general treaty to be signed and ratified by the two countries. It is to be noted that Saudi Arabia has followed the same pattern of frontier delimitation and dividing equally another neutral zone that separated her frontier with Kuwayt a year before. The method of equal territorial division proved to be quite satisfactory to both sides and raised high hopes that it may prepare the way for the reconciliation of other matters. Negotiations concerning larger political issues, though proceeding slowly and cautiously, seem to have already been underway.

## Dispute Between Iraq and Syria Over the Euphrates Water

The Syro-Iraqi ideological conflict, which we have already had occasion to discuss, has been reflected in a number of specific issues since the Ba'th Party came to power in 1968. The dispute over the distribution of the Euphrates water was the most important, but there were other issues—political, economic and otherwise—which have aggravated the tension between the two countries.

The Euphrates, an international river over 3000 kilometers in length, begins in Turkey and flows through Syria and Iraq before it joins the Tigris at a town called Karmat 'Ali to form the Shatt al-Arab which pours into the Gulf. Nearly half of the River Euphrates runs through Iraq.[22] Its basin includes some 350,000 square kilometers, of which 110,000 are in eastern Turkey, 70,000 in Syria and 170,000 in Iraq. The headwaters in Turkey contribute the largest portion of the water supply of the river. There are a few tributaries in Syria which account for the fertility of the Jazira province, but these add little, compared with the tributaries in Turkey, to the basin of the Euphrates. As the river approaches the delta, passing through barren lands, the need for water becomes increasingly more important for both the rural and urban communities of southern Iraq.[23]

From antiquity, Iraq has made full use of the waters of her rivers for irrigation; in modern times, she has more systematically used these waters by means of flood control and increasing use of technology for agricultural production and land reform.

Following World War II, Syria and Turkey began to take an interest in the basin, especially for irrigation and the expansion of hydroelectric power. Syria had already begun the Ghab project and her success

---

22. More specifically the Euphrates is divided as follows: 1040 km in Turkey, 660 km in Syria and 1310 km in Iraq.

23. For a general historical and geographical background, see R. Hartman and Etienne de Vaumas, "al-Furat," *Encyclopedia of Islam* (Leiden, new ed.), Vol. 11, pp. 945–48.

prompted the Government to develop the Khabur River of the Jazira province and plans were laid down for a huge dam on the Euphrates. For this project foreign aid was needed. After unsuccessful negotiations with European firms, the Soviet Union agreed to undertake the construction of a dam at Tabqa and began work on the first stage in 1966.[24] The dam was designed to store water in the depression of Tabqa and create an artificial lake (now called the Asad Lake) of some 80 km in length and covering an area of 630 square km. The water produces hydroelectric power now estimated at 300,000 kilowatts (and ultimately 800,000 kw) and irrigates some 600,000 hectares of land. The first stage of the dam was completed in 1973.[25]

In Turkey a five-year plan (1963–67) to produce hydroelectric power for new industries in eastern Anatolia was started. The Kayban project, designed to produce hydroelectric power, consisted of a dam which would merely change the seasonal flow by eliminating the extreme fluctuations of flow that formerly threatened the property and livelihood of the people inhabiting the neighborhood. Though work on the dam started in 1963, it was not completed until 1973 and the storing of water at Kayban coincided with the storing of water in the Asad Lake in 1974. In that year the amount of water was relatively low and the storing of water in the Turkish and Syrian lakes left Iraq with very little water in the summers of 1974 and 1975.

No sooner had Turkey and Syria started to construct their dams than Iraq began to make proposals about her share of the Euphrates water and an understanding among the three countries about the distribution of waters became necessary, though the Iraqi authorities had shown concern about the matter much earlier. Upon preliminary talks among the three countries in 1963–65, Turkey proposed to discuss with Syria and Iraq not only the Euphrates but both the Euphrates and Tigris waters. While Iraq agreed to participate in principle, she preferred to discuss the Euphrates waters with Syria alone.

Though the preliminary discussion between Syria and Iraq centered essentially on the exchange of information and setting up technical commissions, a number of specific proposals were scrutinized. Several

---

24. The Soviet Union agreed to provide a loan of 120 million rubles (with an annual interest of 2.5 per cent) to cover all costs of the material needed for construction and payment for technicians and transportation. The loan would be paid within 12 years in annual installments after the completion of construction.
25. See Ministry of the Euphrates Dam, *Sadd al-Furat* [The Euphrates Dam] (Damascus, n.d.); Ministry of Information, *al-Haraka al-Tashihiya* [The Correcting Movement] (Damascus, n.d.), no. 15–16.

attempts were made to narrow differences but failed. Iraq maintained that she had for long used the Euphrates water for irrigation and that she should continue to receive the same amount of water in order to keep up at least the existing level of agricultural production. These demands, Iraq held, were legitimate both from the standpoints of equity and law, as she has acquired certain rights known as "prior appropriation," as well as other factors which should be taken into consideration in any future agreement for the distribution of the Euphrates water.[26]

Apart from Turkey's share, Syria demanded that the Euphrates water should be equally divided between herself and Iraq on the ground that Iraq possesses other water resources, especially the Tigris and its tributaries, while Syria's water resources are limited and the Euphrates provides most (over 80 per cent) of the water needed for agricultural production. Of the Euphrates water that flows into Syria, estimated at about 17 billion cubic meters,[27] Iraq demanded 13 billions, thus leaving only 4 billions for Syria. To meet her water needs, Syria demanded that the Euphrates water should be divided equally between the two countries.

Owing to these sharp differences foreign technical commissions—especially a Soviet commission—were invited by Syria and Iraq to study and propose recommendations on the basis of which a certain annual percentage for each country might be agreed upon. Syria, under pressure of an increasing demand for water, felt that the 4 billions cubic meters proposed by Iraq were entirely unacceptable as a billion and a half of it is likely to be lost by evaporation, leaving only 2.5 billion for the Khabur and Euphrates areas which are in need of a greater amount of water.[28]

Negotiations for a settlement of the issues became more difficult when both Syria and Turkey began to store water in their newly formed lakes at Kayban and Tabqa, coinciding with a drought in the region in

---

26. For Iraq's point of view concerning "prior appropriation" see Hasan Ahmad al-Rawi in Tu'ma al-Bandar, *Shihhat al-Miyah Fi Nahr al-Furat* [Depletion of the Euphrates Waters] (Baghdad, 1975), pp. 39–61. See also 'Izziddin 'Ali al-Khairo, *The Euphrates and International Law* (Baghdad, 1976). For Syria's point of view, see National Command, *al-Furat: al-Azama Allati Ifta'alaha Hukkam al-'Iraq* [The Euphrates: The Crisis Created by Iraq's Rulers] (Damascus, 1976).

27. This amount is based on the assumption that Turkey would be alloted 10 billion cubic meters, though no final agreement has yet been reached with Turkey.

28. Syrian experts maintain that the Khabur area is in need of 2 billion leaving only one half billion for the existing area under cultivation in the Euphrates area, estimated at 250,000 hectares, which needs almost five times the amount allotted to Syria. See National Command Information, *Idahat Hawl Mushkilat Miyah al-Furat* [Clarifications Concerning the Euphrates Water Problems] (Damascus, 1975), p. 10.

1974–1975. Iraq maintained that her acquired rights to use the Euphrates water for agricultural production were not respected and reiterated her claims to receive a high percentage. In 1974, Syria agreed to release some of the water stored in the Asad Lake, but was not prepared to do so in 1975, as the drought continued and further release of water from the Asad Lake would affect adversely the operation of the hydroelectric system.

Unable to come to an agreement, Iraq submitted her dispute with Syria to the Council of the Arab League. The Council appointed a technical committee of seven experts to study and report on the matter. The Committee recommended a short-term project to meet Iraq's immediate needs for 1975, which Syria was prepared to accept, but refused to concede Iraq's demand for "prior appropriation" as the basis for a long-term arrangement. Further negotiations, in the course of which Saudi Arabia offered her good offices, helped to narrow the differences, and Iraq seems to be prepared now to accept a settlement on the basis of the formula 60–40 (60 per cent for Iraq and 40 per cent for Syria) as has already been proposed by a number of experts. The ground for a final settlement seems at last to have been set.[29]

The dispute over the distribution of the Euphrates water has become more difficult partly because of the political differences between the two countries and partly because Iraq has embarked on some economic projects considered by Syria harmful to her economy. For instance, Iraq has stopped the pumping of oil through the Syrian pipeline and diverted the oil to the Gulf by the construction of new pipelines. Iraq has also completed the construction of another pipeline through Turkey. These measures, Syria maintains, have been politically motivated and have hampered economic cooperation between the two countries.

## IRAQI-JORDANIAN RELATIONS

From antiquity, the region that forms the kingdom of Jordan today has played with great success the role of a buffer state, and its rulers often acted as honest brokers among their neighbors. In ancient and medieval times, this region served as a buffer zone first between Rome and

---

29. At a meeting in Baghdad (1975) between Saddam Husayn and the Syrian delegation, Saddam is reported to have given his approval for such an agreement. The writer's interviews with Sa'dun Hamadi, Minister of Foreign Affairs (Baghdad, January 9, 1977) and Mukarram Al-Talabani, Minister of Irrigation (Baghdad, January 2, 1977).

Persia, and then between Byzantium and Egypt on the one hand and Iraq (under the 'Abbasids) and Egypt (under Fatimids and their successors) on the other. In modern times, Jordan found herself surrounded by an increasing number of states—Egypt, Saudi Arabia, Iraq, Syria, Lebanon and Israel—which rendered the task of keeping a balance among these rival neighbors exceedingly more difficult. In order to survive, Jordan was bound to follow a moderate and a neutralist policy toward her neighbors and never to take an extreme position on foreign policy issues. If she ever found herself drawn into an alliance with one neighbor or joining a coalition of one bloc against another, she quickly reverted to traditional neutrality and normal relations with all neighbors.

Since her creation as a state after World War I, Jordan's relations with Iraq were particularly friendly as the two countries were ruled by members of the same family—the Hashimi House—who often consulted each other on matters of common concern. The destruction of the Hashimi House in Iraq by the Revolution of 1958 necessarily affected the relationship between the two countries, though Jordan very soon found it necessary to recognize the republican regime of Iraq and normal relations between the two countries were reestablished.[30]

However, there has always existed in Iraq, after the destruction of the Monarchy, an important section of the people who continued to sympathize with the Hashimi House and who looked to King Husayn, ruler of Jordan, as the spokesman and spiritual head of the house. Some may have been sympathetic for purely personal reasons (especially in the case of tribal chiefs with whom the Monarchy always kept friendly relations), but their occasional calls on King Husayn have been looked upon by Iraq's new rulers with suspicion and disfavor. Others, prompted by political or personal ambition, urged King Husayn to lead an opposition and extend his influence or control to Iraq. Though no serious move has ever been made by the King to entertain such designs, the mere circulation of rumors about them is likely to create an atmosphere of suspicion between Iraqi and Jordanian rulers.

The coming to power of the Ba'th Party in 1968 may have added still another cause of suspicion and disenchantment between the two countries. In the past, the Hashimi House has always taken pride in the fact that the Arab nationalist movement (often referred to as

---

30. For Jordan's relations with Iraq under the Monarchy see my *Independent Iraq*, pp. 343–45; for relations after the Revolution of 1958, see my *Republican Iraq*, passim.

Pan-Arabism) was given practical expression by the Arab Revolt of 1916 which the Sharif Husayn, grandfather of King Husayn and founder of the Hashimi House in the Hijaz, had led and whose two sons, 'Abd-Allah and Faysal, founded the Royal houses of Jordan and Iraq. King Husayn of Jordan considers himself as the leader on whose shoulders the mantle of the Arab nationalist movement of today has fallen—a movement stressing liberal ideas and an evolutionary approach to nationalist goals. The Ba'th Party, advocating a revolutionary approach, argues that the Arab Revolt of 1916 which promised independence and unity has failed to achieve those objectives and that the new Arab nationalist movement seeks to achieve not only the objectives of the Arab Revolt of 1916 but also other goals—the goals of an ideology promising Arab unity, freedom and socialism. The Iraqi Ba'th leaders hope to achieve these goals not only for the Arabs of Iraq but also for Arabs of all other lands. In Jordan, as in some other Arab countries, Ba'thist leaders have shown readiness to cooperate with the Iraqi leaders to achieve these goals. For this reason, King Husayn is opposed to the Jordanian Ba'th leaders who sympathize with the Iraqi Ba'th regime just as the Iraqi leaders who sympathize with the Hashimi House have been considered *personae non gratae* to Iraq.

However, as Jordan is an Arab country that has been directly exposed to periodic Israeli attacks, Iraq under Ba'thist rule has shown no less concern for the defense of Jordan than under former regimes and an Iraqi Army to reinforce the Jordanian Army against Israel was dispatched to Jordan in 1968. In theory, the Iraqi Ba'th leaders declared that they would support radical Palestinian leaders on ideological grounds, but in practice the Iraqi military failed to side with the Palestinians against the Jordanian regime in the events of September 1970 (though they did supply them with weapons), when radical Palestinians became involved in a struggle for power with King Husayn.[31] King Husayn, on his part, has reciprocated by offering his good offices to Iran and Iraq to resolve their border dispute on the occasion of the visit of the Shah of Iran to Jordan in 1974. These preliminary steps, pursued by Jordan's Premier in subsequent months, helped to narrow the differences between Iraq and Iran and to lay the ground for the final settlement reached in Algeria in March 1975.

---

31. Though the military acted in accordance with what they considered as Iraqi interests, the Ba'th leaders seem to have been critical of the military and Hardan al-Tikriti, who gave the order to the Iraqi force in Jordan to withdraw and not to fight against the Jordanian Army, was relieved of his position as Minister of Defense (see pp. 59–60, above).

Jordan's efforts to support Iraq in international councils prompted Iraq to cooperate with Jordan in the cultural and economic fields. In 1975 agreements to promote economic, commercial and cultural cooperation were signed and a joint committee to coordinate cultural and touristic activities between the two countries was established.[32] In need of deep seaports in neighboring countries, Iraq offered financial assistance to improve the Port of 'Aqaba, Jordan's principal outlet to the Red Sea, and construct trans-desert roads between Iraq and Jordan. Iraq seems to be disposed to invest capital in Jordan uninhibited by political considerations. On her part, Jordan offered to cooperate with Iraq in all matters of mutual interest, though her cooperation with Syria, with which Iraq is in disagreement, might be looked upon with disfavor.[33] Despite political differences, Jordan's relations with Iraq have become increasingly more intimate in the economic field and both countries have in practice shown willingness to subordinate ideological to national interests.

## RELATIONS WITH OTHER ARAB COUNTRIES

In the wake of the settlement of the frontier dispute with Iran and the termination of the Kurdish war, Iraq turned to other Arab countries to improve her relations with them and assert her role in Arab affairs. On his way back from Algeria in March 1975, Saddam Husayn stopped in Tunisia and Egypt; he promised Bourguiba aid for his country's economic development,[34] and talked with Sadat about economic cooperation. In May Sadat visited Baghdad for further talks, and an agreement of economic cooperation was signed. As a signal of Iraq's willingness to cooperate with Egypt, she contributed one million tons of crude oil as a gift to the Egyptian people and $35 million for reconstruction and rehabilitation. Though dissatisfied with the Sinai agreements, Iraq refrained from criticism of Egypt's drive to arrive at a peaceful settlement of the Arab-Israeli conflict. Iraq also promised aid to the Sudan, Jordan and South Yaman.

The agreement with Saudi Arabia in July 1975, has encouraged Iraq to re-open talks with the Arab Gulf states for possible cooperation, presumably in pursuance of Iraq's wish to play a role in Gulf affairs. It was announced in the summer of 1976 that a conference on Gulf affairs would be held in the fall of that year. Because of Iraq's conflict with

---

32. For text of the agreements, see *The Official Gazette* (Jordan, 1975).
33. See *al-Thawra*, Baghdad, July 29, 1976.
34. In April, 1975, Habib al-Shatti, Tunisia's Foreign Minister, visited Baghdad and it was then announced that Iraq had given Tunisia $15 million as aid for his country.

Kuwayt and suspicion of Iraq's Gulf policy no agreement has yet been reached on possible cooperation when the conference was held in Masqat (Muscat) in November 1976 to discuss Gulf security problems.

The civil war in Lebanon has accentuated the misunderstanding between Iraq and some of her Arab neighbors as she found herself drawn into the conflict. Though Syria supported left-wing groups at first on ideological grounds, she later supported the established regime and right-wing groups in order to maintain public order and keep friendly relations with the Christian population. Consequently, Iraq felt compelled to take the side of left-wing groups and to fault Syria's action on ideological grounds. Though Iraq's move was partly motivated by her ideological conflict with Syria, she aroused the suspicion of other countries, especially Saudi Arabia, with which Iraq had just begun to establish good neighborly relationships. As a result, Iraq's endeavors to play a role in the Gulf and improve her relations with the Gulf states were momentarily suspended and it may take a very long time before her diplomatic initiative could be resumed. However, the Ba'th leaders, believing that time is on their side, seem to be prepared to wait for more auspicious circumstances to persuade their neighbors to agree on an Arab Gulf policy.

## IRAQ AND THE ARAB-ISRAELI CONFLICT

Although not a neighbor of Israel, Iraq has been committed to oppose Zionist designs in Palestine long before Israel was created as a state. From the time of the Palestine wars of 1948–49, she has refused to sign an armistice agreement and still regards herself at war with Israel. Taking such an extreme stand, Iraq was bound to be involved, directly or indirectly, in almost all Arab encounters with Israel. The degree of Iraq's participation depended on how free Iraq was from other preoccupations, domestic or otherwise. Yet no matter how involved Iraq was in those issues, no Iraqi Government could ever remain long in power if it failed to cooperate with other Arab countries whenever they took a joint action against an Israeli attack.[35]

The assumption of power by the Ba'th Party, whose views on the Palestine issue are considered radical, committed Iraq to take an even

---

35. For Iraq's diplomatic or military activities before and after the creation of Israel, see my *Independent Iraq*, pp. 135, 170–71, 273–74, 347–48; *Republican Iraq*, pp. 390–91.

more extreme stand on the issue and to identify the country with such revolutionary regimes as Algeria, Libya and South Yaman. The Ba'th Party has for long considered the recovery of lands taken by Israel as a fundamental national demand and called for Arab unity to mobilize all Arab potentials against the enemy. Iraqi leaders admit that the achievement of this goal might take a very long time, but they maintain that under no circumstances should this ultimate goal be given up or diverted by side issues. Consequently, the Ba'th leaders argue that the Arabs should never accept compromises that might have the effect of subordinating ultimate goals to half-measures like the Security Council resolution of 242 and 338 and others.[36]

Not exposed to direct threats as the confrontation states Iraq could afford to take the long view about the Arab-Israeli conflict; but the Syrian and Egyptian governments, exposed to direct threats and attacks, were bound to consider short-term measures rather than suffer greater losses. Although all Arab countries are agreed on ultimate goals in principle, disagreement on short-term measures has accentuated the conflict between Iraq and other Arab countries.

Not infrequently, the Iraqi leaders have shown readiness to be flexible; they decided to withdraw the Iraqi force from Jordan in September 1970, in the conflict between Jordan and the Palestinians though Iraq was ideologically committed to the Palestinians. The Iraqi leaders seem to have acted in accordance with their country's national interest, though their action became the subject of reproach by opponents to the regime and censored by leading members of the Ba'th Party.[37] But when the October War of 1973 broke out, Iraq had no hesitation to participate by dispatching forces to Syria, even though she had no prior notification about the impending assault on Israel. The Iraqi force seems to have taken an active part first in the drive to force the Israeli Army to withdraw from occupied Syrian territory, and then in defending Syrian territory when the Israelis took the offensive in a drive toward Damascus.[38] Moreover, Iraq participated in the oil embargo and nationalized American and Dutch interests in the Iraqi oil industry. She had already severed diplomatic

---

36. Center for Arab Strategic Studies, *Dawr al-Jaysh al-Iraqi Fi Harb Tishrin 1973* [The Role of the Iraqi Army in the War of October 1973] (Bayrut, 1975), pp. 36ff.

37. See Ba'th Party, *al-Taqrir al-Siyasi al-Sadir 'An al-Mu'tamar al-Qatri al-Thamin* [The Political Report Issued by the Eight Regional Congress], January 1974 (Baghdad, 1974), pp. 181–88.

38. Center for Arab Strategic Studies, *Role of the Iraqi Army in the War of October 1973*, pp. 43ff.

relations with the United States in 1967 and refused to resume them after other Arab countries have reestablished them following the October War of 1973.

Though the Iraqi force that participated in the October war was withdrawn after the cease-fire, Iraq has repudiated the interim-agreements with Israel on the ground that settlement of the Arab-Israeli conflict should follow a victory in the battle field rather than a partial settlement implying recognition of Israeli occupation of Arab lands. To Iraqi Ba'th leaders these agreements have created dissension and conflict among Arab leaders because they were signed in violation of prior commitments to recover all occupied lands. "The only peace agreement that Iraqi would accept," said the Iraqi Foreign Minister to the present writer, "is that in which all the issues relating to the Arab-Israeli conflict would be resolved in a comprehensive peace settlement."[39] The existing interim agreements, the Ba'th leaders maintain, would eventually be repudiated when the Arabs realize that Israel had refused to withdraw from occupied Arab territory. However, the Iraqi leaders, though critical of Arab concessions, are not unaware that the leaders who accepted them had no other choice; they reproached them primarily because they acquiesced to the consequences of the agreements which Iraq considers as inconsistent with Arab national interests. To counteract what is considered as defeatism, Iraq has supported radical Palestinian elements and dispatched volunteers and weapons to assist them in their struggle against the enemy.

As a country which has no common borders with Israel, the Iraqi leaders are justified in taking the long view about a settlement of the Arab-Israeli conflict, provided it is understood that Iraq would continue to play her role as the defender of Arab rights in general after an interim-agreement has been reached with Israel by one or more of the confrontation states. If this strategy were acceptable to other Arab leaders, the Iraqi stand on settlement of the Arab-Israel conflict is not necessarily opposed to the position of the confrontation states. "What they do not accept," the Iraqi leaders argue, "is an approval of the actions taken by leaders of the confrontation states, because such an approval must be construed an abandonment of Ba'thist foreign policy objectives to which Iraq was committed."[40]

39. The writer's interview with Shadhil Taqa, the late Foreign Minister, on July 28, 1974, and Sa'dun Hamadi, now Foreign Minister, in an interview on January 7, 1976.
40. The writer's interviews with top Ba'thist leaders of the National and Regional Commands in 1976 and 1977.

Despite these extremist views, however, Iraqi leaders have often proved quite flexible on matters affecting Iraq's own security and national interests. In the case of the Arab-Israeli conflict, the Iraqi leaders might realize that the achievement of immediate objectives would be necessary before ultimate objectives become a subject for public discussion.

## IRAQI-AMERICAN RELATIONS

Before the Revolution of 1958, Iraq was considered one of the most important strongholds in the Arab World which pursued a pro-Western policy and took an active part in the implementation of defense plans designed to protect the region from Soviet penetration. From the time she achieved independence in 1932, Iraq entered into an alliance with Great Britain and British forces were allowed to use Iraqi territory against any rival power or powers that might threaten the region. In the post-war years, when Britain was no longer capable of undertaking full defense responsibility, the United States began gradually to extend her influence to fill the vacuum created by Britain's withdrawal. Because she was traditionally tied up with Iraq, Britain tried to maintain some form of military cooperation with Iraq in a defense plan for the Middle East known as the Baghdad Pact (1955), which virtually superseded the Anglo-Iraqi Treaty of 1930. However, the real architect of this defense plan, called by American strategists the Northern Tier, was the United States—a plan in which General Nuri, the Iraqi Premier, played an important role both in formation and implementation. But General Nuri's policy, as we have seen, ran contrary to opposition leaders who advocated a neutralist rather than a pro-Western policy. So long as General Nuri was in power and the Monarchy presided over the regime, Iraq pursued a pro-Western policy and played an important role in regional security.

The Revolution of 1958, though it did not completely disrupt Iraq's relations with the West, altered considerably General Nuri's pro-Western policy. Though Iraq did not at once withdraw from the Baghdad Pact—this step was taken a year later—a policy of neutrality was proclaimed which adversely affected her relations with Western Powers. True, the Soviet Union did not replace Britain's position in Iraq, but neutrality proved to be a step toward that objective. In 1959 an agreement to initiate Iraqi-Soviet economic cooperation was concluded, but politically Iraq remained uncommitted to the Soviet bloc, though Sovet influence became noticeable under the Qasim regime. Public opinion, however, was divided on what attitude Iraq should take concerning East-West relationships, because of the sharp conflict between Nationalists and Communists who advocated divergent views about foreign policy until Qasim's fall from power in 1963. For over five years, from February 1963 to July 1968, there were serious attempts at bringing Iraq back to the Western fold by ignoring Iraq's treaty obligations to the Soviet Union and resuming economic and commercial relations with Western countries. Under Premier Bazzaz and the second 'Arif regime (1966–68), the pro-Western elements became so influential that Iraq could no longer be considered in the neutralist camp. Several actions—the agreement to end the Kurdish war in 1966, Premier Bazzaz's visits to England and the United States in 1966 and 1967—contributed in no small measure to promote economic and technical cooperation between Iraq and the West. These steps may have alarmed left-wing parties (Ba'thists, Communists and other radical elements) to whom the "revolutionary process" that was set in motion by the July Revolution of 1958 seemed receding and began to criticize the regime; it was, however, the Six-Day war (1967) and American support of Israel that triggered the revolutionary trend and gave the Army an excuse to overthrow the regime and entrust power in the hands of Ba'thist leaders who pursued a foreign policy opposed to the United States.

The Ba'th Party, committed ideologically to radical views, tried to effect a change in Iraq's foreign policy. Opposed to the recognition of Israel, as noted before, Iraq refused to be involved in partial plans for peaceful settlement. Nor were diplomatic relations resumed with the United States, as Iraq views with suspicion and disfavor the role assigned to Israel to play in regional security.[41]

From 1968 to 1973, Iraq followed an isolationist policy. She nationalized Western oil interests and reduced trade relations with the West, replaced by trade with countries considered friendly because they refused to support Israel in the wars of 1967 and 1973. The beneficiaries of this policy were first the Soviet bloc and then some European and Asiatic countries that had taken a sympathetic attitude toward the Arabs in the October war of 1973.

Iraq's isolationist policy, however, affected adversely her internal conditions, especially after the nationalization of oil industry (1972)

---

41. Ba'th Party, *al-Taqrir al-Siyasi*, pp. 199–212; Al-Thawra Publications, *Qadaya wa Tasa'ulat Mashru'a* [Problems and Legitimate Queries] (Baghdad, 1973); and *al-Mantaqa, Madha? wa Ila Ayn?* [The Region, Why? and Whither?] (Baghdad, 1973).

which reduced the income from oil and impeded the implementation of development projects. As we have seen, first Iraq turned to the Soviet Union and other socialist countries to provide economic assistance and promote trade relations. However, the quality of commodities and technological know-how received from the socialist bloc did not measure up to Western standards. A number of Iraqi experts began to urge the resumption of cultural and economic relations with Western countries on the ground that the Soviet Union, in accordance with the detente policy, herself was engaged in trade relations with the United States. But the top Ba'th leaders, still undecided, were hesitating. The abortive Kazzar coup, eliminating extremists, gave an opportunity to leaders advocating a neutralist policy to review the situation and encourage trade relations with the United States without necessarily accepting American foreign policy objectives in the Arab World.[42] As a result, trade between the two countries, which had almost been interrupted by 1972, began at once to rise from some twenty million dollars in 1973 to over 200 million in 1974 and 1975 and reached nearly half a billion in 1976. Only in arms and armaments did Iraq continue to depend on Soviet supplies.

Improved economic relations with the West, especially with the United States, were not matched by an improvement in official relations.[43] Iraq views American supplies of arms and economic assistance to Israel (while denied to Egypt, Syria and Iraq) as an indirect encouragement to aggression committed by a State-Member of the United Nations that had taken lands by force contrary to the Charter of the United Nations and International Law. Nor was Iraq consulted on plans for a peaceful settlement of the Arab-Israeli conflict, despite several unofficial attempts, because the Ba'th Party has insisted on an overall settlement which the United States has not been willing to accept. Moreover, the Kurdish war, an episode which clouded Iraqi-American relations, has been considered as evidence that the United States sought indirectly to undermine if not to overthrow the Ba'th regime. Mulla Mustafa, supported by Iran, was and is still considered in Ba'thist political circles as an American "agent" who

---

42. See Saddam Husayn's statement to a press conference on April 8, 1974 (Publications of the Ministry of Information, Baghdad, 1974).
43. The number of personnel in the Iraqi and American Interest Sections in the two respective countries have been more than doubled, but diplomatic relations have not yet been resumed despite increasing visits to Iraq by a number of American Congressmen and others in semi-official capacities.

launched his attacks with Western encouragement against the central authority, despite the Ba'th's offer of self-rule—a plan he was prepared to accept from former regimes. His visit to the United States, presumably for medical treatment, must have been an embarrassment for Americans who seek an improvement of relations between the two countries after termination of the Kurdish war.

The civil war in Lebanon, in which Iraq became increasingly involved, affected Iraqi political relations with the United States adversely. Iraq took an uncompromising position in her support for left-wing leaders, partly on ideological grounds but mainly because a victory of left-wing elements in Lebanon would enhance Iraq's position in the Arab world. Syria's intervention in Lebanon, with tacit American approval, tipped the precarious balance between the Lebanese left- and right-wing parties in favor of the latter. Since Syria today is in a sharp conflict with Iraq and has shown willingness to cooperate with the United States, American support for Syria has been construed by Iraq as an opposition to Ba'thist national and ideological objectives.[44] Perhaps a settlement of the Arab-Israeli conflict and a relaxation of tension among rival Arab leaders might eventually lead to the normalization of Iraqi-American relations, as Iraq would find it in her best interest to do, as the agreement on the frontier dispute with Iran demonstrated.

## Retrospect

Ba'thist foreign policy, as noted before, stemmed partly from the Ba'th ideology and partly from Iraqi national interests. In asserting Iraqi interests—independence and friendly relations with neighbors—the Ba'th leaders have followed the pattern of Iraq's traditional foreign policy, namely, an alliance with a Great Power and friendly relations with neighbors in order to protect national interests. For ideological reasons, however, the Ba'th leaders preferred the Soviet Union to be the ally of Iraq rather than a Western power and committed themselves to support revolutionary movements in the Arab world.

In pursuing Iraq's foreign policy objectives, it has been observed that ideological goals have not always been consistent with the country's national interests. For instance, the radical Ba'th views about

---

44. In the eyes of Ba'thist leaders, President Nixon, who had just begun to understand the Arab views, was forced to resign by forces opposed to a reconciliation between Arab and American national interests (see Tariq 'Aziz, *Limadha Istaqal Nixon* [Why Did Nixon Resign] (Baghdad, 1974).

settlements of the Arab-Israeli conflict, which seem to meet the demands of Palestinian extremists, are not in accord with Soviet views which conform to Syrian and Egyptian views. Thus, though an ally of the Soviet Union, Iraq is not in agreement with Soviet views about settlement of the Arab-Israeli conflict concerning which American and Soviet leaders seem to converge. Moreover, the Soviet Union has pursued a detente policy with the United States, though Iraq is ideologically in conflict with American foreign policy in the Arab world.

Does Iraq weigh her policies toward the Soviet Union and the United States in the scale of ideological or national interests? Since the Soviet Union has been prepared to pursue a detente policy with the United States, there is reason for Iraq to pursue a similar policy, separating economic from political objectives, and promote trade relations which are not necessarily opposed to Iraq's foreign policy objectives. Moreover, Soviet support for Syrian Ba'th leaders, with whom the Iraqi Ba'th are in sharp conflict, has prompted Iraqi leaders to pursue their country's national interests apart from ideological considerations. Similarly, Iraq has come to an understanding with Iran, which may not be entirely consistent with Soviet regional designs, and put an end to a longstanding border dispute considered in the national interests of both countries. Having achieved relative internal stability, Iraq seems to be quite prepared to follow an independent foreign policy stemming essentially from her own national interests. How long Iraq can continue to assert an independent policy will ultimately depend on the internal strength and stability of the regime and the achievement of social and economic development considered necessary for public consent and peaceful change.

Chapter VIII

# Conclusion

IN THE final chapter of *Republican Iraq*,[1] I tried to outline the aims of the revolutionary changes in Iraq since 1958 and the emerging trends that might ultimately lead to the establishment of a progressive and enduring political system which would command the greatest public appeal. That political system, it was suggested, should be based on a set of principles that have become overriding in Arab political thinking, such as nationalism and socialism—presumably along secular lines—and a measure of individual freedom. A new form of representation by virtue of which the public can participate in political processes is deemed necessary to provide legitimacy and inspire public confidence. Such a system, if it met the needs of a society that insists on rapid social change, might provide a corrective to the discredited Old Regime by stressing social doctrines that have become fashionable today in the Arab World, derived partly from Arab cultural heritage but mainly from European society. These were the trends of thought in Iraq before the Ba'th Party achieved power in 1968 and its leaders promised to give them practical expression and provide the country with a stable regime capable of achieving cherished national goals.

Has the Ba'th Party accomplished any of these goals during the decade since it achieved power?

---

1. Some of the remarks and conclusions in that chapter entitled "The Unfinished Revolution" are still relevant; readers who are interested in those remarks might wish to see that chapter before reading the final chapter of this work (See *Republican Iraq* [London, 1969], pp. 298–305).

To begin with, Iraq has experienced a series of military revolutions since 1958 which introduced violence as a method of political change and it has become exceedingly difficult to maintain public order and establish an enduring regime. True, even under the Monarchy, governmental changes were frequent, in which some form of violence was occasionally used and the average life of a Cabinet was hardly more than eight months,[2] but the method of change since 1958 has become much more violent and exceedingly difficult to check. Upon achieving power, the Ba'th leaders were determined to put an end to violent changes and erect a regime immune to military intervention. Despite several attempts to overthrow the regime (i.e. the abortive coups of 1970 and 1973)[3] the Ba'th leaders have not only been able to discourage military intervention but have also succeeded in relieving the political process from military pressures. Though it is not unlikely that an adventurist officer might still be tempted to involve the Army in a military action against the regime, the Army as a whole has been closely watched by vigilant Ba'thist eyes and the officers whose loyalty is in doubt are removed from responsible posts. The Ba'th Party endeavors to bring—if it has not already brought—the Army under its control and hopes that its tenure of office will depend on civil rather than military support. The Army seems to have accommodated to party discipline by the recruitment of an increasing number of young Ba'th members into its ranks. Moreover, a number of Army officers has been induced to join the Ba'th Party and a growing fraternization between military institutions and top Ba'th leaders has become noticeable.[4] Today even strikes and popular demonstrations that often recurred and disturbed public order are no longer feasible.[5] For this reason, even political opponents, though they often voice certain grievances against restrictions of political opinion, have paid a high tribute to the Ba'th Party's ability to thwart military interventions and maintain stability and public order.

To stop military intervention in politics, however, may seem only a negative step toward the establishment of an enduring political system; the positive step would be to engage the public in the political process

2. See my *Independent Iraq* (London, 2nd ed., 1960), p. 27.
3. See pp. 53ff. and 63ff.
4. In an effort to foster this relationship, Saddam Husayn has been given a high military rank and military decorations. He has also been given an honorary military degree by the Military College.
5. The Najaf-Karbala demonstrations (February 1977) were allowed on the first day to pass without police intervention, but when it appeared that they might get out of hand, not only the police but also the Army was brought to maintain order (see p. 69, above).

# Conclusion

and establish the regime's legitimacy by some form of representation and the sharing of public responsibility. In both public and private pronouncements, the Ba'th leaders have often indicated the need for political participation and have promised that they will eventually engage the public in political decisions. The recurrence of clandestine activities and the intense rivalry among leaders and parties struggling for power that often disrupted constructive work in the past have prompted the Ba'th leaders to proceed slowly and cautiously in seeking cooperation with rival elements and groups. But in the long run the only sure way to reduce and ultimately put an end to such activities is indeed to widen the popular base by throwing open the door of political participation to all without crippling restrictions.

The first step in the right direction toward political participation was the establishment of the Progressive National Front, composed first of two parties—the Ba'th and the Communist parties—and then of other "progressive" parties and groups. Though in theory the present regime can now claim a much wider popular base than the constituency of the Ba'th Party—indeed, it can claim the loyalty of all elements represented in the Front—in practice, however, the Ba'th Party is alone held responsible for political decisions. As a sign that a wider popular base might be sought to support the Ba'th regime, a number of political leaders and retired officers who had been opposed to the Ba'th and who are not considered by Ba'th standards as "progressive" elements have indicated a readiness to cooperate within the framework of the Front. If a step to enlist the cooperation of these elements were ever undertaken, it would broaden the popular base of the Ba'th regime by the inclusion of a "loyal opposition" within its framework.

Perhaps a more important instrument to enlist popular participation would be a National Assembly in which various shades of opinion could be represented. The Temporary Constitution has indeed provided for such an Assembly but the relevant articles of the Constitution (Articles 46–55) have not yet been implemented. Leaders of various groups and national organizations prepared to cooperate within the framework of the regime seem to be awaiting the opportunity to express their views through an elected organ but plans for the holding of elections have not yet been laid down. Asked by the present writer about the nature and scope of this Assembly, Saddam Husayn, Vice President of RCC, replied:[6] "It will be a democratic institution and a very important branch of the Government. Though not exclusively, its function will be

---

6. The writer's interview with Saddam Husayn (Baghdad, January 9, 1977).

essentially legislative; and the Revolutionary Command Council, now the highest authority in the regime, will be reduced to an Executive Council with some legislative functions." "When will this Assembly be called?" I asked. "It will not be too long—much sooner than some would think—when the plan for calling it has been thoroughly studied and the circumstances for implementation matured," he replied. It is almost taken for granted that representation in the Assembly would be based on corporate and functional principles, though details of the plan have not yet been fully spelled out; political parties, groups and various shades of opinion will also be represented in the Assembly though the percentage of corporate in relation to party representation has not yet been decided upon. This mixed form of representation, combining vertical and horizontal electoral procedures, reflects Ba'thist political methods which seek the blending of collectivist and limited free enterprise doctrines. It is perhaps too early to describe in detail the hybrid political system that is likely to emerge, but in principle it would be a form of social democracy which, as suggested earlier, might have greater public appeal than the two alternatives—traditional liberal democracy and collectivist authoritarianism.[7]

The Ba'th leaders have shown a greater enthusiasm in emphasizing "reconstruction" by planning and economic development than in the granting of freedom and political participation on the ground that no real progress and stability in the country can be achieved before poverty and other forms of deprivation were wiped out. Ba'th socialism, it is held, is designed to improve social and economic conditions as a prerequisite to other ultimate objectives—democracy, freedom and Arab unity. Although in theory the Ba'th ideology promises to achieve all these objectives simultaneously, collectivist measures appear to be overriding in the eyes of Ba'thist leaders and the sudden increase in the wealth and national income of the country has naturally prompted them to seek popular support by an emphasis first on economic development.

In putting forth a program of social and economic development before individual freedom, are the people of Iraq prepared to support the Ba'th leaders in their approach to reconstruction? In other words, are the people in favor of distributive justice or individual freedom? Although a certain balance of the two might be maintained, the people of Iraq—indeed, the Arab people as a whole—seem to be prepared to tolerate restrictions on individual freedom and achieve an equitable distribution of wealth rather than to tolerate disparity between classes.

7. Cf. my *Political Trends in the Arab World* (Baltimore, 1970), Chap. 10.

The Arabs, it is suggested, often speak of freedom and equality as two inseparable words meaning the same thing, but if they were to choose one of the two, it seems that the choice of the great majority would be in favor of equality rather than freedom. Thus a political system that would insure the principle of equality with a minimum of freedom would perhaps command greater public appeal than a system which insures freedom at the expense of equality.[8]

Does this mean that individual freedom should remain indefinitely subordinated to the principle of equality? It is tempting to argue that once distributive justice is achieved, the measure of freedom enjoyed by an appreciable number of individuals would likely to be in greater demand, and some form of a balance between freedom and equality might ultimately be achieved which would insure freedom and prosperity—a welfare state. If the Ba'th regime could achieve a welfare state—indeed a measure of distributive justice has already been achieved, as it is easier than individual freedom—the experiences with developing a political system which Iraq is now undertaking is worth the experiment. The outcome of this system would hopefully lead to a form of "social democracy", combining the principles of democracy and socialism—a blend of diverse, if not conflicting, systems originating from different sources. The framework of such a system has already been defined in broad terms in the Temporary Constitution and other relevant instruments, as noted earlier,[9] but the elaborate structure of the system, like tissues in the organism, would have to evolve gradually on the basis of the needs, conditions, aspirations and experiences of the country if it were ever to endure. In the past Iraq has indeed demonstrated an ability to adapt foreign elements of culture and institutions and create a blend of a native system. Under 'Abbasid rule the Islamic synthesis that emerged remained for centuries a flexible and enduring system which met the manifold needs of the people. If a blend of collectivism and free enterprise could be achieved, it might well emerge as a native form of "social democracy" which combines values and traditions stemming from the national heritage and imported concepts and institutions from contemporary societies.

8. See my *Political Trends*, pp. 260–261.
9. See Chapter 3, above.

# APPENDIX A

# The Interim Constitution[1]

## PART ONE

### THE REPUBLIC OF IRAQ

*ARTICLE 1*

Iraq is a Sovereign People's Democratic Republic: its principal aim is to achieve the United Arab State and establish the Socialist System.

*ARTICLE 2*

The People is the source of authority and its legitimacy.

*ARTICLE 3*

(a) Sovereignty of Iraq is an indivisible unit.

(b) The land of Iraq is an indivisible unit and no part of it shall be relinquished.

*ARTICLE 4*

Islam is the religion of the State.

*ARTICLE 5*

(a) Iraq is part of the Arab Nation.

(b) The People of Iraq is formed of two principal nationalities, the Arab nationality and the Kurdish nationality. This Constitution shall

---

1. Including the amendments of 1973 and 1974 (Official translation). Minor alterations in style and usage, in this and other appendices, have been made by the author.

recognize the national rights of the Kurdish People and the legitimate rights of all minorities within the unity of Iraq.

## ARTICLE 6

The Iraqi nationality and its rulings shall be determined by the law.

## ARTICLE 7

(a) Arabic is the official language.
(b) The Kurdish language, in addition to the Arabic language, shall be the official language in the Kurdish Region.

## ARTICLE 8

(a) Baghdad is the Capital of the Republic of Iraq, and it may be shifted by a law.
(b) The Republic of Iraq shall be divided into administrative units which shall be organised on the basis of decentralization.
(c) The area whose majority of population is from Kurds shall enjoy autonomy in accordance with what is defined by the law.

## ARTICLE 9

The Flag and the Emblem of the Republic of Iraq and the rules pertaining to them shall be specified by a law.

## PART TWO

### SOCIAL AND ECONOMIC BASES OF THE REPUBLIC OF IRAQ

## ARTICLE 10

Social solidarity is the foremost foundation for society. Its implication is that every citizen shall perform fully his duty towards society and that society shall ensure to the citizen his full rights and freedoms.

## ARTICLE 11

The family is the nucleus of society. The State shall guarantee its protection and support, and shall foster maternity and childhood.

## ARTICLE 12

The State shall undertake planning, directing and guiding the national economy in accordance with the following aims:

(a) Establishing the socialist system on scientific and revolutionary principles.

(b) Achieving Arab economic unity.

## ARTICLE 13

National resources and fundamental instruments of production are the property of the People, and the central authority of the Republic of Iraq shall employ them directly in accordance with the requirements of the general planning of the national economy.

## ARTICLE 14

The State shall ensure, promote and support all kinds of cooperation in production, distribution and consumption.

## ARTICLE 15

Public properties and the properties of the public sector shall have special inviolability, which the State and all citizens have to maintain and guarantee their security and protection. Any subversion or attack on it shall be regarded as an attack on the structure of society and a violence to it.

## ARTICLE 16

(a) Ownership is a social function which shall be exercised within the limits of society's aims and the State's programmes in accordance with the provisions of the law.

(b) Private ownership and individual economic freedom shall be guaranteed within the limits of the law provided that individual ownership will not contradict or be detrimental to general economic planning.

(c) Private property shall not be expropriated except for the public interest and in accordance with just compensation in accordance with the provisions of the law.

(d) The maximum agricultural ownership shall be defined by the law and the excess shall be regarded as the property of the People.

## ARTICLE 17

Inheritance is a recognized right regulated by a law.

## ARTICLE 18

Real estate ownership is forbidden to non-Iraqis except in cases specified by a law.

## Part Three

## Basic Rights and Duties

### Article 19

(a) All citizens are equal before the law, without distinction on the basis of race, origin, language, class or religion.

(b) Equal opportunities for all citizens shall be guaranteed within the limits of the law.

### Article 20

(a) The accused is innocent until he is declared guilty by judicial procedure.

(b) The right to defense is sacred in all processes of investigation and trial in accordance with the provisions of the law.

(c) All trials shall be open to the public unless declared *in camera*.

### Article 21

(a) Penalty is personal.

(b) There shall be no offence or penalty except as defined by a law. No penalty shall be imposed except on an act deemed by the law as an offence at the time of its commission. No more severe penalty than the penalty enforced at the time of committing the offence shall be applied.

### Article 22

(a) The dignity of Man is guaranteed. Any kind of physical or psychological torture shall be prohibited.

(b) No one may be arrested, detained, imprisoned or searched except in accordance with the provisions of the law.

(c) Homes are inviolable. They may not be entered or searched except as specified by the law.

### Article 23

Privacy of mail, telegraphic and telephone correspondence shall be guaranteed, and it shall not be violated except for reasons of public security in accordance with the limits and the rules provided by the law.

## Article 24

No citizen shall be prevented from travel outside the country or from returning thereto and no restriction shall be imposed on his moving and residence inside the country except in the cases defined by the law.

## Article 25

Freedom of religion, beliefs and exercise of religious ceremonies shall be guaranteed, provided that this freedom shall neither contradict the provisions of the Constitution and the law nor violate morality and public order.

## Article 26

The Constitution shall guarantee freedom of opinion, publication, meeting, demonstration, forming of political parties, unions and societies in accordance with the aims of the Constitution and within the limits of the law. The State shall endeavour to provide the means required for exercising these freedoms, which run in line with the nationalist and progressive line of the Revolution.

## Article 27

(a) The State shall undertake to eliminate illiteracy and ensure the right of free-of-charge education in various elementary, secondary and university levels to all citizens.

(b) The State shall endeavour to make elementary education compulsory, expand vocational and technical education in all towns and villages and particularly promote evening education which enables the popular masses to correlate knowledge between science and labour.

(c) The State shall guarantee freedom of scientific research, promote and reward distinction and creativity in all intellectual, scientific and technical activities and all kinds of popular genius.

## Article 28

Education shall aim at raising and developing the general cultural level, developing the scientific thinking, encouraging the spirit of research, fulfilling the requirements of economic and social development programmes, creating a free nationalist and progressive generation solid in structure and character, which takes pride in its people, its homeland and its legacy, sympathizes with the rights of all its nationalities and opposes the doctrines of capitalism, exploitation, reaction, Zionism and colonialism in order to achieve Arab unity, freedom and socialism.

## Article 29

The State shall endeavor to provide the means of enjoying the achievements of modern civilization for the masses of the people and generalize the progressive outputs of modern civilization to all citizens.

## Article 30

(a) Public office is a sacred trust and a social service, whose principal attribute is a loyal obligation to protect the interests of the masses, their rights and freedoms in accordance with the provisions of the Constitution and the law.

(b) Equality of employment in public office shall be guaranteed by the law.

## Article 31

(a) Defense of the homeland is a sacred duty and an honour bestowed to the citizen. Service to the Flag is compulsory and the law shall organize the manner of its performance.

(b) The Armed Forces are the property of the people, and they are the People's tool for preserving its security, defending its independence, protecting the people's and the homeland's safety and unity and achieving its national and patriotic aims and aspirations.

(c) The State alone shall undertake to establish Armed Forces, and no body or group shall be entitled to establish military or para-military formations.

## Article 32

(a) Work is a right which the State shall undertake to provide to every citizen capable of it.

(b) Work is an honour and a sacred duty imposed on every capable citizen. It is required by the necessity of participation in building society and its protection, development and prosperity.

(c) The State shall undertake to improve conditions of work and promote standards of living, expertise and culture for all working citizens.

(d) The State shall undertake to provide wider social ensurances for all citizens in case of sickness, disability, unemployment and old age.

(e) The State shall endeavor to organize the programme and ensure the necessary means which enable working citizens to spend their leaves in an atmosphere that helps them to improve their health standards and develop their cultural and technical gifts.

## ARTICLE 33

The State shall undertake to protect public health through continuous expansion of free-of-charge medical services, whether by prevention, treatment or medicine, in all cities, towns and villages.

## ARTICLE 34

(a) The Republic of Iraq shall grant political asylum to all persons persecuted in their countries because of their struggle in the defense of human liberation principles, which the Iraqi People has accepted under this Constitution.

(b) Political refugees shall not be delivered.

## ARTICLE 35

Payment of taxes is a duty imposed on all citizens. Taxes may not be imposed, amended or levied except by a law.

## ARTICLE 36

Any activity which contradicts the aims of the people defined in this Constitution and any act of conduct aiming at undermining the national unity of the masses of the people, provoking racial or sectarian or regional bigotry among their ranks, or violating their progressive gains and achievements, shall be prohibited.

# PART FOUR

## THE INSTITUTIONS OF THE REPUBLIC OF IRAQ

### CHAPTER ONE

#### THE REVOLUTIONARY COMMAND COUNCIL

## ARTICLE 37

The Revolutionary Command Council is the supreme body in the State, which has undertaken since the 17th of July, 1968, the responsibility of achieving the people's public will by stripping power from the reactionary, dictatorial, corrupt system and restoring it to the people.

## Article 38

The Revolutionary Command Council shall exercise, by a majority of two thirds of its members, the following powers:

(a) Elect the Chairman from among its members who shall be designated as the Chairman of the Revolutionary Command Council and President of the Republic.

(b) Elect the Vice Chairman from among its members who shall be designated as Vice Chairman of the Revolutionary Command Council and take the place of the Chairman in case of his official absence or his exercise of his constitutional powers becomes difficult or impossible for any legal reason.

(c) Select new members to the Council from among the Regional Command of the Arab Ba'th Socialist Party, provided that its members shall not exceed twelve.

(d) Accept the resignation of the Chairman or the Vice Chairman or any of the Council's members.

(e) Release any of its members from membership of the Council.

(f) Charge and send to trial any members of the Revolutionary Command Council, or any deputy of the President of the Republic or any Ministers.

## Article 39

The Chairman, the Vice Chairman and the Members of the Revolutionary Command Council shall take the following oath before the Council:

"I swear by Almighty God, by my honour and belief to preserve the Republican Regime and abide by its Constitution and laws, protect the people's interests, safeguard the homeland's independence and safety and integrity of its lands and endeavor with full sacrifice and loyalty to fulfil the Arab Nation's aims of unity, freedom and socialism."

## Article 40

The Chairman, the Vice Chairman and the Members of the Revolutionary Command Council shall enjoy full immunity and no measure may be taken against anyone of them except by prior permission from the Council.

## Article 41

(a) The Revolutionary Command Council shall convene at the invitation of its Chairman or Vice Chairman or one third of its members. Its sessions shall be convened under the presidency of the Chairman or the Vice Chairman and the presence of the majority of its members.

(b) Meetings and discussions of the Revolutionary Command Council are *in camera*; their disclosure shall be subject to constitutional inquiry before the Council. Announcement, publication and notification of the decisions of the Council shall be performed by the manners provided in this Constitution.

(c) Laws and resolutions shall be approved in the Council by the majority of its members, except in the cases otherwise provided in this Constitution.

## ARTICLE 42

The Revolutionary Command Council shall exercise the following powers:

(a) Promulgate laws and decrees which have the power of the law.

(b) Issue decrees required by the necessities of applying the provisions of the enforced laws.

## ARTICLE 43

The Revolutionary Command Council shall exercise, by the majority of its members, the following powers:

(a) Approve recommendations of the Ministry of Defense and public security, initiate laws and adopt resolutions concerning them in respect to organization and jurisdictions.

(b) Declare general mobilization partially or fully, declare war, accept armistice and conclude peace.

(c) Approve the draft of the general budget of the State and the independent and investment budgets annexed thereto and the credit of the final accounts.

(d) Ratify international treaties and agreements.

(e) Provide the internal regulations of the Council, define its cadre, approve its budget, appoint its officials and specify remunerations and allowances of the Chairman, the Vice Chairman, the members and the officials.

(f) Lay down the rules for the trial of its members and setting up the court and the procedures which must be followed.

(g) Authorize its Chairman or the Vice Chairman to exercise some of its powers provided in this Constitution except legislative powers.

## ARTICLE 44

The Chairman of the Revolutionary Command Council shall undertake the following:

(a) Preside over the meetings of the Council, represent it, conduct its sessions and order expenditure therein.

(b) Sign all laws and resolutions promulgated by the Council and their publication in the Official Gazette.

(c) Supervise the works of the Ministers and Institutions of the State, call the Ministers for conferring on the affairs of their Ministries, interrogate them when necessary and inform the Revolutionary Command Council thereof.

## ARTICLE 45

Each of the Chairman, the Vice Chairman and Members of the Revolutionary Command Council shall be responsible before the Council for violating the Constitution, for violating the obligations of the Constitutional oath or for any act or conduct which the Council deems as detrimental to the honour of responsibility which he exercises.

## ARTICLE 46

A Higher Financial Comptrolling Authority shall be established and attached to the Revolutionary Command Council. Its head and the rules of its functions shall be regulated by a law.

## CHAPTER TWO

### THE NATIONAL ASSEMBLY

## ARTICLE 47

The National Assembly shall consist of the representatives of the people in all its political, economic and social sectors. Its formation, manner of membership, process of work in it and its powers shall be defined by a special law, namely, the National Assembly Law.

## ARTICLE 48

The National Assembly must meet in two ordinary sessions each year. The Chairman of the Revolutionary Command Council is entitled to call the Assembly for an extra-ordinary meeting whenever required, and the meeting shall be confined to the subjects for which it is called. Sessions of the National Assembly shall be convened and concluded by a resolution issued by the Revolutionary Command Council.

## ARTICLE 49

Sessions of the Assembly shall be conducted publicly unless it is decided to convene some of them *in camera* in accordance with the provisions of its law.

## ARTICLE 50

(a) Members of the National Assembly may not be questioned over the opinions and suggestions they introduce during their exercise of the tasks of their posts.

(b) None of the members of the Assembly may be pursued or arrested for an offence committed during the meetings without obtaining the Assembly's permission, except in case of being held in the act of crime.

## ARTICLE 51

The National Assembly shall undertake to:

(a) Lay down its internal regulations, specify its cadre, approve its budget and appoint its personnel. Remunerations and allowances of its President and Members shall be defined by a law.

(b) Provide the rules for charging and trying its members in case of their committing one of the acts provided in Article 56 of this Constitution.

## ARTICLE 52

The National Assembly shall consider the draft laws proposed by the Revolutionary Command Council within a period of fifteen days from the date of their arrival to the bureau of the National Assembly's Presidency. If the Assembly approves the draft, it shall be submitted to the President of the Republic, to promulgate it. But if the National Assembly rejected or amended it, it shall be returned to the Revolutionary Command Council. If the amendment were approved by the Revolutionary Command Council, it shall be submitted to the President to promulgate it. But if the Revolutionary Command Council insists on its opinion in the second reading, the draft shall be returned to the National Assembly to be presented in a joint sitting of the Council and the Assembly. The decision issued by the majority of two thirds shall be considered as final.

Article 53

The National Assembly shall consider, within a period of fifteen days, the draft Laws forwarded to it by the President of the Republic. If the Assembly rejects the draft, it shall be returned to the President of the Republic with the statement of the reasons of rejection. But if the Assembly accepts the draft, then it shall be submitted to the Revolutionary Command Council and if it approves the draft, then it shall be liable for promulgation. But if the National Assembly amends the draft, then it shall be submitted to the Revolutionary Command Council, and if it approves the draft, it shall be liable for promulgation. But if the Revolutionary Command Council rejects the amendment or makes another amendment, it shall be returned again to the National Assembly within one week. If the National Assembly adopts the opinion of the Revolutionary Command Council, the draft shall be submitted to the President of the Republic for promulgation. But if the National Assembly insists, in the second reading, on its opinion, then a joint sitting of the Council and the Assembly shall be held, and the draft adopted by the majority of two thirds shall be considered as final, and it shall be submitted to the President of the Republic for promulgation.

Article 54

The National Assembly shall consider draft laws presented by one quarter of its members in affairs other than military matters and public security affairs.

If the Assembly approves the draft law, it shall be submitted to the Revolutionary Command Council to consider it within fifteen days from the date of its arrival to the Council's Bureau.

If it is approved by the Revolutionary Command Council, it shall be submitted to the President of the Republic for promulgation.

But if the Revolutionary Command Council rejects or amends it, the draft shall be returned to the National Assembly. If the latter insists on its opinion, in the second reading, a joint session of the Council and the Assembly shall be convened under the presidency of the Chairman of the Revolutionary Command Council or his Deputy. The draft issued by the majority of two thirds shall be considered as final and shall be submitted to the President of the Republic for promulgation.

Article 55

(a) Deputies of the President of the Republic and the Ministers and those who are in ranks similar to them shall be entitled to attend the meetings of the National Assembly and participate in discussions.

(b) The National Assembly may, after the approval of the President of the Republic, call the Ministers in order to make an enquiry or explanation.

## ARTICLE 56

The President of the National Assembly and every member in it are held responsible before the Assembly for violating the Constitution, perjuring the obligations of the Constitutional oath or for any act or conduct the National Assembly deems as detrimental to the honour of responsibility he exercises.

### CHAPTER THREE
### PRESIDENT OF THE REPUBLIC

## ARTICLE 57

(a) The President of the Republic is the President of the State and the Commander-in-Chief of the Armed Forces. He shall undertake the executive power directly or through the Council of Ministers.

(b) The President of the Republic shall promulgate the necessary ordinances for exercising his powers as prescribed in this Constitution.

## ARTICLE 58

The President of the Republic shall directly exercise the following powers:

(a) Preserve the independence of the country and integrity of its lands, protect its interior and exterior security and protect the rights and freedom of citizens.

(b) Supervise the application of the Constitution, laws, resolutions, judicial decisions and development projects in all parts of the Republic of Iraq.

(c) Appoint Deputies for the President of the Republic and release them from their posts.

(d) Appoint the Ministers and release them from their posts.

(e) Appoint civil and religious judges and civil and military officials of the State, and terminate their services in accordance with the law.

(f) Appoint and accredit Iraqi diplomatic representatives in the Arab and foreign countries, and in international conferences and organizations.

(g) Grant military ranks and medals in accordance with the law.

(h) Hold negotiations and conclude international agreements and treaties.

(i) Accept diplomatic and international representatives and demand their withdrawal.

(j) Approve capital punishments and issue special amnesty.

(k) Direct the control of the work of the Ministries and general institutions and coordinate them.

## Article 59

Deputies of the President of the Republic and the Ministers shall be held responsible before the President of the Republic for their works, and he is entitled to refer any one of them to trial, in accordance with the provisions of the Constitution, for functional errors committed, for taking advantage of, or abusive use of, his powers.

## Chapter Four

### The Council of Ministers

## Article 60

(a) The Council of Ministers shall consist of the Ministers and be presided over by the President of the Republic.

(b) The President of the Republic shall call the Council of Ministers to meet and conduct its meetings.

## Article 61

The Council of Ministers shall exercise the following powers:

(a) Initiate draft laws and refer them to the proper legislative authority.

(b) Issue administrative regulations and decisions in accordance with the law.

(c) Appoint civil officials of the State and promote them, in accordance with the law.

(d) Submit the general plan of the State.

(e) Submit the general budget of the State and the budgets annexed to it.

(f) Conclude and grant loans, and supervise organizing and administering currency.

(g) Declare a full or partial emergency and terminate it in accordance with the law.

(h) Supervise general utilities and official and semi-official institutions.

## Chapter Five

## The Judiciary

### Article 62

(a) The Judiciary is independent and no power shall be exercised over it except the law.

(b) The right to litigation shall be guaranteed to all citizens.

(c) The law shall define the manner of courts formation, their grades, jurisdictions, stipulations for appointing civil and religious judges, transferring and promoting them, litigating and retiring them.

### Article 63

The law shall define the posts of the Public Prosecution, its stipulations for appointing Public Prosecutors and their deputies and the rules for transferring and promoting them, litigating and retiring them.

## Part Five

## General Provisions

### Article 64

(a) No one shall be member of the Revolutionary Command Council and no one shall be deputy to the President of the Republic or Minister except whoever is Iraqi by birth and from Iraqi parents by birth also.

(b) Members of the Revolutionary Command Council, deputies to the President of the Republic and the Ministers shall not exercise a free profession or a commercial business, or purchase from the state properties, sell to the State some of their properties, or barter for them while holding their posts.

### Article 65

(a) The provisions of this Constitution shall remain in force until the Permanent Constitution is promulgated.

(b) This Constitution shall not be amended except by the Revolutionary Command Council by a majority of two thirds of its members.

## Article 66

(a) Laws shall be published in the Official Gazette and shall come into force from the date of their publication except otherwise provided therein.

(b) Laws shall have no retroactive effect except if otherwise provided therein and this exclusion shall not include Criminal Laws and laws of taxes and financial dues.

## Article 67

This Interim Constitution, the laws and judicial decisions shall be promulgated and executed in the name of the people.

## Article 68

All laws and resolutions of the Revolutionary Command Council enforced prior to the promulgation of this Constitution shall remain in force and they may not be amended or abrogated except through the manner provided in this Constitution.

## Article 69

The Chairman of the Revolutionary Command Council shall undertake the promulgation of this Constitution and its publication in the Official Gazette.

## APPENDIX B

# The National Action Charter

Proclaimed By
**President Ahmed Hassan Al-Bakr**
On November 15, 1971

### INTRODUCTION

The Arab Revolutionary Movement in its various contingents and across its protracted militant march, suffered grave defeats and setbacks. From the vast, rich experience accompanying the various stages of its struggle, we may deduce many lessons forefronted by this fundamental fact: Among the paramount factors which secure the ability of Arab revolutionary movements to achieve victory is their consciousness of the role played by the joint action and by the alliance of their contingents. And that among the main factors which led to their defeats and setbacks is the inclination of their various contingents to focus on secondary differences among themselves rather than on the principal controversy existing between them, on one hand and imperialism, Zionism and reaction on the other.

The periods which are characterized by the rising tide of the masses in each part of the Arab homeland and by the intensifying struggle against imperialism, Zionism and reaction as well as by the rising prestige of doctrines, slogans and revolutionary progressive practices are the very periods characterized by the inclination of various progressive and national forces towards cooperation among themselves within specified frameworks and according to specified formulas. Also the periods of regress in the revolutionary tide which were marked by the blowing of the currents of apostasy and its dark regressive ideas, and the multiplication of the imperialist, Zionist and reactionary dangers on the Arab Revolutionary Movement and on the destiny of the Arab people and their liberational progressive accomplishments are the very periods marked by the severe unobjective conflicts between the patriotic, progressive Arab sides.

There is not a shred of doubt that the tendency towards joint action and cooperation among the parties to the national progressive Arab movement was a natural consequence of the heightened political and ideological standard among those parties and their intent to detonate the secondary contradictions among them prior to going into the decisive show-down with imperialism, Zionism and reaction was the reflection of a deterioration in this standard.

The June 5 defeat which inflicted the gravest setback upon the Arab struggle had triggered the onset of a new stage that demands, in the first place, a careful scientific study for the experiences undergone in the outgoing stage and a radical and bold check on its mistakes and aberration and a genuine and decisive revolutionary action to get up to a new standard that rejects the realities of defeat and turns the setback onto the course of victory.

The imperialist-Zionist onslaught on the Arab Nation on June 5 raised the contradiction between the Arab Nation on one hand and imperialism and Zionism on the other hand to extreme degrees of sharpness, a fact which demands on part of the Arab Nation the broadest and deepest mobilization of militant energies for confronting this onslaught and for beating it back and realizing manifest advance in the struggle against the positions of imperialism, Zionism and their ally, reaction. This reinforcement and mobilization operation will by no means be serious and effective unless it embraces the Arab masses, the very masses whose role had been paralyzed by the pre-June regimes and which, by means of coercive and oppressive practices at one time and by demagogical deception at another, had been separated by these regimes from their issues of destiny. This is because it is the masses alone that is the invincible power which is capable of standing up to the imperialist-Zionist onslaught with unrelenting firmness.

Moreover among the exigencies of this stage is that the national progressive forces in every part of the Arab homeland should seek pursuits of cooperation among one another with a view to realizing the highest and strongest possible forms of unity so as to guarantee the availability of the necessary vanguard force which is to lead the masses in the battle. This will serve as a logical and natural answer to the imperialist-Zionist-reactionary alliance which had attained high degrees of compactness and perfection that cannot be confronted, no matter how vast the energies and enthusiasm put up, except by a counter-alliance representing all the forces of Arab liberation and progress hostile to imperialism, Zionism and reaction. Granting that the mobilization of the Arab masses and the cooperation of national progressive masses among one another are two essential conditions for confronting the imperialist-Zionist onslaught and for confronting reaction which aligns itself with imperialism and Zionism—which emerged on the arena after the defeat, trying to inherit the places of the defeated regimes and to regain rehabilitation and positions following long years of retreat and self-indulgence—there is yet another radical condition for placing the cause of Arab struggle at a standard qualifying for victory and warding off the risks of another defeat. This condition provides that the masses and their revolutionary establishments occupy the positions of leadership and guidance, now that the totalitarian, bourgeois and feudalist regimes have failed to stop the imperialist-Zionist aggression on the Arab Nation and failed to realize the Nation's targets of liberation, unity and progress.

The right wing and bourgeois forces which led to the defeat had proved their incapacity and failure by the very fact of defeat; hence, it is neither logical nor reasonable that these forces should continue to monopolize the leadership of Arab struggle at a stage which is more dangerous and delicate, demanding stronger and wider ideological, mobilizational, political and military capabilities.

The unity dictated by the new stage among the various parties of the national progressive Arab movement, whether on regional or national levels, should rest on principles providing for intensification of struggle against imperialism, Zionism and reaction, enabling the masses to lead their battle, the availability of absolute revolutionary democratic atmospheres, liquidation of all manifestations of oppression against the masses and their cultural institutions, liquidation of all forms of imperialistic influence, and closing doors forever against the imperialistic states' heinous attempts at exploiting the current conditions in the Arab homeland to stage a come-back and occupy new political and economic positions. The unity among the parties to the national, progressive movement in any Arab country—to be serious and genuine—is bound to address itself towards the realization of unity among the Arab countries prepared for it. The realistic unity, besides the necessity of being possessing the prerequisites mentioned above, is a unity disposed towards a resolute form of struggle against imperialism. As to the unitary formulas built in the shed of pacifying imperialism, recognizing the Zionist entity and expanding ties with Arab reaction, such unity is not only fictitious one, but in effect, it is also a framework for grouping the forces of apostasy against the progressive forces and for securing passage to the imperialist-Zionist schemings which are categorically rejected by the Arab people.

Among the main fundamental principles for any alliance among the national and progressive forces, whether on the regional or national levels, is the necessity to adopt armed popular struggle as a principal method in the struggle against the imperialist-Zionist enemy and this demands honest and active alliance with the Palestinian Resistance. The Palestinian Resistance, regardless of the divergence of views and evaluations among the ranks of the national and progressive forces about this or that contingent, is a fundamental instrument of our people's struggle against the imperialist-Zionist enemy and its local allies. The alliance with the Palestinian Resistance and the provision of material and moral aids to it in its legitimate struggle, constitutes one of the basic conditions dictated by the new stage—the post-June 5 defeat stage.

Therefore, among the chief assignments of any alliance emerging between the national and progressive forces: the denunciation of all methods of maneuverings and outflanking aimed at encircling the Palestinian Resistance in order to strip it of its militant weapons and to domesticate it in accordance with the imperialist-Zionist-reactionary schemings as well as the resolute struggle against these methods. Also among the chief assignments of this alliance: the exposition of any attempt designed to liquidate the Palestinian issue be it through the setting up of a fictitious puppet state on one part of the Palestine soil or through the banishment of the historical, political and legal aspects of the Palestine issue to portray the issue as a mere question of refugees who deserve sympathy and assistance. The alliance should resist these methods by means of popular struggle. The main target of Arab struggle on the national level is liquidation of the racist, aggressive Zionist entity and enabling the Arab Palestinian people to exercise self-determination on their liberated soil.

Since July 17 and 30, 1968, the Arab Ba'th Socialist Party has led the revolutionary change in Iraq. This change had come at a time in which internal, Arab and international circumstances were characterized by extreme gravity and delicacy. The revolutionary change was born in international circumstances marked by intensification of the ferocious campaign launched by world imperialism headed by the United States of America against the world's nations, particularly the Indo-Chinese peoples, the Arab people and the peoples fighting for freedom and progress in Asia, Africa and Latin America. The same period in which the Revolution was born has been marked by characteristics countering this campaign: the escalated tempo of struggle by the camp of the peoples fighting against the imperialist aggressive camp, particularly in the Indo-Chinese front where the peoples of Vietnam, Laos and Cambodia inflicted numerous and heavy defeats on the U.S. imperialists and on their international and local allies. The period was also characterized by a grave passive phenomenon; namely, the aggravation of division among the ranks of the socialist camp which imposed great damages on the anti-imperialistic human struggle. On the Arab level, the Revolution was born in a gravest stage of the stages of the Arab Nation's struggle—the stage of the June 5 defeat that had led to the Zionist enemy's occupation of the entire Palestinian soil and of other Arab lands of the countries of Egypt and Syria.

If that period has represented a grave military and political defeat it at the same time sparked off a large-scale Arab revolutionary resurgence represented by a developed power of the Palestinian Resistance and by an observable escalation in the determination for struggle against imperialism and Zionism in most parts of the Arab homeland. The period is also marked by intensification of the masses' movement urging for radical change in all political, economic, military, cultural and social conditions, the conditions that had led to the defeat. The July 17 Revolution, in one of its historical aspects, was one of this movement's fruits. On the regional level, the birth of the July 17 Revolution happened in most critical and delicate circumstances prevalent in the country. The national revolution that was led by the people and the army on July 14 had, in the ensuing ten years, retreated to paths far removed from its fundamental objectives and across a long, bitter history of tragedies and disasters until it was ended by the dictatorial reactionary Arifite regime which collaborated with imperialism. The July 17 Revolution, led by the Arab Ba'th Socialist Party, was destined to undertake simultaneously two historical tasks: The first is to complete the aspects of the national revolution which broke out on July 14, 1958, to carry on its march forward and to correct the errors and deviations it had suffered. The second is to realize the assignments of the new stage: the post-June 5 defeat stage.

The 7th A.B.S.P. Regional Conference in its communiqué issued in January 1969 had defined the nature of the stage and described it as the stage of building up a "Democratic Revolutionary Unitary System" as a fundamental and advanced stage of the legitimate struggle's stages for our people in Iraq and in the Arab homeland in quest of building up the socialist, democratic and unitary society. In its historic communiqué, the conference underscored the party and the Revolution's command's consciousness of the importance of cooperation among the national, patriotic and progressive Arab and Kurdish forces inside Iraq in order to accomplish the assignments of this stage—which are enormous, ramified and delicate assignments conducive to polarize fierce animosity of the imperialistic and Zionist circles as well as various categories of the local and Arab reactionary and opportunist forces. This by necessity demands the unity of the forces of struggle which have the real stake in these assignments, both on regional and national levels. The Arab Ba'th Socialist Party which led the revolutionary march forward for over three years looks upon the question of alliance between the national and patriotic progressive forces in Iraq and the Arab homeland from a doctrinal, strategic angle. The assignments of the Revolution on the regional and national levels and the assignments of struggle against the imperialist and Zionist enemy and its local reactionary hirelings, require the amassment of the endeavours and energies of all national and progressive forces in the frame-work of a joint frontal action determined in each country by the country's own conditions. Proceeding from this doctrinal and strategic outlook, the Arab Ba'th Socialist Party, right from the very first days of the July 17 Revolution, embarked upon preparing the appropriate conditions for the emergence of a genuine and powerful unity among all national and patriotic progressive forces by means of the realization of the necessary objective conditions which are indispensible for national unity.

Up this difficult road and in spite of the tenacity of the internal Arab and international conditions, the Revolution, under the leadership of the Arab Ba'th Socialist Party, managed in the course of the last three years, to accomplish or to cross long milestones up the road of achieving the following assignments:

1. Directing a heavy and bold blow to the detachments of agents and spies who continued for long years to impair the country and to

expose its sovereignty and the destiny of its people and its national movements to greatest dangers. Also striking at the imperialistic and reactionary conspiracies which had aimed to overthrow the national authority and to restore the imperialist and reactionary influence in the country.
2. Contributing with capabilities available at the country's disposal, the national battle against the imperialist-Zionist enemy and outstripping the imperialist conspiracies in the Arab Gulf and the ambitions of the reactionary elements in the Gulf and placing all available capabilities in the service of confronting them.
3. The Revolution took a resolute stand against the imperialist conspiracies and schemings which aimed at dominating our oil and mineral resources, particularly the sulphur, and transformed the question of the national exploitation of oil and sulphur from a mere slogan into reality. So far, the major part of the first stage of the national exploitation of oil in the Rumaila Oilfield has been completed. Iraq will begin exportation of national oil with the beginning of next year; meanwhile, the second stage (production of 18 million tons per annum) already got off to a start. Also next year, the national production of sulphur will get off to a start at the rate of 2 million tons per annum. The Revolution also managed to wrest substantial parts of our despoiled rights from the monopolistic companies operating in the country and as a result big increases have been realized in oil royalties on the way for wresting our legitimate rights in full.
4. The promulgation of revolutionary legislations concerning the agrarian question, such as abolition of the principle and right of free choice for feudalists, the free distribution of lands to peasants and the promulgation of the Agrarian Reform Law No. 117 of 1970. This law constitutes a serious and large-scale start to bring about an agrarian revolution emancipating peasantry from the yoke of the feudalist system and achieving an all-out economic and social resurgence in the countryside.
5. Exerting sincere devotion for bringing about fresh and positive atmospheres in the relations between the national and patriotic progressive forces. The Revolution, in its early days, chose to release all political detainees and prisoners and reinstated all of them to their previous jobs. Moreover, the Revolution recently enacted legislation accounting for the dismissal period on political grounds as a service period for promotion and pension purposes.
6. The promulgation of the labour law No. 151 of 1970 and the Pension and Social Security Law No. 39 of 1971. The two laws

realize for the working class important progressive gains and securing for this class the freedom of unionist activity and all fundamental freedoms. The Pension and Social Security Law guarantees a dignified living for the working class within the limits of the possibilities available at the disposal of the state.

7. The Revolution under the leadership of the Arab Ba'th Socialist Party and in cooperation with the Kurdish Democratic Party managed to reach a formula for the peaceful and democratic solution to the Kurdish issue as represented in the March 11 Manifesto of 1970. Since the proclamation of the Manifesto and to date numerous major and basic clauses of it have been realized up the way of completing the implementation of all its clauses, including a self-rule for our Kurdish people within the frame-work of the Republic of Iraq.

8. The materialization of relationships between the masses and the revolutionary authority by means of the participation of the popular organizations in the discussions and study of various basic issues and the promotion of popular rallies and encouragement of the popular voluntary work drives across the country. These drives yielded remarkable results as manifested in the many major agricultural projects and projects of services.

9. The provision of suitable legislative and political conditions for the emergence of the democratic organizations in the country such as the General Federation of Peasants Associations, the General Federation of Trade Unions, the National Union of Iraqi Students, the General Federation of Women in Iraq and tens of vocational, unionist and social organizations. Also the provision of the necessary legislative and political conditions for the emergence of organizations for our Kurdish people in accordance with the March 11 Manifesto, such as the Kurdistan Youth Union, the Kurdistan Teachers Union, the Union of Kurdish Writers, the Kurdistan Students Union and other organizations.

10. The preparation of the largest 5-year Development Plan ever witnessed in the history of Iraq whose appropriations reached about ID. 1000 millions. This plan seeks the realization of all-out development in agriculture, industry, communications, culture, services, public health and all the utilities of the society.

11. Effecting a large-scale economic upheaval represented in the State's perfect control of trade, the provision of the basic commodities for citizens also represented in completing and setting for

operation of many factories whose completion had lagged behind or interrupted and the construction of new factories and expansion of other factories to raise their productive capacities. The development of agricultural conditions and setting up of serious projects and numerous cooperative and collective farms and state farms and putting into practice the slogan of 'Return to the countryside' and the employment of educated manpower in farming.

12. The realization of wide and important reforms in the field of education, particularly in university institutions and higher education establishments and reconsideration of the various curricula in accordance with the principles of the national progressive revolution, encouragement of vocational education to development, the creation of large numbers of schools throughout the country and the establishment of a new University; namely, the Sulaimaniyah University.

13. The construction of cultural and health projects and services and communications projects throughout the country. The last three years have witnessed unprecedented activity in the construction or expansion of hospitals, and the construction of popular clinics as well as in building new roads and improving and multiplying all services to the benefit of citizens and the construction of various cultural utilities.

The Arab Ba'th Socialist Party in presenting the National Action Charter to the attention of the masses and the national forces in this struggling country, now that the Revolution has satisfied the prerequisites for entering a new stage—in which all the people's forces are to be mobilized for confronting the imperialist Zionist and reactionary tide and preparing for exercising popular democracy, it opens the way before all national forces to participate in deepening the revolutionary march-forward and consolidating its foundations to realize the aspirations and great hopes of our people and to transform this country into a huge arena for work and production, also to be an impregnable fortress for steadfastness, a living and genuine model for mature revolutionary action in the Arab homeland and a spring-board for the Arab Revolution.

There is a historic opportunity available before the national forces in the country; this opportunity is dictated by objective circumstances which place them at one trench and is demanding the condition of developing this Revolution and the thousands of potentialities and capabilities with which this country is teeming and to prepare for sacrifice and contribution. These forces can offer much to this noble people through responsible participation that responds to the stage's call. The gigantic national role laid on the shoulder of our country demands placing this country on the road of serious frontal action. The utilization of this country's resources and placing it on the road of socialism necessitates as well the cementation of national unity. Therefore, the proclamation of this charter comes as a realistic reaction to the feelings of the historic responsibility and all-out awareness of its dimensions. The leadership of the Arab Ba'th Socialist Party, whilst presenting this charter for discussion, hopes at the same time that all national and progressive forces and elements express sincere preparedness to turn over a new bright page in the history of their ambitious struggle in quest of our national and patriotic objectives.

## 1. THE POLITICAL SYSTEM

The political system is the legal expression for the interests and aspirations of the social classes and groups it represents. Since the Arab Ba'th Socialist Party represents the interests of the broadest masses from among workers, peasants and other hardtoiling groups, the political system which the party sought to build up in the stage following the Revolution it had led on July 17, 1968 is as defined by the 7th Regional Conference of the Party: a democratic, revolutionary and unitary system. This system will be a phased step up the road of realizing the democratic, socialist, unitary Arab system. The constitution which the Revolution announced on July 17, 1970 had underlined the identity of the political system stating in its first Article: "Iraq is a Sovereign People's Democratic Republic. Its basic objective is the realization of the one Arab State and the building-up of the socialist system." The national coalition advocated by the Arab Ba'th Socialist Party is the broad base for this system and the lasting and dynamic power for it, deepening it and furnishing it with larger moral and material capabilities so that it can realize its assignments as set in this charter and move towards a more advanced stage on the patriotic and nationalist levels.

Therefore, the nature of the system and its constitutional institutions can be defined as follows:

1. The political system built up by the July 17 Revolution under the leadership of the Arab Ba'th Socialist Party, and which seeks the realization of the broadest coalition among all the national,

patriotic and progressive forces and elements is a democratic, popular and unitary system.

2. The political system guarantees all democratic freedoms for the people's masses and their national and progressive forces including the freedom of political parties, social and vocational organizations, trade unions, freedom of the press, opinion and belief and other fundamental freedoms, in accordance with the laws promulgated by the State.

3. Both the legislative and executive authorities shall be exercised throughout the current transitional period by the public institutions provided for in the Interim Constitution. The National Assembly shall be formed in accordance with the provisions of the law and in the light of the principles set forth in the charter.

4. Putting into application local administration formulas and popular councils in all administrative units of the Republic of Iraq. These councils shall have the right to exercise supervision, inspection and criticism, concerning the state officialdom in accordance with the law governing their formation which shall be promulgated by the Revolutionary Command Council and the National Assembly.

5. The end of the current transitional period shall be fixed after the enactment of the permanent constitution and its endorsement by a popular general plebiscite. Hence, this charter regards the preparation of a draft permanent constitution as a priority assignment of the forthcoming stage on which depends the completion of the objective conditions necessary for consolidating the democratic popular system and for building up its national institutions.

A. *THE POPULAR MOBILIZATION:*

The people's masses, from among workers, peasants, students and intellectuals, are the base of the Revolution and the object of its struggle. The Revolution cannot realize its phased and long-term assignments except through the road of full mobilization and amassment of all its capabilities for building up the revolutionary, popular and democratic society and for standing up to the imperialist, Zionist and reactionary conspiracies against our country and the Arab homeland. The organization of workers, peasants, students, intellectuals, women associations, unions and federations is not only a legitimate right confirmed by this charter, but it is also a fundamental national exigency and an essential cornerstone in the new revolutionary society.

Therefore, the Revolution unflinchingly encourages, with all capabilities and energies at its disposal the labour and vocational unions, the peasants associations and the students and women organizations and all other social organizations so that they can play their vanguard, active role in expediting the revolutionary social transformation and realizing the largest possible accomplishments in all aspects of the political, economic, social and cultural planes.

The Revolution regards the question of youth organization, males and females, in broad youth organizations as an exigency and a target it seeks to accomplish in order that youths may be able, within the framework of their brisk, democratic organizations, to perform their duties towards the process of revolutionary building and in safeguarding and developing the Revolution's gains as well as in the nationalist battle of destiny against the imperialist and Zionist enemy and all those coveting any part of the Arab homeland. The Revolution regards as an essential matter the large-scale participation of women in trade unions associations and other existing institutions and it resolutely supports the women's organizations, so that the woman can occupy her proper place and perform her effective role in the process of revolutionary buildup and in the national battle. The Revolution, likewise, guarantees to all women of Iraq all political, economic, social and cultural rights enjoyed by man.

B. THE ARMY AND ARMED FORCES:

The slogan of establishing national armed forces was in the forefront of the requisites of popular struggle in the era of imperialist domination. When the will of our people was imposed on the imperialists and their supporters from among local rulers the national army was formed. Those imperialists and their supporters tried with all conceivable means and methods to banish the army from the people and their national and patriotic movement and transform it into an isolated establishment whose basic assignment was to protect the reactionary system and the imperialist interests. But the overwhelming majority of soldiers and officers composed of the sons of peasants, workers and the middle class, did not submit to the will and strategies of the imperialists and their henchmen; on the contrary, they expressed their full adherence to the aspirations of the people and their longings for freedom, progress and nationalist unity as well as their complete rejection of all forms of oppression and high-handedness. The imperialists and their reactionary henchmen failed to turn the army into an instrument in their hands to strike at the mounting national and patriotic movement. On more than one occasion across the history of our national struggle, the army expressed its alignment to the side of the demands advocated by the popular movement for liberation from the imperialist domination and from the prevalence of the reactionary, exploitationist and corrupt classes. The army's glorious two revolutions on May 5, 1941, and July 14, 1958, serve a living testimony to this effect. And, in the shed of the Revolution led by the Arab Ba'th Socialist Party on July 17, 1968, in which the revolutionary, military regiments and a conscious, and courageous part and, in this very stage—the stage of building up the democratic, revolutionary and unitary society, and of the struggle against the imperialist and Zionist enemy—the adherence of the army to the popular movement and the performance of its national and patriotic duties in a most consummate manner has been accentuated more than at any time before.

1. The prime function of the army and the armed forces is defending the country, its sovereignty and its integrated unity. Besides, among its greater functions is the pioneering contribution to the nationalist struggle for the liberation of Palestine and all the usurped Arab territories, and for repelling all the conspiracies and ill ambitions aimed at any part of the Arab Homeland.

    Such enormous functions require continuous supplies of modern arms and equipment for the army, raising the combatant, scientific, and technological standards for all of its members, raising the alertness and discipline among its different standards and developing the military schools and institutions and building up a national military industry. It would also require particular care in the private soldier so that he will be an awakened and effective element with full prestige and health in the army of which he constitutes a basic foundation.

2. As it is a fundamental part of the people and one of its pioneering detachments struggling for its freedom and advancement in all political, economic, social and cultural fields—and because of its set-up and aspirations being attached to the interests of the sweeping majority of the sons of the people; peasants, workers and the middle class—the army has the responsibility of contribution in the comprehensive national work for building up the new revolutionary society in accordance with the slogan raised by the revolution, i.e. "The Army is for War and Reconstruction," therefore, the army's contribution to the popular work drives and

to all other popular efforts which are aimed at raising the economic, social and cultural standards of the masses, is one of the fundamental conditions for preserving its popular struggle and protecting it against isolatory, bureaucratic and haughty tendencies which the imperialists and their allied forces and the elements lagging behind the revolutionary transition are trying to nourish. Besides, such contribution is a great national must for the realization of advancement in the country as quick as possible and in all fields.
3. To secure the army performing its sacred tasks in war and reconstruction and to insure its consolidation with popular movement and with the interests of the masses, it requires continuous work on deepening the nationalistic, democratic and progressive feelings amidst the ranks of the army. It would also require protecting its integrity against the deviations of the adventurous cliques who think only in their private interests at the expense of the army's fundamental targets and the higher interests of the people stimulated by the imperialistic and reactionary circles who are the enemies of the people.

The solidarity of the army and all the national armed forces, and their firm support of the Revolution and its principles and leadership—also their firm undertaking to defend the Revolution and the gains of the people against any form aggression, conspiracy or sabotage—are fundamental and indispensable factors, and the leadership of the Revolution is the only side responsible for securing such conditions.

As to the police and the security organizations who, before the Revolution, were an immediate tool in the hands of the reactionary and dictatorial authority, whose prime function was to oppress the masses and their national and patriotic progressive forces and who constituted an organization that in conduct constricted the fundamental rights of the masses and their legitimate aspirations in democracy and progressiveness—today, and under the banner of the Revolution and national coalition, have radically different tasks. The fundamental functions of the national police and security forces at present are to protect the safety, security and properties of citizens against any form of aggression or violation, protecting the country against the trifling of the spies, the agents and the saboteurs, and standing firmly against the counter revolutionary groups.

Under the banner of the revolutionary regime and national coalition, attention should be given to strengthening the relationships between the police and security organs and the masses and their national forces, and unionist and professional organizations. Care should also be given to clearing these organs from the elements who are corrupt and enemy to the targets of the Revolution and its popular democratic applications, due to the nature of these elements' ideologies and interests.

This would require deepening the national, patriotic and democratic education amidst the ranks of the members of these organs. It would require immense keenness on making the slogan "The police at the service of the people", tangible in the homeland.

### C. The Administration and the Judicature:

The Revolution has inherited the state machinery from the eras of imperialistic, reactionary and dictatorial domination. Naturally, such machinery, which had been brought up in those eras, was influenced, in set up and tendencies, by the eras' interests and backward conditions and by their hostile attitude to the masses and their aspirations towards freedom, democracy and progressiveness.

However, many a disease can still be found in the state machinery, like its expansiveness, its heavy expenditure and its backward means and ways, also the undemocratic and non-personal relations prevailing in it, and its tendency to disdain the masses and sitting aloof from the masses' interests and fundamental aspirations.

Some parts of this machinery play adverse and subversive roles in the stage of revolutionary transitions and with their lagging behind such transitions and with their passive look at these transitions and its dimensions, form a basic obstacle that hinders the progress of such transitions.

The revolutionary stage and the unity of the national and progressive forces require radical changes in the structure of the state machinery and in its relationships with the masses and their political and social organizations. The slogan that should rule and firmly and consciously be applied is that of placing the state machinery at the service of the masses and for fulfilling their fundamental requirements. Besides, it is absolutely necessary that the state machinery should keep up with all the revolutionary and political, social, economic and cultural changes.

Such tasks require deepening the popular, democratic and revolutionary consciousness amidst the state machinery and also require fighting against bureaucratic and haughty tendencies, and liquidating all the aspects of deviation and corruption, particularly bribery and favouritism. It also requires continuous manning of this machinery with the national progressive elements and with the young elements who believe in the Revolution and its targets, as it also requires the removal of the corrupt and disabled elements.

Moreover these tasks would also require the development of the regulations of the State machinery and work traditions, reducing red tape and generalizing the training courses. It is also necessary that subjective scientific norms be worked out for choosing and promoting the personnel, and that the service regulations be coordinated in accordance with the state's possibilities and with the requirements of development. Besides, it is necessary that pre-studied practical steps be made for eliminating the aspects of disguised idleness spread due to the inflation of the administrative machinery, and that the energies surplus in this machinery be directed to productive projects which contribute to the acceleration of development and advancement in all the country's utilities in order that all the national capabilities be used in full.

The judicature occupies a fundamental position amid the state's machinery due to its tasks of establishing justice and equality among citizens, and of settling their disputes in legal ways. Such tasks of the judicature require the development of its machinery and the removal of the antirevolutionary elements and improving its procedures and preserving the prestige and independence of the judicature, in accordance with the provisions of the constitution.

Besides, it would require reconsideration of the laws and legislations which are in contradiction with the principles and targets of the Revolution, and the legislation of new laws and regulations that should govern the relationships in the revolutionary society in accordance with its premises, principles and targets, and should facilitate the application of all the revolutionary programmes.

### D. THE KURDISH ISSUE:

The Kurdish nationalistic issue, for long years, had been on top of the greater national issues awaiting solution. Due to the issue being suspended, our people had suffered many losses and pains and its unity and the unity of the homeland was endangered.

The July 17 Revolution expressing the principles of the democratic and human principles of the Arab Ba'th Socialist Party, has provided wide horizons for a peaceful democratic and final settlement of this issue. The Revolution's efforts, through cooperation between the Arab Ba'th Socialist Party and the Kurdistan Democratic Party, were culminated with the issuance of the historical March 11 Manifesto.

The March 11 Manifesto is the sound framework for securing the legitimate nationalistic rights and aspirations of our Kurdish people, including autonomy, and for securing unity of the homeland and the people and that of its progressive national and nationalist forces, on the path of struggling against imperialism, Zionism and reaction.

In order to continue fulfilling all the requirements of the peaceful and democratic solution of the Kurdish issue, in accordance with the spirit and provisions of the Manifesto and under the national joint work for building up the unitary revolutionary democratic society the Charter defines the following:

1. The alliance between the Arab Ba'th Socialist Party and the Kurdistan Democratic Party, an alliance constituting the foundation stone in national coalition, is based, as to premise and far reaching objectives, on the historical revolutionary alliance of destiny between the Arab and the Kurdish peoples, and in particular, the Arab and Kurdish toiling masses. It is based on these masses and represents their interest and reflects their legitimate aspirations and ambitions.

2. The Kurdish masses practicing their legitimate nationalistic rights, including autonomy, is done within their natural scope embodied through one national policy, one land and one political regime in the Iraq Republic. It is also done on the basis of accepting and believing that Iraq is an inseparable part of the Arab Homeland, and that the potentialities of the Arab Nation and its energies and legitimate and just struggle for full liberation from imperialistic domination and Zionist usurpation, and for the realization of unity and socialism are historical and sure guarantees for the freedom of nationalities and minorities and their legitimate rights.

3. The implementation of the clauses of March 11 Manifesto and acquiring all parts of a peaceful and democratic solution of the Kurdish national quest is consolidated deeply with the existing revolutionary regime and its constant development and consolidating its bases to confront plotting and intrigue, planned by imperialistic, Zionist and reactionary quarters.

    They are also linked with the struggle for the liquidation of suspicious and adventurous forces and elements, moving under the direction of the above-mentioned quarters.

The relationship between the popular, democratic and national revolution, heading towards the attainment of unity and socialism, consolidated by the alliance of the Arab Ba'th Socialist Party and the Kurdish Democratic Party and the union of all progressive national and patriotic forces with the peaceful and democratic solution of the Kurdish question is an indivisible dialectal relationship.

Any partitional outlook to such relationship is liable to serve at the end imperialistic, Zionist and reactionary schemings to strike at the Revolution and devastate our Kurdish people's expectations to practice its legitimate national rights.

4. The revolutionary transitions in all political, economic, social, and cultural fields in the direction of implementing the tasks of popular democratic stage before the attainment of socialism, as well as the justification of the interests of peasants, workers and toiling masses of the people are but objective assurances of a peaceful and democratic solution of the Kurdish question and to consolidate its progressive content.
5. The responsibility of fulfilling March 11 Manifesto and the justification of a peaceful democratic solution of the Kurdish question does not depend on one party, rather it is a common national responsibility that no national party can shun and give up.
6. The ideological and permanent political struggle against chauvinist, isolationist, superior, and secessionistic elements and trends is a fundamental condition to safeguard the peaceful, democratic solution of the Kurdish question, and its development on one hand, and to safeguard national unity and revolutionary transitions aiming at the attainment of national and patriotic goals on the other.

## 2. NATIONAL ECONOMY

Throughout the pre-revolution stage, the national economy was characterized by many features, in the forefront of which the dependence of most of its sectors on imperialist monopolies and states, and its foundation on these bases securing the interests of the exploiting feudalistic and bourgeois classes on the account of the down-trodden majority of people. It was also characterized by backwardness in all fields, instability of economic policies and their contraventions, and mounting of recessions and malversation and backwardness of the economic machinery.

All attempts to emancipate national economy, organizing it, and establishing it on scientific, progressive bases were unstable and incomplete attempts, threatened by retreat as a result of the former regimés nature and their aggressive policies against the people and its progressive national and patriotic forces.

The stage of Revolution and the establishment of national alliance requires active and resolute efforts to achieve tasks of this stage based on building national economy through a unitary scope, which puts down bases and onsets on a basis of a full-fledged Arab economic policy, that will be put as a whole at the service of popular struggle against imperialism and Zionism. Also the tasks of this stage are to be based on the notion that capitalist development course is rejected not only in principle, but also as an incapacitating course to justify tasks of emancipating national economy, and its setting on well-built up bases and to secure prosperity to all countrymen.

The economic path to which the Revolution is adhered necessitated by premises and the requirements of the popular democratic stage and the necessities towards attaining socialism and requirements of the national battle of destiny.

The coming stage requires the accomplishment of elementary tasks in the economy, including:

1. Steady progress, according to well-studied scientific plans, to emancipate fully the national economy with all its sectors from the fetters of foreign dependency.
2. The building up of a full-fledged and varied national economy, to be careful to keep the country away from a unilateral economy, designed by imperialist states and monopolies, and to achieve self-reliance in all possible sectors.
3. The creation of efficient, specialized, and active economic apparatuses which can attain to national and revolutionary objectives, and work diligently and accurately to apply them.
4. To work for the achievement of economic unity and to support the Arab common market.
5. To place national and patriotic interest as the foundations of any form of economic cooperation and dealing with foreign countries, and to work for developing economic relations with friendly and socialist countries according to such foundation.

6. Securing prosperity to all masses of the people, especially peasants, workers, and toiling groups, liquidating all aspects and methods of exploitation and class coercion, and achieving justice among all countrymen.
7. The public sector is the foundation stone of the national economy in all its branches, whether in agriculture, industry, commerce or services. The state takes over the responsibility of steering the economic activity and lays down the principles and laws regulating it. The first of the conditions in the national economic work is to expand the public sector and bolster it in all capabilities which would promote its efficiency and power to realize the duties of the existing stage and the duties of transition to socialism.

    The private sector is still capable of playing positive roles in building the national economy. It is essential to support this sector through the directions and cooperation of the public sector in accordance with the conditions, programmes and laws legislated by the state on basis of this Charter.

    The mixed sector, which is organized by the State, also plays its positive role in building the national economy and arrangements should be made to select the economic branches to be entrusted with this sector.
8. The prerequisites of economic development require the participation of Arab capital in all the projects in which it may take part as specified by the state. Sufficient guarantees should be given for the participation of both capital sources, public and private, in the national economy.

A. OIL AND MINERALS:

Oil, at this stage, constitutes the main source in the country's economy and plays a crucial role in determining its political and economic future. Because of this exceptional importance of oil in our life, the monopolistic foreign companies played serious roles in threatening the independence of the country and in conspiring against its national and progressive forces against the people's aspirations to achieve freedom and progress.

The strategic target of the Revolution would naturally be the full liberation of oil wealth from foreign domination and exploitation, and to place them under all aspects of national sovereignty, put them completely in the service of the people's welfare and to make of them an effective instrument of struggle against imperialism and Zionism.

To achieve these objectives, earnest and scientific work requires constant and permanent perpetuity in the national oil policy adopted by the Revolution which aims first at building a vast, strong and integral oil industry.

The duty of building the national oil industry requires support of this sector in all appropriate material and human potentials, to develop the institutes and establishments which would secure the cadres that are needed in oil industry and to cooperate with socialist and friendly states.

The Charter reaffirms the necessity of keeping on the policy of wresting our rights from the monopolistic companies whether in action through Arab and international organizations or through the arrangements and legislation of the State.

Foremost amongst the targets of this policy is to secure the participation of the state in the capital of the oil companies operating in our country and to take part in their administration as well as planning the production for the utility of our national interests and increasing the price of oil and revenues.

Adopting the same procedure in the field of oil policy, the Charter attaches great importance to continue the exploitation of minerals nationally and directly.

The establishment of a vast mineral industry is a basic element in the operation of building a diversified and integrated national economy which would realize progress and enables the country to fully control its economic resources and put them under the service of its domestic and national interests and causes.

## B. AGRICULTURAL WEALTH:

The Revolution is responsible for affecting a radical change in all political, economic, social and cultural principles and relations for the benefit of liberation and progress movement. Country and agricultural sectors stand at the front of the sectors which require fast and crucial change owing to the sufferings from miserable and backward conditions, and it constitutes the major sector of the people.

The countryside in our land needs an overwhelming revolution which would liquidate the economic, tribal and sectarian relations and all values of backwardness inherited from ages of slavery and which were spread during the monopolistic and feudalistic underdeveloped regime. The radical agrarian reform initiated by the Revolution in the country is but a start of the Revolution's events which transfer the country from its underdeveloped conditions to developed ones.

The achievement of radical agrarian reform requires, in order to reach the overwhelming agricultural revolution, a vast range and constant continuity in the arrangement taken by the Revolution to liquidate the feudalistic ownerships and to distribute the lands among the farmers, to provide them with seeds, fertilizers, machines, loans and to complete major irrigational and drainage projects to increase the area of arable land and to improve its production. It also requires the spread of wide-range enlightenment and to provide material conditions to stop migration from countryside to the city and to expand the counter-emigration and to encourage educated youths to work in the countryside. Amongst the fundamental necessities to create the required revolutionary changes in the country is to combat illiteracy amongst farmers, to include agriculture as a main subject in education, to generalize agricultural schools and institutes, and to establish institutes and laboratories specialized in agricultural services.

The sound and developed framework to realize the agricultural revolution and to raise the standard of living to the former masses and to increase production in accordance with the requirements of the national economy, is to develop the state farms, collective farms and farmers cooperatives which are being generalized in all parts of the country of our home.

## C. INDUSTRY:

Industry is considered a fundamental base of civilization and progress at this age and it is one of the conditions for transition to socialism. Colonialists and their local allies tried to hinder the establishment of an active and powerful national industry for two main reasons:

1. To keep our country backward so that it remains a market for the disposal of goods manufactured in imperialistic states.
2. To prevent the formation of a large working class. When the national will and subjective conditions dictated the establishment of national industry, the imperialists attempted in different ways to "subordinate" it to the imperialistic markets and to restrict it within the complementary and consumption framework.

The revolution faces today in the field of industry two major duties, (1) the completion, the successfulness, the development and expansion of the existing industries and (2) building a wide and varied industrial base which would support national independence and a base for political, economic and social development leading towards socialism.

As the economy of Iraq depends in principle on two important bases, oil and agriculture, it is natural, therefore, for the industrialization process to be directed for the achievement of mutual connection between them and between these two bases.

The main purposes for industrialization in our country are the establishment and development of mining and petrochemical industries and the construction of industries which depend on agricultural materials produced in the country. This will also necessitate the establishment of industries which provide the oil, minerals and agricultural sectors with their requirements for tools and equipment.

The purpose of building a powerful national industry capable of performing its duties in our patriotic and national battles on one hand and in achieving the well being of the masses on the other hand, require the earnestness to create a balance between heavy and production industries without which it is not possible to set down the bases of an independent powerful national industry and between the consumer industries which meet the citizens' requirements with great care to increase and affect development without over-stressing consumer economy.

Amongst the fundamental conditions which accompany the overwhelming operation of industrialization is the expansion of power industry, particularly high tension electric power.

The public sector in industry is the base on which lies the responsibility of leading the private and mixed sectors. The Revolution has to support this sector with all required capabilities and to expand as far as possible. Owing to the country's need for quick growth and to share the citizens in building operations, the participation of the private sector in industrial programmes, particularly in petty complementary and consumer industries, is a very essential question and the state has to encourage it and provide it with all conditions and guarantees for its success.

The work to expand democratic management in industrial and production installations through the expansion of participation of workers in the Boards of Administration in a way which would secure the increase and development of production and lay down sound working relations, is one of the objectives sought by the Revolution so as to provide the country with educated, active and faithful cadres to direct this vital sector.

The completion of these aims requires the development of the machinery of the public sector in industry and the development of machinery of industrial planning, as well as the increase of industrial school and institutes and to seek the help of all national and Arab expertise and those of the socialist and friendly countries.

## D. COMMERCE:

The commercial sector occupies a vitally important position due to its fundamental relations with the question of national economy and national independence on one hand and for being the responsible sector to provide consumer goods to the people on the other hand.

The line to be adopted in commercial policy is to submit the internal and foreign trades to the requirements of national independence, self-sufficiency, the development plan and to fix the trade movement within the directions of its transition from a mediator monopolistic, greedy sector to a fundamental circuit of an integrated and developed national economy aiming at serving the people. This requires a plan which achieves the objectives of complete nationalization of foreign trade and wholesale trade and to make the import and export policy subject to the requirements of development and higher national interests.

While the Revolution is keen in protecting the interests of the toiling masses and in securing the suitable living standards and in liquidating all phenomena of monopoly, greediness and blackmailing, it is at the same time keen to protect the interests of small and middle merchants and it considers that the private sector is capable in the field of trade of playing a positive role if it is placed within the frame of public utility and higher national interest.

The charter calls for the support of the public sector of trade and to maintain it with all means of success, development and expansion so that it could be able to play its role in the operation of fostering the national economy and building a strong economic base in providing the commodities to citizens at suitable prices, far from fluctuation in prices and away from crises which are arranged by monopolistic avarice and the enemies of the people.

## E. FINANCIAL POLICY:

During the past years, the financial policy was disturbed, improvised, and disconnected from the masses' interests and their basic domestic and national causes. In order that the financial policy may play its fundamental role in building the unitary peoples democratic system, it should be based on clear and permanent scientific adherence to the people's fundamental interests and their domestic and national causes of destiny in guiding the means of expenditure from the budget towards the national defense affairs, development, education, health, social securities and general services.

The charter deems it necessary to reconsider the taxation policy to ensure the adoption of a just procedure of taxes and to reduce the indirect taxation on production commodities, drugs and main consumer materials.

The charter also considers it necessary to take steps that help the masses to be enlightened about their participation in the building up of a new society.

### 3. SOCIAL OBJECTIVES

Throughout ages of foreign domination, class persecution, and control of corrupt groups and dictatorship, anomalous circumstances and dangerous ills prevailed over our community, crippled the masses' capability in work, production and creation, and strained them with fetters of injustice and backwardness.

The slogan to eliminate poverty, ignorance and disease was one of the major slogans in our struggle on both the regional and national levels. It is still one of the great objectives of the Revolution, which seeks to justify a radical and an all-out change in the social conditions, as part of a unitary-socialistic-democratic scope.

The premise of a change sought by the Revolution is the deep faith in the masses and their creative role in history-making and building up human civilization. Therefore, the Revolution under common national work to build the new revolutionary society, seeks to secure all necessary social conditions to safeguard the citizen's liberty and pride, to enable him to work, production and creation, and to set him free from all those fetters that incapacitate and human expectations. These tasks confronting the Revolution in this direction can be summarized as follows:

1. Work is to be considered as a right and duty of any citizen who can undertake it, and eliminating entirely all forms of unemployment.
2. Social security is to be made available to all countrymen, and to secure a decent life for them within a plan that keeps pace with the revolution's advancement and the state's capabilities.
3. To secure health care, medicine, to protect countrymen from diseases, and to consider man's life as a fundamental value that must

be protected by all means within the framework of a developing scientific plan that keeps pace with the State's capabilities at each stage.

4. To propagate all branches of education among all countrymen, to link it with its planned form with the objectives of evolution and development as well as with national and patriotic causes, and to base it on foundations that secure raising up a generation according to the requirements of the Revolution's objectives and expectations of the popular masses, within the scope of Democratic-Socialist-Unitary relations and values.

   The aim of the Revolution at its present stage is to implement its plan in compulsory education in the level of primary schooling up to the two successive stages: intermediate and secondary. To eliminate illiteracy is one of the basic conditions to achieve a radical change in social situations towards progress. The Revolution made endeavours to speed up operations to eradicate illiteracy, but this task is still in need of more efforts and energies. The popular organizations, students and educated classes, bear the responsibility of wide participation to complete them as soon as possible.

5. To provide suitable hygienic accommodation for all citizens according to the requirements of the stage and the State's capabilities. At the present stage, the Revolution aims at fixing rental charges in a form which suits the income of the citizen and protects him from avarice and monopoly. It also aims at encouraging the social cooperative organizations which work to provide accommodation for their members. The state is responsible basically for building large residential units all over the country in which good health conditions and security will be available.

6. Woman, who has suffered all types of slavery, monopoly and backwardness in line with our people, has in addition suffered bad conditions which deprived her of her humanity and hindered her free and active participation in human life. Therefore, the special care to transfer the woman to new positions is a basic target of social transition operation.

   The liberation of woman from feudalistic and bourgeois thinking and from the conditions and terms under which she was a sheer leisure or a citizen of the second class, is a patriotic and sacred national duty for which one should struggle faithfully and keenly.

Our society which faces the tasks of struggle against imperialism, Zionism, reaction and retardation and against the perils converging our destiny, should not be deprived of the active role which the woman could play as she represents half of society.

The liberation of woman from all shackles and obstacles is the correct augury to build up a new generation capable of bearing its home and national responsibilities.

### 4. Culture, Art and Information

Culture, art and information are amongst the best fields of the human civilization and a best means of activity and effectiveness devised by man to express his social situation, feeling, aspiration and expectation. Each stage of man's development has its own culture, information and art, by virtue of the dialectical link between these branches and the social, economic and political system practised by man. It is, therefore, natural and legal for the new revolutionary system to have its own culture, information, and art which express its principles and positions of man's expectations and aspirations.

Revolutionary culture, information and art are born in the old community's womb and strive to express themselves and to occupy the effective position among the masses' ranks. When the old community collapsed, and the Revolution takes over power it has to consecrate its decisive and full victory upon the culture, art and information of the old community. Then the relationship between culture, information and art of the old community and the new revolutionary community becomes an argumentative relationship possessing two features: First, the deep historic developmental outlook of heritage. Second: The ambition to create new information, culture and art expressing fully the situations of the new community, its requirements, feelings and aspirations.

The current stage, the stage of building the democratic revolutionary unitive community to reach socialism, provides the following frameworks and tasks in the field of culture, art and information:

1. The Revolution's information, culture and art are those which stem from the national, democratic and socialist outlook interactioned, in general, with the humanitarian culture and, in particular, with progressiveness. It also must have a close tie with the masses and their interests, problems, sentiments, and aspirations, with respect to the freedom of choice of forms and styles of expression and the maintenance of the process of creativeness.

2. The conscious decisive struggle against thoughts, theories, trends and styles which promote sectarianism, chauvinism, racialism, regionalism and the spirit of defeat and libertinism, serving imperialists and their pillars of feudalists and bourgeoisie and all enemies of the revolution; and purging culture and informational establishments of these elements and of those who believe in them and promote them directly or indirectly.
3. Preserving the Arab heritage, and finding out all the humanitarian and progressive meanings in it; taking care in spreading it among the masses and in the world, and also taking great care of the humanitarian heritage of the civilization of Mesopotamia and the Kurdish National heritage and folkloric characteristics of all national minorities in the country.
4. Providing possibilities to build high institutions of art, culture and information and developing them continuously to keep in pace with the spirit of the time and its progress, and spread them on a large scale among the masses, supply them with able persons believing in the revolution and its thoughts and aspiration; and benefiting from all national, Arab and international experience in all these fields.
5. Struggling against passive outlook towards cultural, artistic and informational work, and raising the social status and living standard of those working in these vanguard fields, and encouraging the youth to participate in them.
6. Universities nowadays play an important and vital role in the life of communities as one of the important means of spreading knowledge and preparing scientific cadres of different specializations.

In our country, these establishments have a special role of keeping up with the revolutionary process and supporting it to fulfill all the requirements of social changes for the benefit of the national struggle. On this basis, the Charter considers it important to support universities and institutions of scientific research in the direction which would conform with the masses aspirations of speeding up the process of social and economic transformation to socialism. This will not be achieved save by the "purging" of these institutions from all antagonistic right-wing and libertarian trends which are against the revolution's ideology and against its progress and by the reform of university educational curricula in a form which would conform with the revolution's premises and programmes in development and the dire need to develop and expand scientific and technological studies.

## 5. ARAB POLICY

The Revolution's policy in the field emanates and is defined from its unitary, progressive, people's democratic identity and from its belief in socialism. The historic duty of the Revolution is to participate fully, actively and in the vanguard of the movement of Arab struggle in achieving its objectives which are summed up in building the unified, Arab socialist, democratic society.

As a means of expression of this policy and to realize its objectives, the Charter states:

1. To launch an all-out, resolute struggle using all methods against imperialism, its influence, interests and strongholds, to liberate every part of Arab lands, and challenge strongly their direct and indirect attempts for infiltration into the Arab homeland.
2. To firmly challenge any foreign attempt aiming at wresting any part of the Arab homeland or imposing their domination on it or splitting it. As the Arab Gulf today is exposed to continuous attempts schemed by the imperialistic quarters to obliterate its Arabism and to wrest some parts of it, the struggle against these attempts is, therefore, considered a sacred domestic and national duty.
3. To struggle by all means to achieve the all-out Arab unity on liberal, democratic, popular basis, provided that the masses should be the active instrument in forging historic unity. Also to struggle against forged formed of unity and to expose it as it aims to strike the essence of unity and forms a means of plotting against it.
4. The question of liberation of Palestine from Zionist occupation is a central cause in the Arab struggle. It is dialectically connected with the struggle for liberation, unity and building of socialism and on the basis of the right of Palestinian people to go back to its liberated land to practise its full right in determining its destiny. This means the denunciation of all surrender solutions and projects aiming at the liquidation of the Palestinian cause through partial settlements.
5. To achieve these major national duties the Arab masses are required to gather within active forms of struggle. The popular armed struggle, particularly on the Palestinian front, and wherever

necessary in all other parts of the Arab homeland, is an indispensable and prime method.
6. To realise the unity of joint action between all revolutionary and progressive national forces whether officially or publicly in the Arab homeland and inside the country to provide the biggest and most active energies of struggle against imperialism, Zionism and reaction.
7. To support the revolutionary changes in the Arab countries and to bolster the liberal and national progressive movements in support of the objectives of the Arab struggle and deepen its historic procession.

## 6. Foreign Policy

The foreign policy of the Revolution emerges from its progressive identity against imperialism and is defined on this basis. It also emanates from the belief that the 17th of July Revolution and the revolution in the Arab homeland are a vital and active part of the international revolution against imperialism. During the past stages, the Revolution expressed its identity in the international field in full and earnest alignment to the camp of struggling people against imperialism, aggression and apartheid, backing liberation movements and progressive forces in every part of the world, and consolidating relations with them and with the socialist countries. Among the salient outlooks of this undertaking was the expansion of political, economic and cultural relations with the socialist countries, the recognition of the German Democratic Republic, the Revolutionary Government of South Vietnam, and the government of National Unity in Cambodia, and supporting all struggling forces for liberty and progress in the world.

Preceeding from this stand, the Charter stresses the following in foreign policy.

1. The resolute adherance to the policy of struggle against world imperialism, the rejection of all forms of dependence, and support of nations' rights in self-determination, and condemnation of aggression, and racial discrimination policies.
2. Resistance of aggressive pacts, designs, and military groupings as well as imperialistic policies threatening the security and safety of nations and endangering world peace.
3. Consolidating relations with the peoples and governments of the socialist camp in a manner securing mutual interests, and elevating

the balance of world struggle to defeat imperialism and exterminate its influence.
4. Consolidating the developing relations with patriotic and nationalist liberation movements especially in Asia, Africa and Latin America, and with all liberation movements in the world in general, including progressive labour and popular movements in Europe and the United States of America.
5. Setting up cooperation and friendship relations with all states who adopt positive stands towards our patriotic and nationalist causes and interests.

# APPENDIX C

# March 11 Manifesto on the Peaceful Settlement of the Kurdish Issue in Iraq

The primary *raison d'être* of the July 17 Revolution was that it represented both the denunciation by the Arab masses of all causes and causers of the June defeat and the consensus of the popular opinion of Iraq in condemning the former dictatorial reactionary rule for contributing, by its defeatist attitude, to that nationalist ordeal. That was because the former regime was completely isolated from the people and absolutely incapable of solving the national issues that had always gnawed at the root of the national structure and whose settlement was a precondition for determined endeavours to mobilise human and material energies in Iraq and commit them where they belong—in the frontlines of the battle of the destiny of the Arab nation.

This being so, the Revolution laid before its eyes, right from the very first days, the duty of realising the national unity of the people of Iraq without any discrimination on account of sex, language, religion or social origin, side by side with assuring all political, social and economic conditions required for this unity. In this way, it should be possible for Iraq to direct all of its energies and possibilities to the nationalist battle of destiny which, in the opinion of the Revolution, represents the summit of the bitter historic strife between colonialism, Zionism and their evil designs in the Arab homeland on the one hand, and the interests of the liberation of the Arab nation and its struggle for the achievement of its human progressive aims on the other.

In spite of the legacy of myriad, complicated problems which confronted the Revolution from the day of its inception, the Revolution proceeded with firmness and faith up the road of liberating Iraq from the residues of colonialism, national betrayal and political and social oppression and for providing all prerequisites to build a new Iraq, where actual equality in rights and obligations and equal opportunities shall effectively be established and wide horizons shall be opened to the masses of the people by means of collective loyalty to the unity of the homeland, to the unity of its people and to the unity of its major goal—nationalist unity, liberty and socialism.

The settlement of the Kurdish issue in Iraq stood in the forefront of the national issues which the Revolution faced. This was particularly so as the incapability of the former regimes to comprehend that issue, even the lack of a genuine desire to tackle it and suggest proper solutions to it in those eras, side by side with the concomitant exploitation of the resulting circumstances by imperialism, its collaborators and its agents, have all combined to further complicate the issue to the extent of rendering it something akin to forbidding and insoluble. The situation had further been aggravated as a result of the substitution of violence for brotherly and objective democratic dialogue, which is required by the nature of this national issue and the legitimate and just rights it involved for a section of the Iraqi people.

From its very first days, the Revolution proceeded to deal with this national issue in an atmosphere permeated with a sense of self-responsibility and with the highest degree of adherence to democratic and revolutionary principles.

The Revolution, which is inspired by the theoretical fountainhead of the Arab Ba'th Socialist Party, believes that nationalist rights are, in their essence, democratic rights. They have, among their aims, reviving the cultural heritage, language and tradition, as well as putting free will into practice. The consolidation of such rights among various nationalities, particularly those of the same homeland, requires the realisation of ways and means for organizing relationships between those nationalities in a manner conducive to their collective uplift.

Any plan aimed at undermining ties between them or sowing the seeds of dissension can be of no service to their collective interests. Meanwhile, the organisation and cementation of national and human ties between them and steering such ties to the service progress, will systematically assure the means of the unity of national life in an atmosphere abounding in national fraternity and peace.

Imbued by these principles, the Seventh Regional Conference of the Arab Ba'th Socialist Party, which convened late in 1968 and early in 1969, took steps to delineate the Party's ideological and theoretical positions on this national issue and chart out a settlement of the issue for the Revolution and the revolutionary authority. The resolutions passed by that Conference had this to say, among other things: "The Conference has stressed the conviction that the question of the nationalist ambitions of the Kurds of Iraq comes in the forefront of the problems facing the Arab revolutionary movement. Years have now passed by without arriving at a sound settlement of this issue. Consequently, unspeakable calamities and tragedies came to be inflicted on both Arabs and Kurds as a result of arbitrariness in approaching the issue. The forces of imperialism and reaction and the detachments of agents and opportunists readily put the situation to their own advantage and used the failure of solving the issue as a vehicle for meddling in Iraq's affairs, bringing pressure to bear on it, spinning conspiracies on the rights of both Arabs and Kurds and inflicting the greatest possible damage on the progressive and democratic nationalist gains they had won at a high cost of self-sacrifice and common struggle." The Conference further stressed that our Party which, in its militant struggle and policy always stemmed from its nationalist humanistic, socialist and democratic ideology, has consistently held in high respect the national ambitions of the Kurdish masses as embedded in their own progressive national substance and view them as legitimate humanistic rights. The Conference well appreciated the strong ties between the realisation of those ambitions and the vigour and soundness of the advance of the popular masses in Iraq up the road of liquidating the legacies of colonialism so as to have Iraq's hand free for engaging in the current battle of destiny in Palestine and keeping up the historic struggle for the achievement of Arab unity, liberty and socialism.

The Revolution, sincere to the principles and resolutions of the Party, has recognised for the Kurdish citizens their entitlement to their national rights and to developing their national characteristics within the framework of the unity of the people and the homeland and the country's constitutional system.

As the Arab nation is engaged in a large scale conflict with imperialism, Zionism and local reaction—a conflict placing it in the frontline of the struggle of the peoples of the Middle East, (it being understood that the struggle of the people of Iraq is closely linked with the struggle of the Arab nation for democracy and for combating the forces of reaction on both world-wide and local levels)—the Revolution considers that the first prop of Arab-Kurdish national unity in Iraq lies in the fact that Kurdish national unity, like its Arab counterpart, is a democratic movement directed against the same forces of reaction. In Iraq, it is tied up to the Arab liberation movement by the unity of struggle against imperialism and its reactionary allied forces. It is also tied up to the struggle of the Arab people by the traditions of historic fraternity, the unity of economic interests and the concerted evolution of the Arab and Kurdish nationalities. Any breach of this harmony will, of necessity, inflict immense damage on the common struggle and on the progressive national resurgence in general.

Imperialism has long realised that the unity of the Arab-Kurdish struggle has the effect of reinforcing the Arab-Kurdish liberation movement and enabling it to occupy important positions in the face of the imperialistic-Zionist-Israeli aggressive schemings in the region, particularly in regard to the national battle of destiny currently raging in Palestine and the surrounding Arab countries. As such, the imperialistic and hireling quarters have been trying madly to break cohesion and fraternity between the Arab and Kurdish masses with the purpose of undermining the front of the revolutionary national struggle of Iraq.

The Revolution, understanding the national issue as an integral part of the revolution struggling against imperialism, Zionism and reaction, will necessarily abide, in every step taken towards settling the Kurdish national issue, by the measures conducive to cementing and consolidating the national and the nationalist struggles against those inhuman forces combined.

From this it follows that the exercise by the Kurdish masses of their national rights and the achievement of equal opportunities for free development constitute the two paths leading to the unification and cementation of Iraq's national struggle against the enemies of the people and the enemies of the Arab nation and of the people of Iraq, namely imperialism, Zionism and reaction.

It was by no means a coincidence that the imperialistic-Zionist-reactionary conspiracies against the Republic of Iraq occurred at a time when signs of peace began looming large on the horizon of our beloved North, thanks to the meaningful endeavours exerted by the Revolutionary Government and the sincere response on the part of the leadership of Sd. Mustafa Al-Barazani.

It is public knowledge that the Revolution had taken all necessary measures for the re-establishment of calm and peace throughout northern Iraq. The following steps have been taken:

A) Recognition has been given to the legitimacy of the Kurdish nationality, this being in accordance with the Resolutions of the Seventh Regional Conference of the Arab Baath Socialist Party, and the official and press statements issued by the revolutionary authority. This fact shall be enshrined in a lasting manner in the Interim Constitution and the Permanent Constitution.

B) The Revolutionary Command Council has approved the establishment of a university in Sulaimaniyah and the establishment of a Kurdish academy of letters. It has also recognized the cultural and linguistic rights of the Kurdish nationality, prescribing that the Kurdish language be taught in all schools, institutes and universities, teachers training institutes, the Military College and the Police College. The Revolutionary Command Council further prescribed the wide dissemination of Kurdish literature—scientific, literary and political—expressive of the national and nationalist ambitions of the Kurdish people. It ordered measures to be taken to help Kurdish authors, poets and writers to form a federation of their own, get their works printed and afford them all opportunities and possibilities for developing their scientific and artistic talents. The Revolutionary Command Council also ordered arrangements to be made for founding a Kurdish publishing and printing house and a directorate general of Kurdish culture, the publishing of a weekly newspaper and a monthly magazine in Kurdish and expanding Kurdish programmes on the Kirkuk TV Station, pending the construction of a TV station broadcasting exclusively in Kurdish.

C) In recognition of the rights of the Kurds to revive their traditions and national days and to make it possible for the whole of the people to join in the observance of national days, the Revolutionary Command Council has decreed Nawrooz Day as a National Day in the Republic of Iraq.

D) The Revolutionary Command Council has promulgated the Governorates Law which provides for the decentralization of local administration and for the creation of the Governorate of Dohuk.

E) The Revolutionary Command Council has issued a general amnesty for all civilian and military personnel who had joined in acts of violence in the North so as to do away with all vestiges of former negative and exceptional conditions and lay the new national life on solid foundations of pervasive security and national fraternity.

The Arab Kurdish masses of Iraq received with acclamation and welcome the acts and measures of the Revolutionary Command Council, thereby setting the stage for proceeding with the realisation of the aims which have become the object of popular consensus and on which the will and unity of word of the people came to be centered.

In view of the above, the Revolutionary Command Council established contacts with the leadership of Sd. Mustafa Al-Barazani, Chairman of the Kurdistan Democratic Party and viewpoints were subsequently exchanged. All were convinced of the necessity of accepting and implementing the contents of this Manifesto. The Revolutionary Command Council reiterates its determination to deepen and broaden the effective measures made with the object of achieving the means of cultural and economic uplift and general development, at enabling the Kurdish masses to exercise their legitimate rights and secure their actual participation in the national build-up and the struggle for the realisation of the great nationalist objectives of the homeland.

The Revolutionary Command Council has thus decreed the following:

1) The Kurdish language shall, side by side with the Arabic language, be an official language in the areas populated by a majority of Kurds. The Kurdish language shall be the language of instruction in these areas. The Arabic language shall be taught in all schools where teaching is conducted in Kurdish. The Kurdish language shall be taught elsewhere in Iraq as a second language within the limits prescribed by the law.

2) It has been one of the main concerns of the revolutionary government to secure participation by our Kurdish brothers in Government and eliminate any discrimination between Kurds and other nationals in regard to holding public offices, including sensitive and important ones such as cabinet ministries, army commands, etc. While endorsing this principle, the revolutionary government stresses the need of endeavouring to have the principle achieved in fair proportions with due care to considerations of merits, the population ratio and the deprivations experienced by our Kurdish brothers in the past.

3) In view of the backwardness experienced in the past by the Kurdish nationality in the cultural and educational domains, a plan should be worked out for the treatment of this backwardness. This is to be achieved through:

(a) Implementing expeditiously the resolutions of the Revolutionary Command Council in regard to the language and cultural rights of the Kurdish people and tying up the preparation and direction of special programmes on Kurdish national affairs in the radio and TV network to the Directorate General of Kurdish Culture and Information.

(b) Reinstating students who were dismissed or had to leave school because of former conditions of violence in the area. These students should be allowed to return to their respective schools regardless of age limits or else have a convenient remedy suggested for their problem.

(c) Building more schools in the Kurdish area, elevating the standards of education and admitting, at a fair rate, Kurdish students to universities and military colleges and granting them scholarships.

4) In the administrative units populated by a Kurdish majority, government officials shall be appointed from among Kurds or persons well versed in the Kurdish language as long as these are available. The principal Government functionaries—governor, district officer (Qaimmaqam), director of police, director of security, etc.—shall be drawn from among the Kurds. Steps shall immediately be taken to develop state organs in the area in consultation within the framework of the High Committee supervising the implementation of this Manifesto in a manner insuring its proper enforcement and consolidating national unity and stability in the area.

5) The Government recognises the right of the Kurdish people to set up student, youth, women and teachers organisations of their own. These organisations shall be affiliated in the national counterparts in Iraq.

6) (a) The validity of paras. (1) and (2) of the Revolutionary Command Council's Decree No. 59 dated August 5, 1968, shall be extended to the date of the issuance of this Manifesto. This shall cover all of those who took part in hostilities in the Kurdish area.

(b) Workers, government functionaries and employees, both civilian and military, shall go back to service without this being subject to cadre considerations. The civilian personnel shall be posted to the Kurdish area within the limits of its requirements.

7) (a) A committee of specialists shall be formed to speed up the uplift of the Kurdish area in all respects and provide indemnities for the affliction of the past number of years, side by side with drawing up an adequate budget for all of this. The committee in question shall be attached to the Ministry of Northern Affairs.

(b) The economic plan shall be drawn up in such a way as to ensure equal development for various parts of Iraq, with due attention to the backward conditions in the Kurdish area.

(c) Pension salaries shall be made available to the families of members of the Kurdish armed movement who met with martyrdom in the regrettable hostilities as well as to those rendered incapacitated or disfigured. This shall be regulated in special legislation patterned on the existing laws of the land.

(d) Speedy action shall be taken to bring relief to aggrieved and needy persons by means of building housing units and other projects ensuring work to the unemployed, offering appropriate aid both in kind and in cash and granting reasonable indemnities to aggrieved persons who stand in need for help. This shall be the responsibility of the High Committee, with the exception of those specified in the above paras.

8) The inhabitants of Arab and Kurdish villages shall be repatriated to their places of habitation. As to villagers whose villages lie in areas requisitioned by the Government for public utility purposes in accordance with the provisions of the law, they shall be settled in neighbouring districts and shall be compensated for whatever loss they might have incurred as a result.

9) Steps shall be taken to speed up the implementation of the Agrarian Reform Law in the Kurdish area and have the Law amended in such a way as to ensure the liquidation of all feudalistic relationships, handing out appropriate plots of land to all peasants and waiving for them agricultural tax arrears for the duration of the regrettable hostilities.

10) It has been agreed to amend the Interim Constitution as follows:

(a) The people of Iraq are composed of two principal nationalities: the Arab nationality and the Kurdish nationality. This Constitution recognises the national rights of the Kurdish people and the rights of all nationalities within the framework of Iraqi unity.

(b) The following paragraph shall be added to Article (4) of the Constitution: "The Kurdish language, beside the Arabic language, shall be an official language in the Kurdish area."

(c) All this shall be confirmed in the Permanent Constitution.

11) The broadcasting station and heavy arms shall be given back to the Government, this being tied up to the implementation of the final stages of the agreement.

12) One of the vice-presidents of the Republic shall be a Kurd.

13) The Governorates Law shall be part of the text of this Manifesto.

14) Following the issuance of the Manifesto, necessary steps shall be taken in consultation with the High Committee supervising its enforcement, to unify the governorates and administrative units

populated by a Kurdish majority as shown by the official census to be carried out. The State shall endeavour to develop this administrative unity and deepen and broaden the Kurdish people's process of exercising their national rights as a measure of ensuring self-rule. Pending the realisation of administrative unity, Kurdish national affairs shall be coordinated by means of periodic meetings between the High Committee and the governors of the northern area. As self-rule is to be established within the framework of the Republic of Iraq, the exploitation of the natural riches in the area shall obviously be the prerogative of the authorities of the Republic.

15) The Kurdish people shall contribute to the legislative branch in proportion to the ratio they have to the population of Iraq.

## Kurdish Countrymen!

These accomplishments achieved by the Revolution are nothing more than a step up the ladder of attaining your national objectives in the shade of this beloved homeland and the unity of its great people. History will bear witness that you never had and never will have as dependable brothers and allies as the Arab people.

Masses of our great people!

It is your will in national unity which will triumph in the end. All attempts made to undermine your militant cohesion shall get smashed up on the rock of your maturity and your determination to live up to your historic responsibilities. Your struggling masses are today shedding off the dust of the intrigues spun by the enemies and greedy elements and are proceeding hand in hand vigorously and resolutely for backing up the cause of the Arab nation, namely Palestine, and realise your sublime objective in respect to unity, liberty and socialism.

## Masses of our struggling Arab Nation!

A page of the history of this struggling country is thus folded out and a new bright one is opened by the Revolution and by all free militant strugglers of this homeland. On this beloved soil, the bonds of affection, peace and fraternity are rejuvenated between two nationalities that are held together by a long record of common struggle across history. Today, tomorrow and for ever, they shall have endless honour across history. Today, tomorrow and for ever, they shall have the honour of reviving a common struggle for vanquishing the enemies of the two nationalities and the enemies of peoples and humanity in its entirety, namely Zionism, imperialism and backwardness. They shall have the honour of a joint contribution to backing up man's struggle for liberation and progress and for consolidating the civilization of the age on foundations of right, equality and justice among all peoples.

Forward for the common struggle, common hopes and common nationalist and human victories!

**The Revolutionary Command Council**
**11/3/1970**

# APPENDIX D[1]

# The Iraqi-Soviet Treaty of Friendship and Cooperation

The Iraqi Republic and the Union of Soviet Socialist Republics, being firmly convinced that the further development of friendship and comprehensive co-operation between them accords with the national interests of both states and serves the cause of peace in the whole world and in the Arab area, and the interests of the freedom of peoples and their security and respect for their sovereignty, decided to conclude this treaty and agreed on the following:

Article 1. The high contracting parties solemnly declare that lasting and unbreakable friendship will always exist between them. They will continue to develop comprehensive co-operation between the two countries and their peoples in the political, economic, trade, technical, scientific, cultural and other fields on the basis of respect for state sovereignty, territorial integrity and non-interference in each other's internal affairs.

Article 2. The Iraqi Republic and the USSR declare that they will co-operate closely and comprehensively in ensuring conditions for preserving and further developing the social and economic gains of their peoples and respect for the sovereignty of each of them over all their natural resources.

Article 3. The high contracting parties, in firmly pursuing a policy of peaceful coexistence among states with different social systems and in pursuing a peace-loving foreign policy, will continue to stand for world peace, relaxation of international tension, and for the achievement of general and complete disarmament, encompassing both nuclear and conventional weapons, under effective international control.

Article 4. Proceeding from the ideals of freedom and equality of all peoples, the high contracting parties condemn imperialism and colonialism in all forms and manifestations. They will continue to wage

1. Reproduced from *New Middle East* (June, 1972), p. 42.

an unrelenting struggle against imperialism and Zionism, and for the full, final and unconditional elimination of imperialism, neo-colonialism, racism and apartheid. They call for the immediate and complete implementation of the UN declaration on the granting of independence to all colonized countries and peoples. The two parties will co-operate with each other and with other peace-loving states in supporting peoples' just struggle for their sovereignty, freedom, independence and social progress.

Article 5. In view of the great importance they attach to economic, scientific and technical co-operation between them, the high contracting parties will further expand and deepen this co-operation and will exchange experience in the fields of industry, agriculture, irrigation and water conservation, exploitation of oil and other natural resources, communications, transport, other branches of the economy, and the training of national cadres.

The two sides will expand trade and shipping between their two countries on the basis of the principles of mutual benefit, equality, and most favoured nation treatment.

Article 6. The high contracting parties will further promote co-operation and contacts between them in the fields of science, art, literature, education, health services, the press, radio, television, the cinema, tourism, sport and other fields.

The two sides will promote wider co-operation and direct contacts between government institutions, social organizations, and scientific, cultural and economic establishments in the two countries for a deeper mutual acquaintance with the life, work and achievements of the peoples of the two countries in various fields.

Article 7. Attaching much importance to concerted action in the international field to ensure world peace and security and to developing political co-operation between Iraq and the USSR, the two high contracting parties will hold regular consultations with each other at various levels on all important international issues affecting the interests of the two countries and on questions concerning the further development of relations between them.

Article 8. The two high contracting parties will, in the event of a situation developing which endangers the peace of either of them or constitutes a threat to peace or a violation of peace, hold immediate contacts to coordinate their positions in the interest of eliminating the developing danger and re-establishing peace.

Article 9. In the interests of the security of both countries, the two high contracting parties will continue to develop co-operation in the strengthening of the defense capabilities of each.

Article 10. Each of the two high contracting parties declares that it will not enter into any international alliance or grouping or take part in any actions or undertakings directed against the other high contracting party. Each of the two high contracting parties also undertakes not to allow its territory to be used for any action that might cause military harm to the other party.

Article 11. The two high contracting parties declare that their commitments under the international agreements now in force do not conflict with the provisions of this treaty and they undertake not to conclude any international agreements incompatible with these provisions.

Article 12. The present treaty will be operative for 15 years and will be automatically renewed for each subsequent five-year period unless one of the two high contracting parties expresses its desire to terminate it by giving notice of this to the other high contracting party 12 months before the expiry of the treaty.

Article 13. Any differences of opinion between the two high contracting parties over the interpretation of one or more of the provisions of this treaty will be settled between them in a spirit of friendship, understanding and mutual respect.

Article 14. This treaty is subject to ratification and will come into force on the day of the exchange of the instruments of ratification, which will take place in Moscow at the earliest possible time.

APPENDIX E

# Iran-Iraq Treaty on International Borders and Good Neighbourly Relations*
## [Done at Baghdad, June 13, 1975]

The President of the Republic of Iraq and His Imperial Majesty the Shahinshah of Iran, in view of the sincere willingness of the two parties expressed in the Algiers Agreement of March 6, 1975, to reach an ultimate and permanent settlement of all outstanding questions between the two countries;

And in view of the fact that the two parties have conducted a final re-demarcation of their land borders on the basis of the Constantinople protocol of 1913 and the minutes of the Border Demarcation Commission's Sessions of 1914 and have demarcated their river borders in accordance with the Thalweg line; and in view of their willingness to restore security and mutual confidence along their joint borders;

And in view of the historical, religious, cultural and neighbourly relations between the peoples of Iraq and Iran;

* Reproduced from the *Baghdad Observer*, Nos. 2240–41. Vol. V, June 23 and June 24, 1975. Unofficial. Maps and appendices are not reproduced.

And proceeding from their desire to consolidate the relationships of friendship and good neighbourliness, promote their relations in the economic and cultural fields and enhance the ties between their peoples to a better standard on the principles of territorial security, border sovereignty and non-interference in the internal affairs of each other;

And in view of their determination to establish a new era of friendly relations between Iraq and Iran on the basis of full respect for national independence and equality in national sovereignty and proceeding from their behalf in the mutual implementation of the principles and realisation of the objectives and purposes provided for in the United Nations Charter;

Have resolved to conclude this treaty and authorise their commissioned representatives.

President of the Republic of Iraq . . .

His Excellency Saadoun Hammadi, the Foreign Minister of Iraq;

His Imperial Majesty the Shahinshah of Iran . . .

His Excellency Abbas Ali Khalatbari, the Foreign Minister of Iran.

Who, after exchanging instruments of their full authorisation, which they have found authentic and consistent with governing principles, have agreed to the following provisions:

### Article One

The two supreme contracting parties confirmed that the international land borders between Iraq and Iran are those which have been re-demarcated in accordance with the principles and pursuant to the provisions of the protocol for the re-demarcation of the land border and supplements thereto, appended with this treaty.

### Article Two

The two supreme contracting parties confirmed that the international borders in Shatt al Arab are those demarcated in accordance with the principles and pursuant to the provisions of the protocol for the demarcation of river borders and supplements thereto, appended with this treaty.

### Article Three

The two supreme contracting parties undertake to practice, along the borders in general, firm and effective control for the purpose of stopping all penetrations of a subversive nature, wherever they may emanate, on the principles and pursuant to the provisions of the protocol on border security appended with this treaty.

## ARTICLE FOUR

The two supreme contracting parties confirm that provisions of the three protocols and their appendices mentioned in articles 1, 2 and 3 hereof, supplementary thereto, which constitute an inseparable part thereof, are final and permanent provisions, irrevocable for whatever reason and shall represent indivisible elements for a comprehensive settlement, and consequently any encroachment upon any element of such a comprehensive settlement is contradictory in principle to the essence of the Algiers Agreement.

## ARTICLE FIVE

Within the context of non-encroachment on borders and the strict respect for the safety of national territories of both states, the two supreme contracting parties confirmed that the line of their territorial and water borders is unencroachable, permanent and final.

## ARTICLE SIX

1. In the event of any dispute arising pertaining to the interpretation or implementation of this agreement, the three protocols and appendices, such dispute shall be resolved within the framework of strict respect for the Iraqi-Iranian border line specified in Articles 1 and 2 above, and within the context of safeguarding Iraqi-Iranian border security pursuant to Article 3 above.

2. Such dispute shall be resolved by the two supreme contracting parties, in the first stage, through direct bilateral negotiations within a period of two months, effective from the date of an application by any party.

3. In the case of non-agreement, the two supreme contracting parties shall, within a period of three months, seek the good offices of a third friendly state.

4. In the case that any of the two parties declines to utilise the good offices, or in the case that their arrangements prove ineffective, the dispute shall be resolved by means of arbitration within a period not exceeding one month, effective from the date of rejection or failure.

5. In the case of non-agreement between the two supreme contracting parties on arbitration procedures, any of the supreme

contracting parties shall have the rights, within 15 days effective from the date of non-agreement, to resort to an arbitration tribunal. For the purpose of forming an arbitration tribunal to resolve each dispute, each of the two supreme contracting parties may appoint one of its subjects as an arbitrator, and the two arbitrators shall nominate an umpire. In the case of failure on the parts of the two supreme contracting parties to appoint their respective arbitrators within a period of one month, effective from the date of delivery by any party of a notice from the other, demanding arbitration, or in the case that the two arbitrators fail to reach agreement on the nomination of the umpire, prior to the elapse of the said period, the supreme contracting party which has demanded arbitration shall have the right to call upon the chairman of the International Court of Justice to appoint the arbitrators or the umpire in accordance with the procedures of the Permanent Court of Arbitration.

6. Decisions by the Permanent Court of Arbitration shall be binding and implementable by both supreme contracting parties.

7. The two supreme contracting parties shall equally share arbitration expenses.

### Article Seven

This treaty and the three protocols appended therewith shall be registered in accordance with Article 102 of the UN Charter.

### Article Eight

Each of the two supreme contracting parties shall ratify this treaty and the three protocols appended therewith in accordance with its internal law.

This treaty and the three protocols appended therewith shall become effective as of the exchanging of instruments of ratification, due to take place in the city of Teheran.

Pursuant thereupon, the two authorised commissioners, deputised by the two supreme contracting parties, have signed this treaty and the three protocols appended therewith.

Written at Baghdad on the 13th Day of June 1975.
    Abbas Ali Khalatbari, Foreign Minister of Iran
    Saadoun Hammadi, Foreign Minister of Iraq
The treaty and the three protocols appended therewith have been

endorsed in the presence of His Excellency Abdul Aziz Bouteflika, RCC member and Foreign Minister of Algeria.

Following is the text of protocol on Border Security between Iraq and Iran.

Pursuant to the resolutions of the Algiers Agreement dated March 6th, 1975, and proceeding from the keenness to consolidate security and mutual confidence along joint borders;

Proceeding from their determination to exercise firm and effective control along the borders to cease all infiltrations of a subversive nature and establish close cooperation between them, with a view to preventing any infiltration or illegal passage through their common borders, with the purpose of subversion, rebellion or mutiny;

With reference to the Teheran protocol dated March 15, 1975, minutes of the Foreign Ministers meeting concluded in Baghdad on April 20, 1975, and minutes of the Foreign Ministers meeting concluded in Algiers on May 20, 1975;

The two contracting parties have agreed to the following provisions.

### Article One

The two contracting parties shall exchange information related to the movement of subversive elements which may penetrate into either of the two countries with a view to committing acts of subversion, rebellion or mutiny in that country.

The two contracting parties shall take appropriate measures in respect to the movements of elements referred to in article one hereof.

Each shall notify the other immediately of the identity of such persons; it is agreed that they shall utilise all measures to prevent them from committing acts of subversion.

The same measures shall be adopted against the persons who gather in the territory of any contracting party with a view to committing acts of sabotage or subversion in the territory of the other party.

### Article Two

Versatile cooperation established between competent authorities of both contracting parties shall be applicable in respect to border closure with the purpose of preventing the penetration of subversive elements, at the level of border authorities of both countries, through to the highest levels of Ministers of Defense, Foreign Affairs and Interior in each of the contracting parties.

### Article Three

Potential penetration inlets which may be conducted by the subversive elements have been specified in the following manner:

1. Northern borders area: From the juncture point of Iraqi/Turkish-Iranian borders through Khanaqin-Qasr Shirin (inclusive — 21 points).

2. Southern borders area: From Khanaqin-Qasr Shirin (exclusive) through the Iraqi-Iranian borders — 17 points.

3. The penetration points specified here above are detailed in the appendix.

4. Inclusive with the points specified here above shall be any other penetration point to be discovered in the future, which should be closed and controlled.

5. All border passage points, except those currently assigned to customs authorities checkpoints, shall be subject to a passage embargo.

6. In view of the significance of developing versatile forms of relations between the two neighbourly countries, the two contracting parties have agreed that in the future, in accordance with mutual agreement, other passage points be specified to be under customs authority control.

### Article Four

1. The two contracting parties undertake to assign necessary human and material facilities for effective border closure and control against any penetration of subversive elements through the passage points specified in Article three above.

2. In the case that experts, due to experience acquired on the subject, consider that more effective measures should be adopted, means thereof shall be specified through monthly meetings of border authorities of both countries or through contacts made, when necessary, between such authorities.

Results of such meetings, together with their minutes, shall be forwarded to the supreme authorities in each party; in the case of a dispute between border authorities, competent heads of department, in Baghdad and Teheran, shall meet to reach entente and the results of such meetings shall be listed in special minutes.

### Article Five

1. Arrested saboteurs shall be handed over to the authorities concerned of the party in the territory of which they are arrested, and shall be subject to the legislations in effect therein.

2. The two contracting parties shall notify each other of the measures adopted in respect to the persons referred to in para. 1 hereof.

3. In the case of border crossing by wanted saboteurs, the authorities of the other party shall be notified, which shall take all necessary measures to help arrest the persons mentioned above.

### Article Six

When necessary, by agreement between the two contracting parties, embargo areas may be specified with a view to preventing saboteurs from attaining their ends.

### Article Seven

For the purpose of establishing and developing useful cooperation between the two parties, a permanent joint committee consisting of heads of border administrations and representatives of the Foreign Ministries of both parties shall be set up. The committee shall hold two annual meetings at the beginning and middle of each calendar year.

However, at the request of any party, extraordinary meetings may be held to consider the most appropriate utilisation of moral and material facilities for border closure and control and for the effective and good implementation of the basic provisions of cooperation stipulated in this protocol.

### Article Eight

Provisions of this protocol pertaining to the closure and control of borders shall not affect special agreements between Iraq and Iran related to grazing rights and a border commission.

### Article Nine

For the purpose of safeguarding the security of joint water borders in Shatt al-Arab and precluding the penetration of subversive elements from both parties, the two contracting parties shall adopt effective measures, notably by establishing checkpoints equipped with patrol boats.

Written at Baghdad on the 13th of June, 1975.
  Saadoun Hammadi, Foreign Minister of Iraq
  Abbas Ali Khalatbari, Foreign Minister of Iran
This protocol was endorsed in the presence of His Excellency Abdul Aziz Bouteflika, RCC Member and Foreign Minister of Algeria.

The following is the text of the re-demarcation of land border protocols between Iraq and Iran;

In accordance with what was agreed upon in the Algiers Communiqué dated March 6, 1975, the two contracting parties agreed upon the following provisions:

### ARTICLE ONE

The two contracting parties confirm and realise that the re-demarcation of international borders between Iraq and Iran has been conducted on land by the joint Iraqi-Iranian-Algerian Committee on the basis of the following:

1. The Constantinople Protocol of 1913 and the minutes of the Turkish-Persian Border Demarcation Commission of 1914;

2. Teheran Protocol dated March 17, 1975;

3. Minutes of the Foreign Ministers meeting concluded in Baghdad on April 20, 1975, which approved, *inter alia*, the minutes of the Committee entrusted with the re-demarcation of land borders concluded in Teheran on March 30, 1975.

4. Minutes of the Foreign Minister's meeting concluded in Algiers on May 20, 1975.

5. Descriptive minutes of the demarcation of land borders between Iraq and Iran written by the Committee entrusted with the demarcation of land borders dated June 13, 1975. These minutes constitute Appendix No. 1 to this protocol.

6. Maps scale 1/50000, on which the territorial border line is demarcated together with the locations of old and new crosslines. These maps make up Appendix No. 2 which is an inseparable part of this protocol.

7. Description cards of old and new crosspoints.

8. Document related to projection lines of border pegs.

9. Aerial photographs of Iraqi-Iranian border surroundings with the locations of old and new peg points.

B. The two parties undertake to finalize demarcation of border points between peg points fourteen and fifteen within a period of two months.

C. The two contracting parties shall cooperate to produce aerial photographs related to Iraqi-Iranian territorial borders, to be used for the demarcation of border lines on maps, scale 1/25000, together with demarcation of peg positions, within a period not exceeding one year, effective May 20, 1975. This should cause no prejudice to the implementation of the treaty of which this protocol constitutes an inseparable part.

As a result of this, the descriptive minutes of territorial borders, mentioned in Para. 5 above, shall be amended.

Maps clarified in accordance with provisions of Para. C shall replace all presently available maps.

### Article Two

The international Iraqi-Iranian border shall follow the line specified in the descriptive minutes drawn on the maps mentioned in Para. 5 and 6, Article 1 above, with due consideration of provisions of Para. C of the said Article.

### Article Three

The border line defined in Article 1 and 2 of this protocol shall also demarcate, in a vertical direction, the air space and underground of both countries.

### Article Four

The two contracting parties shall set up a joint Iraqi-Iranian committee to settle the position of real estate property, buildings, technical installations, etc., whose title deeds will change accordingly as a result of the re-demarcation of Iraqi-Iranian borders, in a spirit of good neighbourliness and cooperation, by means of re-purchases, compensation or any other satisfactory form, with a view to avoiding any source of dispute; the committee shall carry out such settlement of public property within a period of two months. As for claims related to private property, the committee shall submit, within a maximum period of two months, a report denoting that the position of such private property will be settled within the subsequent three-month period.

### Article Five

1. A joint committee from the authorities of the two countries has been set up to survey border peg points and authenticate their positions.

Such survey shall be conducted annually in the month of September by the above mentioned committee in accordance with a time table to be drawn up thereby, reasonably prior thereto.

2. Any of the two contracting parties may apply in writing to the other party for the conduct by the committee of an extra survey of the peg points; in such case the survey shall be commenced within a maximum period of 30 days from the application date.

3. The joint committee undertaking the survey, shall write down minutes related thereto and submit them, duly endorsed thereby, to the competent authorities of both countries. The committee may decide to establish new peg points, when necessary, with the same specifications of present pegs, provided that such action should not be conducive to changing the course of the border line. In such case, the competent authorities of the two countries shall check the peg points and projection lines on relative maps and documents mentioned in Article 1 of this protocol.

4. The two contracting parties shall jointly afford the cost of peg maintenance.

5. The joint committee shall replace pegs moved out of their places, rebuild destroyed or lost pegs in accordance with maps and documents mentioned in Article one of this protocol and adhere strictly not to change the position of pegs under any circumstances. The joint committee shall, in such cases, write down minutes on the works concluded, to be submitted to competent authorities in both countries.

6. Competent authorities in both countries shall exchange information related to the condition of border pegs, with a view to securing the most appropriate means and techniques for their protection and maintenance.

7. The two contracting parties undertake to adopt all the necessary measures to protect the pegs and punish individuals who may commit the crime of moving them from their positions, destroying or damaging them.

## Article Six

The two contracting parties have agreed that provisions of this protocol, which has been concluded without any reservation, will organize from now on any border question between Iraq and Iran, and officially undertake to respect accordingly their mutual and final borders.

*Appendices*

Written at Baghdad on the 13th of June, 1975.
Abbas Ali Khalatbari, Foreign Minister of Iran.
Dr. Saadoun Hammadi, Foreign Minister of Iraq.

This treaty and the three Protocols appended therewith have been endorsed in the presence of H.E. Abdul Aziz Bouteflika, RCC Member and Foreign Minister of Algeria.

Following is the full text of Protocol on the demarcation of Iraq-Iran Water Borders:

Pursuant to the agreement incorporated in the Algiers Declaration dated March 6, 1975, the two contracting parties have agreed to the following provisions:

### ARTICLE ONE

The two contracting parties confirm and realise that the demarcation of international water borders between Iraq and Iran has been conducted in accordance with the Thalweg Line by the Iraqi-Iranian-Algerian Committee on the basis of the following:

1) Teheran Protocol dated March 17, 1975.

2) Minutes of the Foreign Ministers meeting concluded in Baghdad on April 20, 1975, which approved, *inter alia*, the minutes of the committee entrusted with the demarcation of water borders, concluded on board the Iraqi vessel *al-Thawrah* at Shatt al-Arab on April 16, 1975.

3) The joint water maps which, after checking on land, rectification and transfer of geographical projection lines of border lines of 1975 thereto, have been signed by specialised technicians on water affairs, affiliated with the joint technical committee and also by the heads of Iraqi, Iranian and Algerian delegations to the committee. The maps mentioned above enumerated hereunder have been appended to the Protocol and thus constitute an inseparable part thereof.

Map No. 1: Shatt al-Arab inlet No. 3842, published by the British Admiralty.

Map No. 2: Internal Embankment through Point Keda No. 3843, published by the British Admiralty.

Map No. 3: Keda Point, through Abadan, No. 3844, published by the British Admiralty.

Map No. 4: Abadan through Um Taweela Island, No. 3845, published by the British Admiralty.

## Article Two

1) The border line at Shatt al-Arab shall follow the Thalweg Line, i.e. the medial line of the main channel, navigable when the water level is at its lowest navigation level, beginning from the point where the territorial border line is projected at Shatt al-Arab, through to the sea.

2) The border line defined in the manner specified in Article one above shall vary in accordance with variables emanating from natural reasons in the navigable main channel of the river; the border line shall not vary according to other variables, unless the two contracting parties reach a special agreement in that connection.

3) The variables mentioned in Para (2) above shall be authenticated jointly by the competent technical bodies of both contracting parties.

4) In the case of any shift in the river's main channel or/and Shatt al-Arab basin, due to natural phenomena, with the resulting effect being represented in a change in the national title to the territory of each of the two countries, the immovable property, buildings, technical installations or other, such border line shall continue to represent the Thalweg Line according to the provisions of Para (1) above.

5) Unless the two parties resolve by joint agreement that the border line should follow from now on the new stream, the water stream shall, at the mutual expense of both parties, be restored to the line of 1975, depending thus on the demarcations on the four maps specified in Para. (3) Article (1) hereof, if any party requests within the two years subsequent to the incidence of notice thereof by, any party; meanwhile, the two parties maintain the right to navigation and utilisation of water in the new main channel.

## Article Three

1) The water borders at Shatt al-Arab between Iraq and Iran, as defined in Article Two above, have been demarcated in the line specified in the joint maps mentioned in Para. (2) Article (1) above.

2) The two contracting parties have agreed to consider the end-point of water borders as located on a straight line connecting between the ends of both shores on the Shatt al-Arab Basin at the lowest ebb level (water level gauged by astronomical measures). This straight line is drawn on the joint water maps mentioned in Para (3) Article (1) above.

## Article Four

The border line defined in Articles One, Two and Three of this Protocol also defines, in a vertical direction, the air space and underground of both countries.

## Article Five

The two contracting parties shall set up a joint Iraqi-Iranian committee to organise, within a period of two months, the position of real estate property, buildings, technical installations, and other, whose title deeds have changed as a result of the Iraqi-Iranian water border demarcation, either by purchase, compensation, or any other appropriate manner to avoid any source of dispute.

## Article Six

In view of the finalisation of survey works at Shatt al-Arab and the drawing up of the joint water map mentioned in para (3) Article (1) above, the two contracting parties have agreed to conduct a joint survey of Shatt al-Arab once every ten years, from the date of concluding this Protocol. Each party shall have the right to conduct, jointly, new surveys prior to the elapse of the ten-year period.

Both contracting parties shall equally share survey expenses.

## Article Seven

1) Commercial, government and military vessels belonging to both contracting parties shall enjoy navigation freedom in Shatt al-Arab, regardless of the line demarcating the territorial waters of each country in all parts of navigable channels situated within the territorial waters and leading to the Shatt al-Arab main channel.

2) Vessels belonging to a third country and used for commercial purposes shall enjoy navigation freedom in Shatt al-Arab on equal footing and without discrimination, regardless of the line demarcating the territorial waters of both countries in all parts of the navigable channels situated in the territorial waters leading to Shatt al-Arab's main channel.

3) Each of the contracting parties may permit entrance into Shatt al-Arab to foreign military vessels to visit its ports, provided that such vessels shall not belong to a country in a state of hostility or armed

dispute or war with any of the contracting parties, and that the other party shall be notified beforehand, at least 72 hours prior, to such a visit.

4) The two contracting parties shall, under all circumstances, deny permission for entry into Shatt al-Arab to commercial vessels belonging to a state hostile, or in armed dispute or at war with any of the two parties.

## ARTICLE EIGHT

1) Rules for navigation in Shatt al-Arab shall be defined by a joint Iraqi-Iranian committee in accordance with the principles of equitable navigation rights of both countries.

2) The two contracting parties shall set up a committee to draw up rules for the combat of, and control over, pollution.

3) The two contracting parties undertake to conclude subsequent agreements on matters mentioned in Paras. (1) and (2) hereof.

## ARTICLE NINE

The two contracting parties realise that Shatt al-Arab is mainly an international navigation route; therefore, they undertake to refrain from any exploitation that might impede navigation in Shatt al-Arab and the territorial waters of each country in all parts of the navigable channels situated in the territorial waters and leading to Shatt al-Arab's main channel.

Written at Baghdad on the 13th of June, 1975.

Abbas Ali Khalabari, Foreign Minister of Iran

Dr. Saadoun Hammadi, Foreign Minister of Iraq

This Treaty and the three Protocols and Appendices have been endorsed in the presence of H.E. Abdul Aziz Bouteflika, RCC Member and Foreign Minister of Algeria.

H.E. the Iranian Foreign Minister, in a statement on the occasion, pointed out:

"I have the honour to assure Your Excellency, that in accordance with our agreement on the conclusion of the treaty pertaining to the international borders and good neighbourly relations between Iraq and Iran, together with the three Protocols and Appendices, namely:

1 — Agreement on navigation in Shatt al-Arab

2 — Agreement on grazing rights

5 — Agreement on border rivers

4 — Agreement on the rights and terms of reference of border commissions;

The two supreme contracting parties are bound to draw up and conclude the same simultaneously within a period of three months as from today.

Kindly accept my respects."

Abbas Ali Khalatbari

Foreign Minister Saadoun Hammadi's message reads:

"It honours me to acknowledge the receipt of your letter dated June 13, 1975, and confirm that, according to our agreement on the conclusion of the Treaty on International Borders and good neighbourly relations between Iraq and Iran together with the three Protocols and Appendices, namely:

1 — Agreement on Navigation in Shatt al-Arab
2 — Agreement on grazing rights
9 — Agreement on border rivers
4 — Agreement on the rights and terms of reference of border commissions:

The two Supreme Contracting Parties are bound to draw up and conclude the same simultaneously within a period of three months as from today.

Kindly accept my respects."

Saadoun Hammadi<br>Foreign Minister of Iraq

H.E. the Minister,

It honours me to confirm to Your Excellency that, in accordance with the agreement we have reached today, the two supreme contracting parties undertake to conduct, within a period not exceeding one year, all formalities related to the ratification of the treaty on international borders and good neighbourly relations between Iran and Iraq, together with the three Protocols and Appendices, in accordance with the international law as an arbiter to each party.

Kindly accept my sincere respects.

Abbas Ali Khalatbari<br>Foreign Minister of Iran

H.E. the Minister,

It honours me to acknowledge the receipt of your letter dated June 13, 1975, and confirm that, according to the agreement concluded today, each contracting party undertakes to conduct, within a period not exceeding one year, all formalities related to ratification procedures of the Treaty on International Borders and Good Neighbourly Relations Between Iraq and Iran, together with the three Protocols and Appendices in accordance with the international law of each party.

Saadoun Hammadi<br>Foreign Minister of Iraq

# Index

'Abadan, 148
'Abd al-Jalil, Ghanim, 62, 63n.
'Abd al-Karim, Tayih, 62, 63n.
'Abd-Allah, 'Amir, 98
'Abd-Allah, Hamza, 92
'Abd al-Nasir, President Jamal, 15n., 16, 26, 125; and Ba'th Party, 47; Impressions of Saddam Husayn, 74
'Aflaq, Michel, 6, 16, 18, 39; writings of, 8n.
Agrarian reform, 85, 97, 117ff., 129; planning and research, 112ff.; under the Old Regime, 117; and Revolution of 1958, 117ff., 122ff.; Higher Agricultural Council, 121
Ahali (Populist) movement, 3ff.
Ahmad, Ibrahim, 81; and KDP, 92f., 107
'Akrawi, 'Aziz, 93
Algeria, 151, 169
Algiers Communiqué, 151f., 166
al-'Ali, Salah 'Umar, 62
al-'Allaf, Jar-Allah, 43
al-Alusi, Dahham, 11n.
Al-'Amara, 63
'Amili, 'Izzat-Allah, 55
'Ammash, Salih Mahdi, 11, 25n., 67, 155; and Persian dispute, 56; and rivals, 57ff.
al-Ansari, Ibrahim Faysal, 31f.,
Arab-Israeli War, 18, 81, 127n; and oil policy, 128; and foreign policy, 142ff., 168
Arabistan, 148
Arab League, Council of: Euphrates dispute, 164
Arab nationalism, 47, 78, 142; and Progressive National Group, 96; and Kurds, 102; and Hashimi House, 166; see also Pan-Arabism

Arab Revolt of 1916, 166
Arab Socialist Union, in Iraq, 20
Arab unity, 47, 142; the view of Saddam Husayn, 75
'Arif, 'Abd al-Rahman, regime of, President (1966–68), 17ff., 80, 172; and the Army, 22ff.
'Arif, 'Abd al-Salam, 130n.; and 1958 Revolution, 11–12; rivalry with Qasim, 13ff.; death, 17; regime (1963–1966), 17
Army, 21f; 38, 45, 86f., 172; factionalism in, 18; failure to support PLO, 59; under Ba'thist control, 32, 75, 178; and Kurds, 107, 109f.
al-Arsuzi, Zaki, 9
al-Asad, Hafiz, 48
Asad Lake, 162, 164
Ashdari, Babakr, 94
al-Aswad, Muhammad Sa'id, 10n.
al-'Aysami, Shibli, 39, 90n.
'Aziz, Tariq, 14n., 15n., 63, 98
al-Azzawi, Muzhir, 95f.

Baghdad: demonstrations in, 19, 59
Baghdad Pact, 141, 148, 171
Baghdad Treaty, 152f.
al-Bajari, (al-Bachari), 'Abd al-Hadi, 51f.,
Bakhtiari, Gen. Taymur, 55n.
al-Bakr, Ahmad Hasan, 11, 16, 18f., 23f., 28f., 39, 50, 58, 61; Cabinet, 25–26n., 31n.; President (1968), 25; Prime Minister, 31, 153; Kazzar uprising, 64ff.; personality and character, 69ff.; and Mulla Mustafa, 109; on economic reform, 130
al-Barzani, 'Ubayd-Allah, 94
Basra Petroleum Company, 127f.
Ba'th Party, and NDP., 4, 23f., 26f; and

261

Communists, 4, 79, 179; basic principles and origins, 6f.; military members, 11; overthrow of Qasim, 14f.; Regional Command and RCC, 25; overthrow of Nayif, 30; role in government, 36ff.; structure of, 40n.; and bureaucracy, 41f.; dissension within, 47f., ch. 4; and Kurds, 93f., 102ff.; and Progressive National Front, 97ff.; and Agrarian Reform, 119, 121; and industrialization, 129ff.; and social reforms, 137; and education, 139f.; and Soviet relations, 144ff.; nationalization of oil, 123, 125; Iran policy, 149; Kuwayt policy, 155; Jordan policy, 165; and Arab-Israeli conflict, 168ff.; accomplishments of, 178ff.
al-Baytar, Salah al-Din, 6, 16
Bazzaz, 'Abd al-Rahman, 51f., 172; Premier, 17f.
Brazil: Petroleo Brasileiro contract, 128
Britain, see Great Britain
Bubyan, 154, 157ff.

al-Chadirchi, Kamil, leader of NDP, 4, 77n., 95n.
Charter for National Action, 97ff., 137
Civil leadership, ascendency of, 60f.
Communism, Communists, 3, 5, 6, 47, 53, 92, 137, 172; activities of, 79ff.; conflict with pan-Arabs, 13; Qasim and, 13f., 79; and Progressive National Front, 41, 87, 97ff.; Kazzar and, 64; Policies and objectives, 84ff.; and Soviet Union, 145, 147
Constantinople Protocol of 1913, 152
Constitution, 97; temporary constitutions, 32ff., 179, 181; revision of, 59
Cooperative societies, see Agrarian reform
Coups d'etat, aborted attempt (1970), 53ff.

al-Damarji, 'Abd al-Hamid, 51
al-Damin, 'Abd al-Rahman, 10
al-Dawud, Col. 'Abd al-Rahman Ibrahim, 22ff., 50, 56; fall of, 28f.
Development Board, 112; see also Planning Board
Development plans, 97f., Ch. 6; dates of, 113; irrigation, 134; Kurds and, 105; Agrarian, 118ff.; Industrial, 129ff.; see also Economic reforms and social reforms
al-Duri, 'Abd al-Sattar, 11n.
al-Duri, 'Izzat Ibrahim, 62, 63n., 66

Economic assistance, 144f.
Economic reforms and plans, 97ff., ch. 6, 180; planning and research, 112ff.; Revolution of 1958, 111; Revolution of 1968, 112; Agrarian, 118ff.; Industrial, 130; see also Development plans and Social reforms
Education, 112, 139f.
Egypt: relations with, 167

Factionalism, 13, 49f., 58
Fadil, Muhammad, 66
Fahd, Crown Prince, 160
Faw (Fao), 154
Foreign policy: Charter for National Action and, 98; and oil, 126; and trade, 132f.; Nuri's, 141ff.; Soviet assistance, 144; Iraqi-Soviet Treaty (1972), 145ff.; Shatt al-Arab dispute, 148ff.; Treaty with Iran (1937) 148f.; Baghdad Treaty, 152f.; relations with Kuwait, 153ff.; relations with Saudi Arabia, 159f.; relations with Syria, 161ff.; relations with Jordan, 164ff.; and other Arab countries, 167f.
France, 21, 128; and IPC, 127
Free officers, 71, 97

Ghab project, 162
al-Ghanim, Wasfi, 9
Ghaydun, Sa'dun, 11n., 22, 25n., 29, 59; and Kazzar uprising, 64ff.
Great Britain: presence in the Gulf, 90, 153f.; relations with Iraq, 141, 143, 149, 171; and oil, 126

Haddad, Na'im, 11n., 62, 63n., 90n.
Hadid, Muhammad, 95n.
Haditha, 129
al-Hajj, 'Aziz, 80f.
Hamadi, Sa'dun, 10, 62, 63n., 126, 158
Hammudi, Ja'far Qasim, 11n.
al-Hamdani, 'Adnan, 62, 63n.
al-Hani, Nasir, 26; assassination of, 50f.
Hasan, Hashim, 93
Hashimi House, 160, 165f.
Hashim, Jawad, 114f.
Health Services, 112
High Committee (HC), composition of, 99f.
Hiwa Party, 91f.; see also Kurds
al-Hub, Jawad Abu, 11n.
Husayn, 'Abd-Allah, 166
Husayn, Faysal, 166
Husayn, King, 151; and Iraqi relations, 165f.

Husayn, Saddam, 29, 39, 90n., 98, 145, 151, 160, 164n., 167, 178n., 179; and Kazzar uprising, 63ff.; and nationalization of IPC, 125ff.; on industrialization, 134; personality and character, 71ff.; Secretary of IRC, (1964), 16; Secretary General, (1966) 17;
Husayn, Sharif, 166
Huwayda (Hoveida), Amir 'Abbas, 152

Ideological groups, struggle among, 77ff.; *see also* Political Parties
Ilyas, Yusuf al-Hajj, 95n.
Imperialism, 84, 89f., 145
Independent Democratic Group, 95f., 99
India, 128
Industrialization, 111, 129ff.; planning and research, 112ff.; *versus* agriculture, 123; *see also* Organization for Public Industries
Industry, nationalization of, 87, 112, 123ff., 170; *see also* Oil
Iran: Kazzar uprising, 66; Kurds and, 101, 107, 110, 173; oil production, 125; plot of 1970, 54f.; relations with, 141, 153; Shatt al-Arab dispute, 148ff.
Iraqi Company for Oil Operations, 127
Iraqi National Command, 16, 38n., 39n., 47f., 66; and Kurdish problem, 102
Iraqi National Oil Company (INOC), 26n., 28, 123f.
Iraqi Oil Tankers Company (IOTC), 124
Iraqi Regional Command, 16, 38ff., 44, 47, 69; composition, 40; and Kurdish problem, 103
Iraqi unity, 102
Iraq Petroleum Company (IPC), 19, 27f., 123ff.
Iraq-Syria: differences over Jordan policy, 59; Ba'thist disputes, 67f.
Irrigation, 112, 119, 121, 134ff., 161ff.; under the Old Regime, 117, 134
al-'Isa, Sulayman, 9
Islam, 33f., 181; Communism and, 91
Isma'il, 'Abd-Allah, 94
Isma'il, Fa'iz, 9
Isma'il, Su'ad Khalil, 10
Israel, 84, 89, 128, 142, 166; and the Arab-Israeli conflict, 168ff.; and Iraq-U.S. relations, 172ff.
Istiqlal (Independence) Party, 6, 77f., 95

Jadid, Salah, 18
al-Jadir, Adib, 26n.
Jamil, Husayn, 95n.
Jamil, Muhammad, 9
Jasim, Falih, 69

Jawad, Hashim, 50
Jawad, Hazim, 11n.
al-Jazrawi, Taha, 44n., 54, 62, 63n.
Jews, espionage trial (1969), 51
Jordan, 28, 144; Iraqi support of PLO, 59, 169; relations with, 164ff.
July Revolution, *see* Revolution

al-Kamali, Shafiq, 11n.
Kanna, Khalil, 50, 52
Karim, Habib Muhammad, 80
Karmat 'Ali, 161
Karu, Abu al-Qasim Muhammad, 9
Kayban project, 162
Kazim, Shamsi, 10n.
Kazzar, Nazim: background and character, 63; plot against government, 64ff.
Kazzar uprising, 63ff., 173
Khabur River, 162f.
Khaddam, 'Abd al-Halim, 68
al-Khalkhal, Hamid, 11n.
Khanaqin, 106
Khasawna, Mustafa, 9n.
Khattab, Dia Shith, 32, 33n.
al-Khudayri, 'Abd al-Khaliq, 10
Khurays, Yusuf, 9n.
Khurramshahr, 148, 150
Kirkuk, 106f., 127
Kosygin, Premier Alexei, 124, 145
Kubba, Muhammad Mahdi, 95n.
Kubba, Salih, 28
Kurdish Democratic Party (KDP), 21, 81, 109; and the Progressive National Front, 41, 99ff.; origins and development of, 92ff.
Kurdish Progressive Group, 94
Kurdish Revolutionary Party, 93
Kurdish War, 17, 87, 93; and Iraqi-American relations, 174f.; termination of, 67, 88, 167
Kurds and Kurdistan, 19, 27, 33, 52f., 56, 85, 97, 145, 147, 152f., inter-factional clashes, 20f.; Kazzar and, 64; political parties of, 91ff.; problem of, 101ff.
Kuwayt, 60, 126; relations with, 153ff., 168

Lebanon, 168, 174
Libya, 126, 169
Lutfi, 'Adnan, 9n.

al-Majid, Hamdi 'Abd, 11n.
Mandali area, 150
Maoism, 89
March Manifesto, 93; principal points of, 103ff.

Militia, civil, 43f.; *see also* National Guard *and* Popular Resistance Force
Minorities, 91; *see also* Kurds
Mobil Oil Corporation, 128
Mu'alla, Tahsin, 11n.
Muhammad, 'Aziz, 80, 91, 94, 98; at Second National Convention, 83; at Third National Convention, 88f.
Muhyi al-Din, Husayn, 32
Muhyi al-Din, Taha, 94
Munif, 'Abd al-Rahman, 11n.
Mustafa, Adham, 9
Mustafa, 'Izzat, 10, 62, 68f.
Mustafa, Mulla (of Barzan), 17, 27, 52f., 100, 153, 173; appeal to deGaulle, 21; Kazzar attempts to assassinate, 64; promise to al-Hajj, 81; and split of KDP, 92f.; and March Manifesto, 105ff.; surrender in Iran, 109

Najaf-Karbala demonstrations, 67ff., 178n.
al-Naqib, Hasan, 11n., 61
Nasir, President, *see* 'Abd al-Nasir
Nasirites, 95f.; in the military, 17, 20
National Assembly, 20, 34ff., 45, 179f.
National Command, *see* Iraq: National Command
National Council for the Revolutionary Command (NCRC), *see* Iraq: National Command
National Democratic Party, (NDP), 3, 5, 77f., 95f.; *see also* Ahali
National Guard, 43
National Union Front, formation of, 78
Nationalism, nationalists, 6f., 13, 172; and Arab socialism, 7; Communism, 91
al-Nayif, Col. 'Abd al-Razzaq, 22ff., 50, 56; fall of, 28f.; Premier, 26
Nayif-Dawud group, 25f., 50; fall from power, 28f.; relations with Ba'th leaders, 27f.; and Western support, 144
Non-alignment policy, 142, 172
Nuri al-Sa'id, Gen., 52, 78n.; Kuwayt dispute, 153; pro-Western policy, 171f.

Oil, 19, 87, 112ff.; nationalization of, 123ff., 169, 172f.; Soviet assistance for, 124; Hungarian assistance for, 124
Organization of Petroleum Exporting Countries (OPEC), 125; Algiers meeting (1975), 151
Organization for Public Industries, 130f.

Palestine, Palestinians, 84, 89, 144, 166, 168f.

Palestinian Liberation Organization (PLO), 59f.
Pan-Arabism, 166; and Kurds, 102
Pan-Arab movement, 46f., 78; influence on Arab Socialism, 6
Parliamentary system: re-establishment advocated, 20
Persian Gulf, 90, 127, 129, 155, 167; Iraq-Saudi Arabia and, 160
Pesh Merga (Kurdish militia), 106
Planning and research, 112ff., 130
Planning Board, 112; membership and organization, 114ff.
Political Parties, 41, 77f.; pre-Revolutionary period, 97
Popular Resistance Force, 43
Port of 'Aqaba, 167
Progressive National Front, 41, 67, 90, 95, 145; creation of (1973), 53, 79, 87f., 97ff., 179; Kurdish representation, 94; *see also* High Committee
Progressive National Group, 96, 99
Provincial Law, new, 105
Public Law 69, 127
Public Law 80, 20n.; 28, 123ff.

Qadduri, Fakhri, 10
al-Qadir, Anwar 'Abd, 24
Qasim, 'Abd al-Karim, 11–12, 69, 130; overthrow of, 14; regime, 50, 171f.; and moderate parties, 79; claim on Kuwayt, 153f.
al-Qatifi, 'Abd al-Husayn, 149n.

al-Radi, Husayn ('Adil, Salam), 80
Ramadan Revolution, *see* Revolution (Feb. 8, 1963)
Rashid 'Ali uprising, impact on Saddam Husayn, 72
Rashid, Taha 'Ali, 9n.
al-Rawi, 'Abd al-Ghani, 18, 53, 55
al-Razzaq, 'Arif 'Abd, 17
Regional Command, *see* Iraqi Regional Command
Regional Congress, 67
Republican Guard, 22, 24, 29
Resolutions 242 and 338; 169
Revolution: July Revolution (July 14, 1958), 11, 78, ch. 2; and Saudi Monarchy, 160; and Jordanian relations, 165; altering of pro-Western policy, 171f.; Ramadan Revolution (Feb. 8, 1963), 14; Revolution of 1968, 21ff., 27; events preceding, 17ff.
Revolutionary Command Council (RCC), 25, 32f., 34, 127, 180; members,

25n.; composition of, 35n., and Planning Board, 116
Revolutionary Court, 42f.
Rida, 'Ali, 54
al-Rikabi, Fuad, 11, 14n.
Riyad, Mahmud, 156
Royal Dutch Oil Company, 128
al-Rubay'i, Tahir, 11n.
Ruzkari (Liberation) Party, 92; see also Kurds

al-Sabah, Shaykh Jabir al-Ahmad, 157
al-Sabah, Shaykh Sabah Salim, 153
al-Sabah, Shaykh Sa'd al-'Abd-Allah Salim, 155f.
al-Sabbagh, Col. Salah al-Din, 73
al-Sa'di, 'Ali Salih, 10n., 14n., 15f.
al-Sa'di, Salim, 11n.
al-Sahhaf, Kamil, 11n.
al-Sa'igh, 'Abd al-Ghaffar, 11n.
Sallum, 'Abd-Allah, 11n., 62
al-Samarra'i, 'Abd al-Khaliq, 65f.
al-Samarra'i, Fa'iq, 95n.
al-Samarra'i, Col. Salih Mahdi, 53, 55, 62
al-Samita, 156
Saudi Arabia, 125f., 164; relations with, 159ff., 168; Kuwayt boundary, 161
Shah of Iran, 151, 166
Shammar tribes, 159
Shanshal, 'Abd al-Jabbar, 59
Shanshal, Siddiq, 95n.
Sharash (Revolution) Party, 92; see also Kurds
Sharif, 'Abd al-Sattar Tahir, 94
al-Sharkarchi, Taha, 61
Shatt al-Arab, 54, 65, 147, 154, 156, 161; dispute with Iran, 148ff.
al-Shawi, Hisham, 96
al-Shaykhli, 'Abd al-Karim, 16, 62, 63n.
Shell Oil Company, 128
Shihab, Hammad, 22, 25n., 32, 59; and Kazzar uprising, 64ff.
Shi'i community: and al-Najaf-Karbala demonstration, 68; and Saudi relations, 159
Shim'un, Mar, restoration of citizenship, 56
Shintaf, Karim, 11n.
Sidqi, Bakr, 69f.
Sinjar and Duhok, 106
Sipahi, Muhammad 'Ali, 11n.
Socialism, 32, 47, 86, 180f.; and development plans, 113; and industrialization, 129ff.; and education, 140
Social reforms, 136ff., 180; planning and research, 112ff.; see also development plans and economic reforms
South Yaman, 90, 167, 169

Soviet Union: 98, 162; cooperation of, 67, 130n., 173; and Iraqi Communists, 83f.; al-Hajj criticism, 81; treaty with Iraq (1972) 88; and Iraqi oil, 124, 126, 128; relations with, 143ff., 171ff.; and Kurdish problem, 147
Spain, 124, 128
Special Revolutionary Court, 43
Standard Oil of New Jersey (Exxon), 128
Sudan, 167
Sulaymaniya, 106
Sultan, 'Abd-Allah, 11
Syria, 1, 174; Ba'thists, 16, 18, 44, 47, 67f.; support of PLO in Jordan, 59; al-Najaf-Karbala demonstrations, 68; Kurds in, 101; conflict over Euphrates, 129, 135, 161ff.; relations with, 143

al-Talabani, Jalal, 81
al-Talabani, Mukarram, 80n., 93f., 107
Talib, Col. Naji, 18
Tigris-Euphrates: irrigation, 135; Iraq-Syria dispute, 161ff.
al-Tikriti, Hardan, 11n., 24, 28, 29n., 32, 50, 67, 144, 155, 166n.; and rivals, 58f.; assassination of, 60
Tunisia: relations with, 167
Turkey: Kurds in, 101, 107, 110; pipeline through, 129; Euphrates irrigation plan, 135, 161ff.; relations with, 141

Umm Qasr, 147, 154ff.
Unayza tribes, 159
United Arab Republic, 18, 47; Ba'thist view, 78; Communist attitude towards, 13
United National Front, 4n., 11, 97
United Nations: and Iraqi-Iranian dispute, 56, 150f.
United States, 26, 84f., 90, 169; relations with Iraq, 171ff.; and Iraqi oil, 128, 170
al-'Uqayli, Gen. 'Abd al-'Aziz, 18, 51f.

Wahhabi, 159
al-Wandawi, Mundhir, 11n.
Warba, 154, 157ff.
West, Western, 28, 51, 115; and Iraqi Communists, 83f., 88; Iraqi policy towards, 30, 141ff., 171

Yahya, Gen. Tahir, 18, 21; resignation, 20
Yasin, Yahya, 10n.
Yusuf (Fahd), Yusuf Salman, 80, 91

Zadah, 'Abd al-Khaliq Bushehri, 55n.